CLERGY WIVES' STORIES

Fifteen Oral Histories from the 1950s to the Present Day

Recorded and compiled
by Sheila Rowe

About the Author

Sheila Rowe was a clergy wife for thirty years and has four children and five grandchildren. She has been widowed for fourteen years. She was originally trained as a nurse and midwife and a Person-Centred-Counsellor and has a Masters in Oral History.

Published in 2013 by The Plynlimmon Press.
plynlimmonpress@uwclub.net

Copyright Sheila Rowe 2012

ISBN No: 978-0-9552222-2-1

A catalogue record of this book is available from the British Library.

Typesetting, repro, layout and styling by Tony Crowther of ARC Design, West Sussex Tel: 01903 871238 Email: info@arcdesign.me

Printed and bound in the UK by Juniper House of Print, Lawford Manningtree, Essex. Tel:01206 230884 Email:richard@jhprint.co.uk

This book is dedicated
to my late husband,
a parish priest.

ACKNOWLEDGEMENTS

I would like to express my gratitude to all the clergy wives whose stories are recorded here, for allowing me to tape their histories and giving me permission to reproduce them. Many gave me photographs to enhance the text, some sepia, some black and white and some in colour. They are reproduced throughout as given by each contributor and help to reflect the changes taking place in their lives.

All of the contributors have made a huge emotional commitment and remained enthusiastic about having their stories told and have been patient in the time it took for the telling.

I am also grateful to the Rev. Simon Holland for his initial inspiration and to John Quartly who transported me to some of the clergy wives' homes and for his encouragement and some editing.

CONTRIBUTORS

Those who wish to remain anonymous are recorded by a pseudonym and some requested Christian names only to be used.

Clergy wives who were daughters of priests

Jean Ash, née Topping. *'I never wanted to marry a clergyman'*

Mary Nagel, née Thomas. *'I had a pretty good idea what it would be like married to a priest'*

Clergy wives who married curates

Margaret Riddelsdell. *'It's been an interesting life. I am glad I married a missionary'*

Sylvia. *'My children have to come first'*

Margaret. *'I think what I've always tried to be is a good church-woman'*

Clergy wives who married ordinands

Ann. *'Curates' wives sit over there in that corner'*

June. *'I adapted to being a clergy wife quite easily'*

Hazel Treadgold. *'I was determined never to look like the conventional clergy wife'*

Gill. *'I certainly didn't feel privileged at being a clergy wife'*

Wendy Carr. *'I've got to go the way of the Lord'*

Clergy wives who married laymen who later became priests

Claire Lunney. *'We gave ourselves to the people and they gave themselves to us'*

Hilary Smith. *'I'd rather work in the background'*

Sue Howden. *'God what do you want me to do here?'*

Florence. *'And so I made my commitment to Jesus'*

Maureen. *'I used to scream at God sometimes'*

Places Served by Their Husbands

Jean Ash
St. Andrew's Plymouth, Devon
St. Augustine's Bromley Common, Kent

Sylvia
A parish in West Sussex
St. Margaret's Isfield, East Sussex
Ashley Green, Buckinghamshire
A village near Salisbury in Wiltshire
A town in South West Ayrshire
Stratford St. Mary and Higham in Suffolk

Claire Lunney
Westerfield & Tuddenham St. Martin
with Witnesham, Suffolk

Ann
A parish in Worcestershire
A parish in Dudley, West Midlands
Reading Street Broadstairs, Kent
Holy Trinity Church, Selhurst, Croydon
St. Mary's Church, Sutton Valance, Maidstone
Fishbourne, West Sussex

Margaret Riddelsdell
Mombasa, Malindi, Maseno and
Limuru near Nairobi in Kenya
St. Andrew's, Islington

Hilary Smith
Cheadle, North Staffordshire
Blakenall Heath, Walsall
Knutton, Newcastle-Under-Lyme
Return to Blakenall Heath, Walsall
St. Michael's and St. Mary's, Lichfield
St. Andrew's, West Bromwich

June
A parish in Mid Derbyshire
A parish between Nottingham and Derby
St. Andrew's, Guist, Norfolk

Hazel Treadgold
Southwell Minster, Nottinghamshire
Wollaton, Nottingham
St. Cuthbert's, Darlington
St. George's Windsor and The Royal Chapel in The Great Park
Chichester Cathedral

Sue Howden
Wigmore Parish, Chatham
Doddinghurst Bradwell, Essex
Pleshey Parish and Retreat House
Wickham Bishops, Essex

Gill
A parish near Leeds
A parish in South Lincolnshire
A large parish and a group of villages near Lincoln

Florence
A town parish and a village parish near Chelmsford
A seaside parish in Essex

Wendy Carr
Tonbridge, Kent
Cheadle Hulme, Cheshire
St. Mary's Widford with The Church of The Holy Spirit, Chelmsford
The Church of St. Thomas, Dagenham, Essex
Holy Cross & St. Andrew's, Basildon

Margaret
Poulton-Le-Fylde, Lancashire
The Church of St. Nicholas, Marton Moss, Blackpool
An industrial village near Blackpool
Chichester Cathedral
Boxgrove and Tangmere, West Sussex
Westbourne, West Sussex
East Preston with Kingston, West Sussex

Maureen
A parish in London
Two parishes in Essex

Mary Nagel
Chiswick, West London
Horsham, West Sussex
St. Richard's Aldwick, West Sussex

Contents

'Oral history gives history back to the people in their own words. And in giving a past, it also helps them towards a future of their own making.'

(Paul Thompson. *The Voice Of The Past, Oral History*. Published 1988 by Oxford University Press, page 265.)

"My dear, I'll give you a bit of advice, keep your mouth shut and your door open."

(Advice given by the Bishop of Lancaster's wife to Margaret when she became engaged to a curate, page 192.)

INTRODUCTION

The clergy wife had a troubled history as she made many attempts to enter a world in which celibacy ruled. In spite of the fact that St. Peter was a married man, celibacy became the rule for the priest. The argument raged through the centuries. Should priests remain Christ-like and single or be married like St. Peter? If allowed to marry should they have children or leave all and follow their calling, as the Apostles were asked to do, and devote themselves to the needs of the church?

The Bible in 1 Corinthians, chapter 7 verses 32 to 33 says 'He that is unmarried careth for the things that belong to the Lord, how he may please the Lord…But he that is married careth for the things that are of the world, how he may please his wife.'

Fast forwarding to the Reformation, Henry VIII declared himself the Head of the Anglican Church and in spite of his own personal extravagance in wives refused to legalise clerical marriages, enforcing celibacy. Following his death priests were allowed to marry again until the rule of Mary Tudor who established strict rules and punishments for married clerics who refused to divorce their wives, including burning at the stake. After Mary's death in 1558 Queen Elizabeth the First conceded to clerical marriages under ecclesiastical law but not the law of the land. The latter was finally established by James the First in 1604 and has remained so ever since and having a wife and family became no hindrance to preferment.

In the latter part of the eighteenth and early nineteenth century many famous sons and daughters emerged from privileged educated clergy families. They include Ben Johnson, Sir Christopher Wren, Lord Nelson, Jane Austen, Alfred Lord Tennyson, the Brontë Sisters and Cecil Rhodes to name a few.

As the twentieth century imposed its wars, social changes and economic stringency on idyllic country rectories, they became relics of a bygone era, beautiful but somewhat dilapidated mansions which were difficult and too expensive to heat, surrounded by neglected gardens. To maintain her home a clergy wife needed boundless energy and enthusiasm. She moved from the Victorian parent of eleven, twelve or more children to the two or three of the neo-Georgian era. At first it was still possible to employ a useful nanny or servant at a very low wage but as the years progressed she found herself coping alone.

This book is a record of the life and role of the clergy wife from the 1950s to the present day. Each one was interviewed and recorded personally by the author. Their oral histories reveal the transition from the old style traditional wife to the working wife and mother as they keep pace with their contemporaries. Most are revealed as nomads, moving from antiquated vicarages impossible to heat to more modern houses that they can never own and keeping open house on a restricted budget. Their individual stories demonstrate unique approaches to the tasks they are expected to fulfil within the system. Their marriages reveal long term lasting relationships with men of God who are their husbands, fathers of their children and their priests. How do they feel about the controversial changes within the church culminating in the ordination of women priests and gay bishops?

As each one opens her door to us, we step beyond the façade of her professional life to find a heart that helps to keep the parish alive with its warmth and humanity. As she takes stock of her memories and reviews her joys, achievements, strengths, weaknesses and sorrows we find the 'alter ego' behind the clerical collar.

In the history of the Church of England their voices speak of courage and dedication to a demanding role as they are held fast by the richness and depth of their own faith. Come with me as we bear witness and hear their stories.

CLERGY WIVES' STORIES

*Fifteen Oral Histories
from the 1950s
to the Present Day*

JEAN ASH

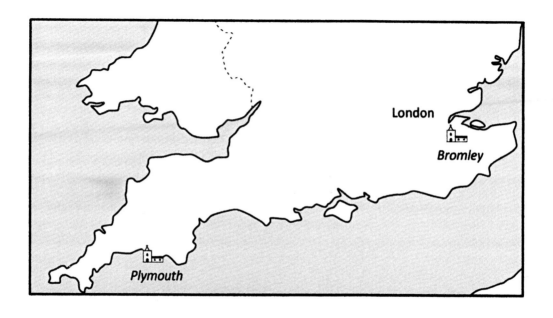

JEAN'S STORY

'I never wanted to marry a clergyman'

My name is Jean Ash and I live in Leigh-on-Sea; my maiden name was Topping. I was born in Islington in 1931. My father was a curate at St. Jude's, Mildmay Park. After a second curacy in Old Harlow Essex, he accepted a Living in Stratford in the East End of London. We lived there until I was five and I have only vague memories of that period of my life. They include the Bishop of Barking coming to lunch wearing gaiters, the gift from a parishioner every Christmas of a wonderful cake in the shape of a detailed house with a garden, a large portrait of George V on the wall that I kissed "Good night" each evening, part of the ceiling falling down just as I left the room, playing in a sandpit in the garden and being terrified by the smoke from a train which enveloped us as we were taken over the bridge for a walk. It took me a long time to get over that.

Because my parents were so involved in parish work we used to have someone living with us rather like a nanny, to look after my sister and me. Her name was Beatie and she was greatly loved by us all. She stayed with our family for several years. It was quite the norm in those pre-war days, even for a clergy family; I was very fond of her. My mother still had time to enjoy being with us. She did bath us and put us to bed and gave us rides on her back from chair to chair in the sitting room. She was an accomplished pianist and we had sing-songs around the piano which I repeated with my own children in later years.

My sister Joyce is four years my senior and because of this relatively large gap I played a lot on my own with Ludo, marbles and various other games. My favourite toy was a Noah's Ark with many pairs of animals. They were walked across floors, up stairs and across tables. I liked the different sounds they made on the surfaces. A friend, still of many years standing, often came to play and we would create clothes for our paper dolls, acting out all sorts of imaginary stories with them.

Prior to being ordained, my father was in the Territorial Army and when the First World War was declared in 1914 he embarked as a captain into France. During the Battle of the Somme he was wounded by a piece of shrapnel in his back. Because of the risk of it shifting to his heart he was floated down a river and kept flat on a raft and then had to be lifted onto the boat by a crane to get back to England. When he was fully recovered he enlisted in the Indian Army and joined the Ghurkhas guarding the Khyber Pass on the North-West Frontier. It was after all this that he went into the Ministry.

In 1936 we moved to Westcliff-on-Sea in Essex when I was five, to live in a small 'semi', ostentatiously calling itself St. Andrew's Vicarage. After we left eight years later, the Diocese bought a double fronted detached house in the same road as the church, a much better investment. Whilst we were there my parents ran an annual sale in the hall and a gift was contributed each year by the Queen Mother and the congregation gave us many handmade articles. One of the curates' wives made little pink bows that she tied on to small tree branches and they were sold. My mother made lamp shades and she was a great knitter, she was always busily knitting.

In 1939 the war started and I vividly remember my father standing in the pulpit on September the 3rd announcing that war had been declared on Germany and suggested we should all return to our homes. My sister Joyce had stayed at home and heard the announcement on the radio.

She put two buckets of water by the front door and started rather unsuccessfully to try to dig an Anderson Shelter in the small back garden. She was soon to be evacuated with the Westcliff High School girls up to Chapel-en-le-Frith in Derbyshire, where they stayed for the whole of the next four years.

After a while I went with my mother to stay with my grandmother who lived in Crowborough in Sussex, where the fear of invasion was not so great. We were there for quite a long time. My father had to stay behind to look after the parish. He said it was like a ghost town with most women and children gone.

Above: Me (left) with my sister Joyce
Left: My father

My cousins came to stay alongside us at my grandmother's and they are happy memories. I played with my cousins and we dressed up in costumes provided by my grandmother, enacting little plays before the adults. I can remember a German reconnaissance aircraft very slowly coming out of the clouds one day when I was standing in the garden, I saw the black crosses clearly on its wings, and it was a frightening moment. I was told later it was no doubt filming the Army barracks nearby but I felt safe there.

We stayed there for about two years when I remember moving with my mother to a friend's huge house in Bishop's Stortford in Hertfordshire, where there were six boys as well, evacuated out of London. After a while I took and passed the Eleven Plus exam, so on returning to Westcliff I was immediately evacuated to Derbyshire joining the High School and my sister. So I was whipped away from my parents for the first time, I hated it and was very miserable. I cried every night for a fortnight. My mother sent my teddy bear so that calmed me down a bit and I had very kind foster parents who looked after me well.

My sister thoroughly enjoyed it because she liked the independence. She got a bit upset when she didn't know where I was living in the village, but she found me eventually. The school had taken over some huge mansions which were used for both classrooms and billets for those not in a local home. I really hated Derbyshire and in subsequent years when we went on holiday with our children we visited Chapel-en-le-Frith to kill the ghost of my dislike of such a beautiful county. I was only there for six months because the authorities decided to return the whole school to Westcliff. We came back to be bombarded by doodlebugs with that never to be forgotten and terrifying noise. That was awful. Sadly one of my school friends was killed when one of them came down on her house. We were at Westcliff until 1944 when I was thirteen. Then we moved into the depths of the country near Harlow in Essex to a little hamlet, called Magdalen Laver.

My father had charge of Magdalen Laver and High Laver for the next sixteen years. High Laver is famed for being the burial place of John Locke the philosopher (1632-1704). I loved it there and I return to visit whenever I can because I've never been so happy in a place. My grandmother lived with us until her dying day, when she was buried in Magdalen Laver at the ripe old age of ninety one. The Hamlet appears to be in a time warp as nothing has changed apart from the building of a new village hall. In the old one I used to enjoy playing snooker and darts and winning prizes at Whist! During our stay in Westcliff we had no war damage but no sooner had we settled in Magdalen Laver than a V2 rocket dropped in the field opposite and blew several windows out. My sister was in the bedroom with the wardrobe door open, which fell on her when the rocket went off. My mother was calling out "Joyce, Joyce where are you?" We heard this muffled sound and found she was inside the wardrobe. We were cheek by jowl with the fields and I used to go out and help with the harvest and ride on the back of the horse drawn carts which I thoroughly enjoyed.

Before the war ended German prisoners of war used to come and help with the harvest on the farm and I talked to them. The farm manager who was my father's church warden said "If you're going to start fraternising with the enemy I shall have to tell your father," but it was all very innocent. I only chatted with them but we struggled to understand each other. I cannot remember if I obeyed the farmer! Anyway I loved it there and I would cycle the four miles unaccompanied to Harlow for the Youth Fellowship on a Friday evening but there were no lights on the road at all. You could in those days without fear. Later when I had passed my driving test I was allowed to take the car.

The Rectory was a huge house with a moat all the way round and we had ducks, chickens, goats, cats and a dog. We used to have to milk the goats, one of which was called 'Grandma' because she was very old. She would kick you when you were milking her so you had to use one hand to hold her leg and milk with the other one. There was no gas or electricity in the house, so we used Tilley lamps and candles. Often in the winter there was ice on the inside of the windows and in the bitter winter of 1947 virgin snow lay thickly on all the fields. It was a beautiful sight. Magdalen Laver church is virtually in the middle of the fields, so it took some getting there. In order to get to Herts and Essex High School in Bishop's Stortford we were taken the four miles by car to Harlow Station to get there by train.

During 1947 we had to take a shovel to dig our way through the drifts or not go at all. The only heating in the Rectory was a Rayburn in the kitchen with small open fires in the other large rooms. My mother washed the clothes in a brick-built boiler with a fire underneath. We had two very large walk-in larders, containing my mother's home-made jam and bottled fruit in Kilner jars. In the old Rectory, half way up the stairs, was a green baize door and the toilet was behind the door and two empty rooms where my father stored the apples and pears from the orchard. This was originally the maid's quarter, but we had no maid or nanny.

Above the baize door was a blue glass window shedding an eerie light which made it all rather scary because like Jane Eyre we feared what was behind the green baize door. When my friend came to stay, we would wake each other up if we wanted to go to the toilet in the night but as I say I loved it there. Later the old rectory was sold and a new one built for us but it lacked the character of the old one.

My father was there for sixteen years taking all the services, ringing the bells, stoking the boilers and bringing some of the congregation to church in his car. My mother and I shared the playing of the organ at Magdalen and High Laver. It was operated by a hand held pump, if the person pumping got

The church at Magdalen Laver

The church at High Laver

distracted the music would end with a wail. It was from there that I left to go to college to train as a Junior school teacher in Darlington for two years. During the holidays I used to go home to the newly built Rectory at Magdalen Laver, where in the summer vacations I would help with the harvest again. Sadly the horses were no longer there but I still used to love helping on the farm driving the tractors, spending many happy hours from early morning buzzing around the country lanes.

On leaving college I went to teach in Tonbridge at Sussex Road Primary School. The headmistress was a committed Christian who encouraged and supported me as I struggled in my first year both spiritually and as a teacher.

The old Rectory at Magdalen Laver

My father's new Rectory at Magdalen Laver

It is only with hindsight that I have seen the hand of God in my life in people who have carried me through doubts, and the experiences I have had. Whilst there I belonged to an evangelical Church and became a leader in the Youth Group called 'Campaigners'. They are similar to Guides and Brownies but with a much stronger Christian link. I took classes and occasionally spent a week-end away at camp. On October 3rd 1953 I went to a youth meeting in London run by The Church Mission Society in Salisbury Square. When I was talking to the area secretary I asked him if he knew of any CMS activity in the Tonbridge area. At that moment Brian Ash walked past and we were introduced. He said "This is the man you need to meet. He is running a local group." I had met my future husband!

As it happened both of us belonged to the Tonbridge Philharmonic Choir but hadn't actually met before, although I had spotted him across the Chancel of the Church where we rehearsed. From then on our relationship developed and we were married on August 25th 1956 by the Rev. Raymond Fountain just outside Tonbridge at Hildenborough church. At the time Brian was a bank clerk.

I never wanted to marry a clergyman neither did my sister Joyce. I've never really understood why we felt like that because we had a happy childhood. It may have been the financial stringency, far worse in those days than today. It could have been the lack of privacy, your home was never your own because the needs of parishioners were paramount. My father's parish was in a rather deprived area of Westcliff and I remembered the stringency of my parents' lives combined with living through the terrifying years of the war. All this may have contributed to the feeling that I never wanted to become a clergy wife.

I was dead against Brian becoming a clergyman although I knew he wanted to explore the idea. We were on very good terms with the vicar Raymond Fountain and his wife Anne in Hildenborough and they often used to invite us up there, we had many happy hours sharing meals together. They had known Brian for several years before we met and knew of his desire to enter the Ministry and were very concerned that I did not share his feelings on the matter. One time when we were there for lunch Raymond said to me "Would you mind coming into the study with me to have a chat?" So, I went in there. I can't remember a word he said but I walked out of that room with a totally different attitude.

*Our wedding
in 1956*

David and the twins in 1962

It must have been the Holy Spirit at work in me because from then on I accepted it. So in October 1959 Brian became a theological student resident in The London College of Divinity in Northwood, Middlesex, for the next three years. Our idea was to start a family after he was ordained but things did not turn out that way! David was born in January 1960 and the twins Nicholas and Jacqueline arrived in March 1962.

Unlike life today students were allowed home only at half-term and for the married men an extra week-end during the second half of the term. Fortunately I had very supportive in-laws just around the corner who came to our bungalow most days to help me. My parents were still in their remote parish but they came to stay when they could and friends invited me round, so life was not too stressful.

Eventually Brian was invited to serve his curacy in the large city centre church of St. Andrew's, Plymouth, in Devon. So, waving goodbye to his parents with a mixture of apprehension and excitement, Brian and I set off in our Morris Minor Traveller overnight with three children under two tucked down in the back. Our clergy life was about to begin! At six o'clock in the morning we arrived in front of an enormous double fronted terraced Victorian house with five bedrooms, three reception rooms, a large kitchen and scullery. The rooms were high with embossed ceilings and without central heating. We were about to face the bad winter of 1962 to '63 feeling freezing cold. It was one of the worst on record.

St. Andrew's was the main parish church with five curates. Soon after we arrived another curate and his wife and baby son joined the staff. Their flat was all frozen up so they had to come and live with us for a fortnight. In the kitchen there was a Welsh dresser from floor to ceiling and a Rayburn above which were two airers on pulleys. All three babies were in nappies, which had to be washed, so it was like a Chinese laundry as they hung above our heads. The Rayburn in the kitchen did its best to keep us warm and the vicar gave us an oil stove to put in the hallway but it made a pitiful impact. The cold spell lasted for about six weeks and flocks of sheep were found frozen together on Dartmoor.

On Sundays Brian would go off early to the church. I would have to get all three children ready and set off the good mile down the hill with the twins in their push chair and David trotting along beside. In spite of all this I think it was another one of the happy places I've lived in and still keep in touch with friends made there. I loved the moors, I loved the sea and when Brian was working I'd 'tootle' off on a day trip to the beach. Our days off together took us further a-field over the Tamar bridge or onto remote moor-land where we enjoyed climbing the rugged tors of Dartmoor.

The total number of children amongst the four curates was about seven, which rose to eight when Elizabeth our youngest was born in our house on September 21st 1965. The midwife who attended her birth was a member of The Elim Gospel Hall, and as soon as she was born she said "Shall we pray over her?" A lovely thought.

As I had rather a large family I was not expected to take on any parochial duties except for hosting a Young Wives' Group in our house and occasionally sharing activities with the Youth Group. They turned out to make wonderful baby-sitters, enjoying it more if the twins woke up!

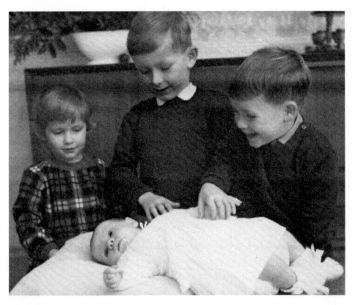

*Our complete
family in 1965*

Brian, now a vicar

Sadly in 1966, after four short years there, Brian felt called to work for the CMS as area Secretary, this involved going round to different parishes to give talks about the missionary society. That was the unhappiest time in my clergy life. We went to live in a village called Loose near Maidstone, a delightful little place. It was the first time in my life that I had lived in an ordinary house in an ordinary street and I felt very unsettled. Brian would be away at conferences or out for a lot of week-ends and evenings preaching from one end of Kent to the other, thus making it impossible for him to attend church with us as a family on some Sundays. It was a lovely house with a lovely garden because it was all much more compact and manageable. The children enjoyed their schools and their friends but I felt rootless and out on a limb. I did some part-time teaching when Liz was about three. The headmaster let me take her with me and she would sit in the class with the children. They thoroughly enjoyed looking after her whilst I was teaching. I tried three different churches in Loose and Maidstone, sometimes doing a little Sunday school teaching. Eventually I came back to the little church I'd first been to in Loose for the rest of the seven years we were there.

We were then about to take the biggest step of our lives by moving to Bromley in Kent to St. Augustine's church on Bromley Common. It was the first time that Brian had been a vicar and the first time that I had been a vicar's wife. We were to be there for twenty four very happy years, it was where the children grew up and were launched into their careers of nursing and teaching. Eventually they all married and produced seven grandchildren for

us. I was very nervous when we arrived; I shall never forget Brian's induction service. I expected to go unobtrusively into the church but as soon as I stepped through the door with the children in tow, the church wardens with their wands paraded us down to the front of the church. I could feel every eye upon me, but I need not have worried, everyone was very friendly and made us feel at home. A large flower arrangement greeted us at the vicarage and future friends came to help us make the beds. The garden was very big and needed a lot of attention. A big mansion had been on the site many years before which had burnt down. Following that, another large house was built which was bombed later during the war. Having decided to build a Church and Vicarage on the site, the consequential rubble was bulldozed back, flattened and grassed over.

We spent seven years on most days off clearing tons of rubble and creating flower beds, thus making it possible for us and the parish to use it for many different functions such as garden parties and family weddings. The Play Group in the Church Hall came out to play and enjoyed rolling down the slopes, whilst bouncy castles sprang into life on several occasions. Since we left on our retirement in 1997 the vicarage has been extended.

Above:
St. Augustine's
Church Bromley
Common

Right:
Our new vicarage
at Bromley

We could have done with that extra space as my mother came to live with us after my father died and we still had four children at home. We had to make Brian's study into her bedroom and he moved into the church office. We were not too far from Brian's parents in Hildenborough, so we were able to enjoy their visits until they both died.

As the children grew up and became more independent I decided to do some part-time teaching. First I went to a local Junior school in the parish occasionally doing supply teaching which was not so enjoyable. Eventually I spent seventeen years teaching music in an International Junior Boarding School in Chislehurst just ten minutes from home. A friend had asked me if I played the piano and as a result I joined the staff of this Methodist-based Christian School. I taught recorders and took singing classes but eventually landed up producing a musical each term. Christmas and Easter were on Biblical themes and in the summer I produced secular ones such as 'Alice Through the Looking Glass,' 'Mary Poppins,' 'The Wizard of Oz' and a few from the BBC productions.

Above: Our garden, after all our hard work, used for many different functions

Left: The choir at St. Augustine's, where as the need arose, I became mistress and organist

I tried to use every child in the school, encouraging their ability to sing and to act. It was another one of the very happy periods of my life, and we still have quite regular contact with some of the staff.

I was fully involved in the life of the church and in the role of vicar's wife. My first opportunity was to help run a Junior Choir on Thursday afternoons after school. The idea was that as soon as they were confident and if they wished to, they became full members of the regular Sunday Choir. Having helped with that, after a time I not only became a member of the choir myself but as the need arose became choir mistress and organist. I indulged my interest in music and drama by producing Christian musicals that were enacted in church. One producer would take the drama, one would be the choreographer and I would lead the choir and music. I also helped with the Youth Group called Pathfinders, teaching on Sundays and occasionally going away with them for week-ends to various camp venues.

At the vicarage we'd sometimes get desperate people needing help in all sort of ways, including a great variety of tramps. One of them always announced himself as Thomas the Tramp, another wore a deaf aid and shouted his orders before you'd hardly opened the door "Cup o' tea and a cheese sandwich." Some made you weep with their inadequate situations, dressed in the thinnest of clothes on a freezing night. We kept a supply for them but sometimes Brian's had to be used when nothing else was available.

The tramp we got to know best was Frank, a broad Scot who lived in a shed in the garden of a neighbouring vicarage. He helped us to recreate our neglected garden. Although 'down and out' Frank was a clever man. He knew each flower by its Latin name and sat doing the Times crossword over his tea at the kitchen table. Sadly we heard he had died whilst on the road some years later.

I couldn't help being slightly amused once when I found myself entertaining in the kitchen over an afternoon cup of tea a drug addict who claimed to have beaten up a policeman and robbed banks and jewellery shops to get money for his habit. It was a very sad situation because he came from a very respectable home in Chislehurst.

Ian was a young man who was found sleeping rough under the railway bridge. We gave him a bed for several weeks at the back of our garage and through gentle handling and placing of Christian books when he came in for meals, he showed an interest and eventually became a Christian, which makes all the hassle worth going through. We once had to foster a young child of five who needed rescuing from a dire home situation for a few weeks. She is now about forty and still keeps in touch at Christmas to see how 'Uncle Brian and Aunty Jean' are getting on.

Being a vicar's wife means sharing your husband with many other people. You might be in the middle of a conversation or just about to put a meal on the table, when the phone or door would go and he'd be called away. I enjoyed the variety of ways for which the garden was used, as previously mentioned. Our planning, digging and creating have reaped their reward. However, unlike most families whose husbands go out to work, we were able to eat most of our meals together and share broken time, so when he retired it wasn't such a shock to have him around all the time, he was the one who experienced the greatest difference.

Our children were all involved in Pathfinders and the choir in their younger days. As a result of going to Christian camps in the summer they each made a Christian commitment to follow Christ in their turn. Now in retirement it is no longer life at the vicarage but it is still a life of fulfilment as we seek to serve God in our local church and community here in Essex. Brian takes services during interregnums and has preached in our own church in Rayleigh on several occasions.

We are still a close family and use birthdays and Christmases as an excuse to get together. David and his wife are fully involved in their church in Birmingham leading Taize services with David belonging to The New English Orchestra Christian Choir. We have both joined the church choir and the local Bach Choir. I occasionally play the keyboard for the informal service and have taken on the role of Choir Mistress whilst waiting for a new organist. Nick has been ordained as a Non-Stipendiary Priest, teaching part-time in the local Church school, well supported by his wife and two daughters.

Jacky, Jonathan and their family of two children are fully involved in their local church but having ME Jacky is unable to do as much as she would like. Liz and Chris met when they were both members of the community in the Lee Abbey Christian Holiday Conference Centre in Devon. They now belong to their local Kings' Church, where all three boys help to lead the worship in a variety of ways. We pray constantly for them as our grandchildren grow up in this very different and uncertain world.

Now as Brian and I look back on our three score years and twenty, I can honestly say that I'm glad I became a vicar's wife, as it gave me greater confidence in myself and a trust in Our Lord from whose shared Ministry we never retire.

SYLVIA PERRY

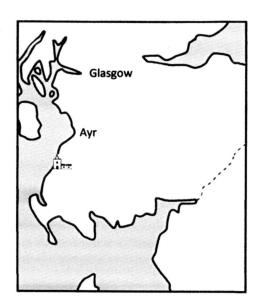

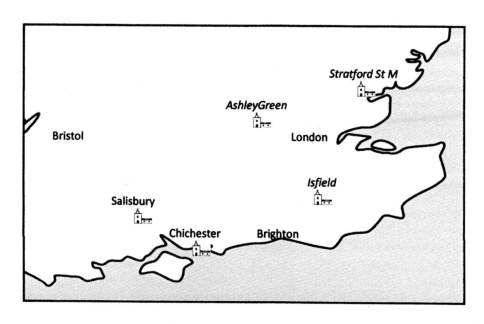

SYLVIA'S STORY

'My children have to come first'

My name is Sylvia Perry, not my real name but how I wish to be known. I was born in 1928 into a poor family. My father was a chef on Pullman trains but during the great recession of the 1930s he lost his job and then worked as a bus conductor. He had been a sailor but had left the navy to stay with his wife and family. He wasn't a religious man but one of my abiding memories of him is his frequent singing of two hymns 'Eternal Father, Strong to Save, Who's Arm Doth Bind the Restless Wave' and his other favourite 'Abide With me, Fast Falls the Eventide, the Darkness Deepens, Lord With me Abide'.

My mother was a devoted member of the church and dad was happy for her to go regularly to Evensong. Her motto in life was 'All things work together for good to those who love God.' When we were old enough she took us with her and my brother Keith was in the choir as soon as he could sing. I was sent to Sunday school on a regular basis and loved all the social life it held for us, the annual Sunday school outings, the parties and sales.

We never had any holidays because we couldn't afford them and we lived in a small two up and two down rented house, but the coastal town where we lived in Sussex provided everything I needed for a happy childhood.

My brother was two years older than me and was my role model. He passed The Scholarship, as it was in those days, and attended the local Grammar School. When I passed two years later my father insisted I should also be educated and sent me to the local High School for Girls. None of my friends from primary school came with me and I found myself in a different world. Part of the clothing grant from the local authority had been used to kit out my brother and I didn't have the right colour coat. I felt I had come into a crowd of rich people and felt ashamed of our poverty.

The whole family was deeply affected by war. My mother had lost her fiancé Fred; he was killed at the Somme in 1918 and had been destined to be a priest.

Upper: Fred, killed at The Somme

Centre: My mother as he knew her

Lower: My father in World War One

She talked of him often and I still have his photograph. I have a feeling that he still had an influence on our lives, as you will see.

My father, whom she married eight years later, had run away to sea at the age of fourteen and become a Petty Officer. He witnessed the Battle of Jutland from a Destroyer in 1916 and was present at the Dardanelles in the naval engagement at Gallipoli in 1915. He never talked to me about his experiences but did tell Keith about them.

The Second World War affected us all very deeply. Keith and I were evacuated in 1940 when France fell to the Germans. We were sent to Hertfordshire but separated by eighteen miles because we went with our schools. My father was made redundant again, because so many people had left the coast there were not enough left to keep all the buses going. He joined the National Fire Service, living in the Fire Station for two nights out of three. At every air raid they had to deal with the fires and dig people out of the rubble.

My mother visited us once in 1941 and then sadly she died when I was twelve. Ten days later Keith was run over by a lorry and not expected to live. Apparently he regained consciousness when a ward service was in progress. The Dean of St. Alban's Abbey came over and said to my thirteen year old brother "When you are dead I shall pray for your soul." Keith however survived and when he was well enough he went to the Abbey to show himself to the Dean, who then said to him "God has given you your life back, what are you going to do with it?" Perhaps he was sowing a seed because much later Keith was to become a priest. During these dark days his recovery was a miracle that lifted me out of a state of desperate pain and despair. I felt my mother must have been watching over him and God had appointed her as our Guardian Angel, a philosophy that stayed with me for the rest of my life. Sometimes, though, I think she went off duty for a while but always seemed to come back in time to prevent total disaster. I was away for four and a half years, but that is another story. An important thing to say here though, is that my experiences of war initiated a loss of church life for me and put my faith on hold.

My foster parents were kind enough but they blasphemed a lot and didn't believe in God. They were from the East End of London and had been given a Council House on a huge Estate under a re-housing scheme. I tried going to the main parish church but the vicar was a very old man with a reed-like voice and no one spoke to me at all, just left me sitting by myself. So I tried another church, which was quite a long way from where I was billeted, but no one spoke to me there either, so I gave up.

Before my mother died she had put me in touch with a private nursing friend she knew from church who was looking after an old gentleman in the town but she was too evangelical for me and every time we met she just kept asking me "Do you love the Lord Jesus?" As I was so unhappy it gave me no comfort and anyway I felt if there was a God how could He allow this terrible war with all its devastation and cruelty? Then the nurse moved away when her patient died and I never saw her again. My foster parents got into a habit of sending me down to the back door of the pub on Sunday mornings to collect their beer and I was ashamed to meet my school friends as I struggled home with a bag full of heavy bottles but even that experience didn't persuade me to go back to church.

After I returned home I lived with my grandfather for a year and then my father remarried and I stayed with him and my stepmother in her house for a year and a half working as a telephone operator at a huge Post Office switchboard. I went back to the church my mother had taken me to and joined a Youth Club which the new vicar set up for all the young people returning from the war and there I found my faith again and became confirmed. The previous priest who had seen us all off when we were evacuated had been sent to a country parish after the vicarage, a few yards along the road from our house, was bombed tragically killing his two year old daughter Deidre. I found a lovely boyfriend at this church Youth club and my brother, who had been working in London and separated from me for years, came back to live as well and also joined the church.

When I left for London to start my training at King's College Hospital in Camberwell my boyfriend gave me up because I had moved away and my brother felt I had deserted him again but after a few months had passed he left his job and went to The London College of Divinity to train as a priest under Dr. Coggan. The College had been evacuated to Surrey, so again I saw very little of him because I was too involved with my training as a nurse. Whilst I was at King's, Father Tate at St. John the Divine church in Kennington held meetings for young student nurses who were trying to come to terms with the human dramas they were encountering on a daily basis on the wards. He was just there to listen to us as we learned to deal with healing and death. I have never forgotten him, sitting there in his cassock in his own house and offering us coffee and a space in a totally relaxed way.

I also trained as a midwife and Queen's District Nurse and was sent to work in Seaford in Sussex as a Queen's Nurse Midwife. This meant we carried out general nursing as well as midwifery. Whilst I was there a colleague and I attended the local parish church and also decided to join the church Youth Group for older members run by the curate. The first evening we went there was a dance and, corny as it may sound, as we walked into the room the music was playing 'Some Enchanted Evening you will see a stranger, you will see a stranger across a crowded room.' I looked across the room and found the curate holding my gaze.

After that during his sermons I would try to catch his eye and then he developed an infection and I was sent to his lodgings to give him penicillin injections as it was administered in those days. The rest as they say is history.

Very early on Easter Sunday morning in 1954, before the eight o'clock communion service, Leonard came and put an engagement ring on my finger and we were married on September 18th by his vicar who advised us to move to another parish as every eye would be upon us in the small town where we were so well known. My father gave me away and seemed so proud that his daughter had become a professional person and married into the church.

For my husband Leonard it was a second marriage. He had originally been a maths teacher but when war broke out he went into the medical unit of the RAF. He was stationed just outside Coventry and was there

My husband in World War Two

during the Blitz. He married a girl he met at St. John's Church but sadly she was dead within three months. When he left the Forces after six years he went to Kings in the Strand on a course for ex-Service men and became ordained under Bishop Bell of Chichester. When his mother heard he was to become ordained she realised he would never make much money and perhaps she would have preferred him to have an easier time financially than she herself had had as a war widow. Our wedding was slightly marred by the fact that she died unexpectedly six weeks before, but it all went ahead as planned because we felt that is what she would have wanted. His father was killed at the Somme in March 1918 when he was a year old but he did have one

sister Minnie, three years older than him. She remained unmarried and very much in touch with us for the rest of her life and has recently died at the age of ninety seven. To me Len was a minor polymath not just a priest, he loved the sciences, nature, the universe, literature and drew me into all these interests. He was my soul mate but he was also a man of his time and did not expect me to work and also we decided we wanted to start a family straight away. I realised that I could not cope with the huge responsibilities of my work, marry a priest and have a family so I went along with that. We also agreed to take the vicar's advice and move to another parish. He was offered another curacy in West Sussex. My brother who was also ordained by then was working as a curate in London. He got married ten days after us and we came back a couple of days early from our Honeymoon in Sidmouth so that I could be a Matron of Honour.

I must admit that whilst we were engaged I never really thought about what it would entail exactly to be the wife of a priest. Len made some attempt to explain it all, but as we were only engaged for six months and so bowled over by events and finding time to be together at all with our busy lives, it wasn't a great topic. We went straight from our Honeymoon to this lovely house called Rose Garden that had been bought for the curate. When we arrived at this spacious house our sticks of furniture seemed to disappear. It was a bit spooky but I revelled in its space. We had no fridge in those days but a larder with a slate shelf to keep everything cool. The garden had a soft fruit area covered in

Opposite:
Our Wedding Day

Left:
Our lovely curate's house

broken net but its most striking feature was the pond and it also had a large conservatory. I was woken up on our first morning at about five o'clock. I had been roused by a wall of sound, the sound of bird-song; a glorious dawn chorus that made me feel I had been transported into another world. It was coming from the bird sanctuary at nearby Pagham and it held me in thrall.

Every day Leonard said Evensong regularly at five o'clock and whatever was happening he went to the church to say it there. In the parish was a Deaconess whom I held in some awe and we got off to a very difficult start. One day Leonard and I had our first disagreement. I have no recall what it was about but I do remember that torrential rain was falling as he left the house to say Evensong. Our differences had not been ironed out and as he left I cried my eyes out. Then of course the door bell went but I was in no fit state to answer it. I heard somebody go round the back and open the conservatory and then leave. When I went to investigate a large bunch of flowers had been left. Of course it was the Deaconess coming to introduce herself and when she met me a few days later, she told me she knew my husband would be out and came to have a chat. She could see I was in because a light was on and "You wouldn't have left a dog out in that rain." I couldn't bring myself to explain. It would have felt like a betrayal to admit that priests and their wives occasionally fell out. I've never forgotten the experience and it made me realise that whatever the emotion or problem you have to be ready to answer the door. I had already had professional training, so I should have known better. However I soon had a similar experience myself. The vicar was a very rich man and in fact his family had built the church themselves. The first time I called to meet his wife and introduce myself I took a bunch of flowers but the door was opened by the butler who simply stated "Madam is not at home." I never tried to call on her again so that was another difficult start. I was left with a feeling that we were not destined to be happy there.

I had learned to ride a bike late in life because I never had one as an evacuee child. I was issued with one to use in London as a pupil midwife on the District and as a Queen's nurse in training but we only covered small close areas. I never enjoyed riding the thing and always pushed it down steep hills as well as up. After we were married Leonard bought me one because we could not afford a car. There was a Billy Graham Crusade several miles away during February 1955 and we were given instruction before taking part. I was engaged as a counsellor for those who came forward and interviewed converts from age eleven to forty-five as they made their commitment to follow the way of Christ. I felt I was able to deal with that but it was the bike rides that bothered me. I couldn't understand why I felt so exhausted after the long ride home until it dawned on me that it was too much for me because I was three months pregnant.

I joined the Young Wives' Group but just as a member because the existing leader was happy to stay in office. I was lonely and realised that by moving to the new parish so soon after our wedding I missed my colleagues and friends and neither of us had a mum to visit and comfort us, so I was glad to be an ordinary member of the Young Wives'. I was asked to become the Enrolling Member of The Mothers' Union and felt very nervous in my heavily pregnant state when I turned up for the Service to be officially installed. Leonard told Mrs. Vicar how I was feeling but her only comment was "She'll soon get used to it," and so I did but it also dawned on me that Leonard was not happy with his situation either and had asked Bishop Bell for a move. Although he had requested to move when we married Len did not find it easy to tolerate the frustrations of this curacy. In the previous one he had been given a lot of responsibility, he had had war service and been widowed and felt he was being treated like a youngster from college. The Bishop was understanding and offered him to be Priest-in-Charge of Isfield and part of a team Ministry in Uckfield and Horsted Parva. We went to view the house and situation but because my baby was due we could not move until after the birth. The house at Isfield had been empty for eighteen months and was festooned with cobwebs, hanging in great loops, so at least the delay gave us the chance to clean it up a bit.

Meantime the Young Wives' were lovely and held a Baby Shower for me giving me lots of presents for the baby. I took to taking an afternoon rest as the summer got hotter and hotter in the lovely garden by the pond in the shade. There I saw pond life at its best. I watched fascinated as dragon flies emerged from their pupae and frogs from tadpoles and I saw a snake eat a small frog whole. I made jam from the fruit in the garden and became absorbed in becoming a mother. Leonard was happier and looked forward to the birth and a fresh start in a new parish. Our son Stephen was born in August 1955 during the night at The Zachary Merton Hospital. Len of course was sent straight home when I was admitted as no husbands were allowed anywhere near a delivery in those days. I found myself in the next bed to a young woman who was very distressed because she had given birth to a Thalidomide baby with no arms and felt she couldn't keep him. The nurses asked me to comfort her and try to persuade her to take him home but I can't remember the outcome.

We had served in the last curacy for just one year and on the day in September in 1955 when we moved into a house named Greenways in Isfield, Stephen screamed his head off because my milk had disappeared completely with the stress of it all. Greenways lived up to its name as the house was surrounded by and immersed in greenery. Here Leonard and the team leader in charge of Uckfield parish and one other priest worked well together managing several services between them and only once turning up at the same time to take the same service.

We still had no car but the house was opposite the railway station and as Stephen grew up there he spent a long time looking out of the front window at the steam trains. One day he called me urgently, "Mummy, mummy you must come." I ran into the lounge and he wanted me to see the first Diesel train to go through. The church was isolated from the village, the story being that at the time of the Black Death in 1348 the priest burnt down the houses in an attempt to stop the spread of the disease. It was a beautiful church, very peacefully painted white inside with an outstanding tomb.

Whilst we were there our second son Kenneth was born in August 1957. He was delivered at home whilst two year old Stephen went to tea with one of the parishioners and this time there was no escape for Leonard as he helped the lone midwife bring his son into the world. Although we had no family to help us the parishioners were very kind and flooded me with flowers and gifts for the baby. We had been there for just two years when Kenneth was born and Bishop Bell offered Leonard a move when he was just four days old and I was still in bed. I felt unable to move again so soon after a birth but Leonard went to see the two churches of Pycombe and Newtimber and then turned them down. Later I realised that he had been very influenced by me in a post natal state and felt very guilty about it. It made me determine never to stand in his way again whatever the situation. I think if he had gone there we would have stayed buried in the heart of Sussex for the rest of his working life but as you will see things turned out very differently. In Isfield with a baby and a toddler, the nearness of the train station was a great asset. I was able to take the pram in the guards van to go shopping in Uckfield. It was a deep welled old pram with Kenneth inside and Stephen sitting safely perched on a seat at the end.

We stayed in Isfield another two years until June 1959 when we moved to Ashley Green, a parish in Buckinghamshire near Berkhampstead. Here we lived at the heart of the village green, very close to the church and school. The house was enormous with eight bedrooms and no central heating. There were three stoves that needed constant refuelling, one in the huge hallway, one in the study and one in the lounge but most of the heat disappeared up the central well of the house. However it was a lively parish and they made us very welcome. Leonard bought himself a Scooter as we still had no car and he had a second small parish to serve. There was an old caravan in the glebe next to the garden and one of the church wardens informed us that we had inherited a lodger because there was nowhere else for him to go, assuring us he would be no trouble, which he wasn't until the weather got cold.

I still maintained the office of Enrolling Member of the Mothers' Union but had no one to look after the boys when I took the meetings. After trying to keep them quiet one day I rebelled and told Leonard it wasn't fair on the children and I would not be taking the Mothers' Union any more. He quite agreed and suggested I visited someone he thought might like to take over. It was the local builder's wife but he had recently died. She asked me in and said "Come and see Dad" and there he was in the lounge in a coffin with the lid off, which was common practice in those days. I paid my respects to him but didn't mention the MU. However when she got over her loss she took it on and it became a major part of her life.

As time went by I felt the strain of our poverty and decided to do something about it. The top third floor of the house in the distant past had been the servants' quarters and was shut off by a staircase so I turned it into a flat and rented it out to the second teacher at the school. We became friends and I am still in touch with her at Christmas. I also turned the glebe at the back of the house into a place to rear hens. I bought a small piece of equipment called an electric hen and placed the day old chicks under it until they were strong enough to run in and out of a barn onto the village green and glebe. I reared seventy-six at a time and sold them at sixteen weeks at point of lay. One had something wrong with her so I took her into the kitchen and nursed her until she recovered and then had to keep her as a pet. She ran with the others but always came and laid me an egg in a box by the back door. We also kept a goat which I milked every day. One day she escaped and took off down the village past the school when the children were out to play with Leonard in hot pursuit. They all ran to the railing laughing their heads off but were reprimanded by the Headmistress for laughing at the vicar, but he could see the funny side of it and fortunately managed to catch the goat and bring her back. Although the house was so big and unmanageable I was enjoying making use of the top floor and the glebe and the boys loved the hen and the goat Suzy. With the pocket-money from selling eggs and hens we were able to buy our first television set from an auction sale when I was thirty-three years old.

One of the parishioners said "Now you'll have time for nothing." But she was proved wrong because I started a Young Wives' Group which I could manage more easily because it was held in the evening.

Greenways, the house at Isfield

The church at Isfield

Ashley Green house

Everything seemed to be going well with our lives there until we were hit by the severe winter of 1962 to '63. Len came off his scooter as he tried to negotiate the ice on the way home from a Christmas morning service at Whelpley Hill, a hamlet with the second church in the Parish. We were all waiting for him to eat our Christmas dinner and although he didn't appear to be badly hurt apart from a cut knee it was the beginning of a disastrous chapter for him health-wise. The snow fell and lay all around us in deep drifts. The lodger in the caravan could not keep warm so we let him in to warm himself by the stove in the hallway. Then as it got deeper he couldn't get over to us so I found myself taking dinners over to him.

It was a great struggle to keep our house warm enough when suddenly Leonard became desperately ill on the first of February with bronchitis, pleurisy and a viral pneumonia. Two doctors came to see him and decided he could not be moved to the hospital so I would have to nurse him at home and because they queried TB at the time I could not let the boys into the bedroom. They would wait at the door whilst I was in the bedroom. I could no longer cope with the chickens and the goat and had to quickly find another home for them all. I also had all the stoking to do to keep us alive. The church warden was a very unsympathetic man and agreed to arrange the services for one Sunday only when Leonard was first taken ill and then left the arrangements to me.

One Sunday I realised that the priest who was coming to take Evensong had not turned up, so I asked Leonard what I should do. "Why you will take it yourself of course" he said with about ten minutes to go. "You won't be able to give the blessing and you have no sermon prepared, so just stand in the front pew and lead Evensong." In those days the church was pretty well attended for the evening service. I struggled across to the church in the snow and did as he asked and was so pleased when the head teacher at the school said to me as she left the church "You know I really enjoyed that." We had no family to help us, Minnie was in Sussex and working for Lewes County Council but a very kind parishioner called with home made cakes and colouring books for the boys. Of course the snow went away and Leonard began to recover. I sat on the bed and cried as I realised he was going to make it. He stroked my head saying "Just let it all come, it's the most natural thing in the world."

The Bishop came to see us, I can't remember his name but he was a darling. He said that Leonard was to have a convalescent holiday and then he would arrange a move to the West Country because he needed to get out of this cold house and work in a warmer part of the country. So in April all four of us went to Torquay for a convalescent holiday for two weeks and on the seventeenth of May Len resumed work, three and a half months after he had been taken ill. The Bishop was as good as his word and first we were offered a Living near Yeovil but did not accept because the house again was huge, it had no central heating, a huge glebe area to maintain and a second parish that needed a car to get to and we still didn't have one.

Another offer was made and this time we accepted a small country parish near Salisbury with a beautiful Rectory that had been designed by the architect Butterworth. We moved on 9th October 1963 after three years and three months at Ashley Green. It was a difficult move to manage with no car, so Len decided to travel down in the moving van and sent me off in a bus with the two boys to travel by train. The bus stopped right outside the village school where the children were all out to play. Stephen's best friend Nicky saw us and ran over to the fence to say goodbye. As we boarded the bus he called out "Mrs. P don't forget to remind Steve when my birthday is!" As the bus drew away they waved frantically to each other and Stephen broke down, sobbing loudly. I felt such a 'heel', so when we arrived in London and had to wait a while for a train I took them both to the station cinema for a treat to watch cartoons.

Whilst we were in there I suddenly realised I'd not made a note of the hotel Len had booked for the night in Salisbury because the furniture would be stored and unloaded the next day. I rang home just in time as Len was about to leave the house to get into the van and he told me it was The White Hart. He also said he had forgotten the lunch I'd left in the oven for him until the moving men asked what was burning and it was too late to save. We arrived at The White Hart and I put the boys to bed and sat in the window waiting for the van to arrive and drop Len off. When he hadn't come by ten o'clock I began to get worried and could see myself as homeless with two small boys with no money and no furniture but of course the van was just a bit late due to a hold up and when he eventually arrived he was a bit tired but none the worse for wear. We were to spend four productive years in this small parish. At first it was a question of recovering and getting used to a new environment.

The house lent itself to our needs but again had no central heating but a Rayburn in the huge kitchen and stoves in the study, lounge and dining room. The kitchen looked across the fields to the river and was the hub of the house where we ate unless we had company. Its one drawback was the floor which consisted of paving stones that needed scrubbing on my hands and knees. It was huge and just like scrubbing the pavement outside. The massive front door was painted blue and studded. Just inside in the hallway years later we were to discover ancient murals that had been covered over. They read: 'Unless The Lord Build The House, Their Labour Be But Lost That Build It' and 'As For Me And My House, We Will Serve The Lord.'

The small green corrugated iron church hall was at the side of the garden. The boys went along to the village school and found soul mates. Kenneth our second son had his tonsils out during another bout of snowy weather trapping us in the village but we were rescued this time by a parishioner who came along with chains on his car wheels determined to get me into hospital to see my boy. He then, poor dear, died himself a few months later. After seven months there we were able to buy an 'old banger' from a neighbour in the village for twenty five pounds. It was a huge car for me but I had not forgotten my driving skills and my licence was still valid by a few months, which made me realise we had been over nine years without a car. With cushions all around me I found a new freedom and we shared it amicably.

In this parish one of the church wardens' wives ran the Mothers' Union and I started a Young Wives' Group. Len started a group for the village children and grew in strength from day to day. We always had the church annual fête in the Rectory garden and one year as we stood in the front doorway, watching everybody disappear at the end of the day and closed the huge studded door shut in a state of exhaustion we hadn't noticed that Kenneth was standing beside us with one of his hands on the doorpost until I realised that we'd shut the great blue studded door on his wee fingers. We rushed him straight to the Casualty department in the car. Fortunately only one nail was badly damaged and he still bears the scar today.

Len had fully recovered his vigour and took us to Poole in Dorset to visit his aunt, his mother's sister. We found her lonely and unwell and decided to take her in to live with us and gave her the study for a room downstairs and converted the dining room into a study. She loved the boys and every week when she drew her pension she would see what was left from the week before and give them some pocket money telling them to run to the village shop and buy sweets. It worked well because I loved her too and she became for me I suppose the mother figure I didn't have and another woman in the house. Unfortunately she died in my arms one evening after I'd put the boys to bed. It was they who comforted me the next day with their arms round me "Don't cry mummy she has gone to heaven now." When she was buried in the churchyard two kind parishioners came along to the service although they had hardly known aunty.

Before Len's illness we had decided to adopt a baby and had our names on the waiting list of an overseas project. Our names had been down for over two years so we assumed it would never happen, but as Len recovered, he wanted to go on with the idea. Eventually a little Chinese girl arrived on the 20th December 1963 aged two and a half years. A neighbour in the village had an adopted daughter and boys of her own and came to give me support and advice which I needed as this already formed strong little character took charge of our lives. One of the old ladies in the parish asked my husband how long it would take her to become white.

In 1964 in June we were invited by Billy Butlin to a free holiday in Skegness; he took on Clergy families and my brother Keith and his family went for the same week. It was a lovely change for us because apart from the convalescent break we had only managed two locums in Sussex at Hastings. These were great but took a lot of organising. We had to make sure our own parish was covered and take the services, funerals and weddings where we went plus domestically leaving everything spick and span for the locum covering our place, getting used to other people's domestic arrangements and hoping the children would not damage anything. So after these experiences a Billy Butlin holiday was a gift indeed and to see my brother and his family was wonderful.

Later on we did another locum exchange with our three children. This time we landed up in a huge Victorian vicarage in Clacton, looking after St.Paul's church. Whist we were still lying in bed one morning Kenneth came into the bedroom looking very sheepish and said the window had fallen out on to the lawn. Of course I looked at him in horror and said "What have you done, what have you done?" I ran into the bedroom and sure enough there was an enormous hole in the wall where the large bay window had been but of course poor chap Kenneth hadn't done anything, apparently it had just decided to fall out.

Len phoned the priest who had taken over our house with five children and he said not to worry he knew it would happen sometime as the wood was rotten and they hadn't got round to informing anyone but he had been about to ring us to say "Your safe in church has been rifled as though with a tin opener and all the vessels are stolen!" I don't think we hurried back but did enjoy the seaside with the children. Later on we did locums in Yorkshire and Southampton.

By 1965 the village school had become too small, with very few children due to attend in the next academic year from the village, and the local authority was discussing closure and bussing the children to a larger school nearby. We realised our boys were not doing well and were bored, so we transferred Stephen to a large Church Aided School in Salisbury and Kenneth to a larger neighbouring primary where Len had been going to take RE and assembly. As he was Chairman of the School Managers this didn't go down well but he knew the school was destined for closure and we saw Stephen change overnight and become a different boy. Whatever was happening in the parish I felt that my children must come first. We weathered the storm but it was a difficult time because, however small, a handful of mothers wanted their children to stay at the village school and felt we should have fought to keep it open, but the decision was out of our hands.

In 1965 we took in another child Razia for adoption. She was born in this country in a Mother and Baby Home to a young South American Indian girl who was unable to keep her. Now we felt our family was complete, but on February 23rd 1966 the adoption agency phoned to say her mother was coming to collect her the next day as she intended to run away to Gretna Green in Scotland and marry the father. Although we could see it would be better for her to go to her birth parents it was a time of very mixed emotions for us all as she had become an integral part of our family and it took me months before I could consider filling the empty pram.

Our completed family, Hannah, Kenneth with Laura and Stephen

Then the adoption agency telephoned to say they had another baby for us to consider and baby Laura came to us in November 1966, at last our family was complete. A period of peace settled for a while as the family and parish settled down. It was a very busy time for us all. Len had become Priest-in-Charge of another church and been made Chaplain to a large elderly person's home.

However it wasn't long before we both felt a change was inevitable as this small parish had only been looked upon as a time of recovery and renewal. But when Len asked me if I would like to live in Scotland I replied "You must be joking!" I soon realised that he was really serious.

Unfortunately when negotiations were on the way for our move I had become unwell and was in need of surgery. I had a hysterectomy and whilst still recovering from this we moved to a coastal town in South West Ayrshire in October 1968. Laura, our youngest, by this time was two years old, both our sons were attending Bishop Wordsworth Grammar School in Salisbury and Hannah was still at the primary stage. We had served in the Wiltshire parishes for six years. I had made friends in the parish but found it was impossible to single anyone out as a special friend. I never had time to feel this was a major problem and there were always people in the village and church we could turn to and them to us.

Because of my surgery I had been unable to travel to Scotland to see the house or parish but trusted Len to take us to somewhere reasonable. The journey was long and painful for me, mainly because my two year old daughter spent most of it sitting on my sore tummy. Eventually I asked to take over the driving for some relief and as we drove through an autumnal Stranraer the tears streamed down my face because it was so beautiful. When we arrived before the furniture the kind church treasurer took us out to eat. He treated us all to a slap up meal and booked us into a hotel for the night.

An hour or so later we were invited to one of the church wardens' houses for tea, which turned out to be the biggest spread imaginable with roast beef and all the trimmings and lots of cakes and pastries to follow. I was expecting a cup of tea and a cake and although I'd eaten a hearty meal earlier I knew I had to do it justice, so as not to offend. After this welcome we found our way to the church and house to take a look at our new home. It was a large house with four bedrooms heated by night storage heaters downstairs and nothing on the next floor. From the old ill-fitting sash window in the bathroom Ailsa Craig was in full view capped with snow.

The next day when we moved in the children thought it was spooky. I took the girls round to the local shop to stock up with food leaving Hannah outside to look after Laura in her pushchair as the shop was small and crowded. When I came out I found the girls surrounded by a gang of children gazing at them and calling them names and Hannah begged me as we walked back "Take me home mummy, take me home."

Meantime Kenneth had been sent to buy meat at the butchers but came back with nothing because none of the butchers in town could understand what he was asking for. We didn't know that sausages were called 'lights' and all our English cuts were also foreign. We comforted them by taking them all to a toy shop I'd spotted at the bottom of the road and allowing a tiny present each. Then we bound up their eyes so they could all play Blind Man's Buff in the large passages and rooms downstairs. In spite of this hiccup we found all the parishioners delighted to have us.

I was bought a new gas stove by the church council to supplement the ancient Rayburn for cooking. The parish paid part of our stipend and I found myself involved with a large Women's Guild which met in one of our three reception rooms. After ten minutes of their arrival the room was foggy with smoke as they all lit up like troopers but there was a toughness and genuineness in these women that I came to admire.

The boys had to attend the local Academy, where some of the children were so poor the Head could not insist on uniform. Stephen had to rearrange his language options and in our interview with the headmaster he told us straight "When you come to these outlandish parts, you have to put up with what you get." Hannah had the choice of two schools, the local Presbyterian or Roman Catholic Primary. We chose the Presbyterian for her which later proved to be disastrous. The church was well attended by Scottish Episcopalians and English people living in the area. After the first morning service we were invited to tea by an English lady who had bought a Scottish castle and lived in a small cosy part of it but the children thought this was wonderful and ran wild in the grounds and ruins.

After a while we were invited to a large house in the heart of Edinburgh where the Episcopal Church had set up a centre for distributing clothing that had been donated to priests' families. So once a year we made this trip to this wonderful city, taking all the children and found something for each one of us.

We found a loyal and devoted congregation and also the meaning of religious strife. The Scots who spoke in a broad dialect defeated me at first and one day a woman came to the door and kept repeating "The wain's greetin on the brie! The wain's greetin on the brie!" By the time I found out that she meant my child was crying on the bridge it was too late to help Hannah, she wasn't there any more. When she came home from school her shoes would be all scuffed and one day she came home at lunch-time saying she would never go back. I took her back on the spot and asked to see the Head. The headmistress to my surprise told me that I must take Hannah out of her school because she was being mobbed by the children in the playground and on the way home from school. She defended her pupils by saying they were not used to coloured children and coming from an Episcopalian family was also a problem. We had no choice but to do as she suggested and send her to the R C Junior School. They turned out to be more cosmopolitan and one of the nuns took Hannah under her wing and gave her the odd crafty sweet from her habit pocket and was generally encouraging. We never forgot Sister Mary. By the time Laura was three years old and the dust was settling I asked permission to start a Play Group in the large manse. This would enable pre-school children from all denominations to get together and help them and Laura to mix and find friends. I found some strong helpers from the congregation and one a trained actress Rita played the piano and helped the children sing.

We had room in the garden for swings and a sand-pit under cover. Twelve children were registered to meet for the five days if they wished and I decided it was a great success when a little boy who was an only child living in an isolated spot saw me shopping in the High Street and called the length of it "Aunty Sylvia". The three loyal people who helped me five mornings a week and I received a few pounds each month for pocket money.

*The Playgroup
in the Rectory*

After a year or so of having a bit of pocket money I decided I must try to return to work to help our dire financial situation and to retain my brain cells. Len had moved with the times and was in full agreement. I sent for a Social Studies Correspondence Course by Wolsey Hall under the supervision of London University. The only time I had to study was between ten and twelve at night, after the children had gone to bed, but I managed to keep up most of the time and was occasionally visited and supervised by a tutor who flew from London.

Eventually I started work in a very small way travelling twenty-two miles for three sessions a week of three hours as an assistant hospital social worker. The play group was taken over by a Scottish lady and many years later I heard it was still surviving.

One of the three-year olds at the play group was the son of the local Presbyterian minister and I became friendly with his wife. When it came to our turn at St. John's to host The Women's World Day of Prayer I asked for her help. She agreed to come and asked if she could give the talk from the pulpit to which I agreed and took on the task of taking the Service and sending out all the invitations.

When I sent one to the Roman Catholic Priest he telephoned me and said it had never happened before, so I replied "Well, it's happening this time and we so look forward to seeing some of your ladies." Much to my joy two nuns turned up, as well as Methodist ladies and various Presbyterian Guilds were also represented.

Len had amongst his flock an eminent lady from a nearby coastal resort who was married to a Presbyterian and at her request and with the husband's consent and the agreement of the local people it was arranged that he would take an Episcopalian Service in the small Presbyterian Chapel and her husband agreed to attend and play the organ. Len was really excited about this and realised he had made history as it had never happened before.

When Laura was ready to start school at the age of four and a half we sent her to the R C school which had managed to absorb Hannah. It was situated on the opposite side of the road to the Presbyterian infants. When I went to collect her at the end of her first day I said with the usual trepidation "How did you get on today Laura?" She replied "We are not allowed to spit across the gate at the Protestants." As the horror of this statement sunk in it confirmed my growing understanding of what we were up against. The Orange men came over the narrow divide from Ireland to march every July in their hundreds through the town. We were living on the edge of sectarian strife and in the end it was to overwhelm us. It wasn't just a local affair but it was at a parish and personal level that we were deeply affected.

However in October 1971 the worst disaster of all took place. Our sons attended a local Youth Club of mixed affiliation and one evening went in for a badminton tournament. On the way home Kenneth was assaulted by some of the other members who were Presbyterians. He was pulled to the ground by his hair, which was long in those days and kicked in the face. Stephen was powerless to help him. As he entered the house I was upstairs preparing for bed but could see from the top of the stairs that his face was black. I ran down and cushioned his head in my lap. Someone had witnessed the attack from their house and phoned the police and eventually there was a Court Hearing.

Right & opposite: The Orange Men from Ireland marching through the town in 1969

A schoolmaster from the Academy called on us and offered his apology for the assault but for me it was the last straw and I told Len I could no longer stay, my children must come first. He sent for the Bishop but when he came he seemed to have no real comprehension of the situation and said to Len he would not help him return to England. "You have a flock and you must stay with them!"

As I heard this I left the room and the house quietly by myself to hide the tears and went and sat on the beach. It was warm enough there in the autumn on a nice day provided you had enough warm clothing. There was no one about and as I sat on the hard stones and gazed out to sea, I knew I felt unable to stay in Scotland but at the same time I knew I couldn't leave Len and take the children back because firstly I still loved him dearly and I had no money and would have no home to go to. I went back and told him that we needed to seek the help of our English friends and he agreed. I was a close friend of an Archdeacon's wife in East Anglia. We had been evacuated together and I was her bridesmaid and godmother to her eldest son. So Len wrote to Bishop Leslie and explained the situation. He was a darling who proved to be very understanding of our situation and promised to help us.

He made us an offer but was very angry with the local PCC when they turned us down on the grounds that we would not want to do all the entertaining that was needed for the musicians that came and performed in one of the churches. However Bishop Leslie was faithful to us and kept his word and made us another offer but it took us from October '71 to July '72 to finally move back to England. I have never forgotten Bishop Leslie who invited us to the parish where we were to spend the next twelve happy years.

On the day we were to come down to East Anglia for interviews with the PCCs we had made elaborate arrangements to have our children looked after

in our absence by a church warden's wife, a lovely lady who had twins herself but she agreed to come and stay in the Rectory and look after them all until we came back. As it was a Sunday there was a service in the morning so we planned to leave after lunch but whilst we were eating it with the radio on we heard that a train strike had been declared and there were no trains from Glasgow until further notice. We had bought expensive tickets for the train but could see we would never get to the interviews unless we jumped into the car and drove down.

A sketch of Higham Church by John Constable

There were no motorways in those days but we did get there in time to see those concerned that evening. The introductions went well and we were welcomed to join the parishes but somehow had to get back. We started the drive late that evening and as we approached Doncaster about half way I realised I wasn't going to make it because I felt exhausted and unwell. I had a dear friend living there, so we found our way to her place and threw stones up to tap her bedroom window at one in the morning. Down came Eileen in her dressing gown and in spite of the shock of seeing us standing there she took us in and made up beds for us on her two settees, built up her fire and made us hot drinks, a true friend indeed.

Finally on the eighth of July 1972 we moved to the Livings of Stratford St. Mary and Higham in Suffolk, where we were to spend twelve happy years. Of course we were sad to leave the friends we had made in Scotland and one of Stephen's again made the most poignant farewell. Stephen had been sent on ahead to stay with his aunt because we couldn't get the cat, Woody, who we had taken in as a starving abandoned kitten, and everyone and everything into the car. His best friend came round whilst we were packing the car to leave unaware that Stephen was no longer there. He stood in the empty house in a state of grief and my heart went out to him. I gave him a glider Stephen had made that would have been very difficult to pack anyway.

As we locked the door to drive off he remained in the doorway waving frantically and looking bereft. The evening before all the furniture except beds had been taken and the girls were settled in an empty room when two of the nuns from the school came round to say goodbye to them, I was very moved as I watched them bending over them.

Our cat Woody hated the car, we knew this and had put him in a cardboard

The beautiful interior of Higham church

box the vet had supplied with a tranquilliser, saying he would never get out of that. Little did he know our Woody. After several hundred miles of scrabbling he leapt out of the box on one of the children's laps and landed on my back when I was taking a turn at driving. He was terrified and clung on to my clothes with his claws scratching my back, so I was also in agony and eventually under great stress I screamed out "Throw the cat out of the window." Of course I didn't mean it because I loved Woody dearly. Kenneth, who had a way with animals managed to prize him off me and he put his head inside his jacket and held him close calming him until he went to sleep for the rest of the journey. When the Bishop came to see how we were settling after we moved in and commented on our lovely puss, our youngest piped up "My mummy told us to throw him out of the car window." No comment.

Again this was all new territory. I had never been to East Anglia in my life and had heard that it was a bleak cold place in the winter and very flat. But as we drove our exhausted brood into Suffolk the greatest impression was one of peace and beauty and this stayed with me throughout our sojourn there. We had come to the heart of Constable Country. The house was modern compared with all the others we had inhabited but still had no central heating.

We decided to ask the Dilapidations Board if they would consider putting it in after a long Interregnum of eighteen months and to our surprise they did. So for the first time we would be warm in the winter.

One slight hiccup occurred when we first moved in when a member of the PCC phoned and told me they had been waiting eighteen months for a new rector's wife to come and arrange the flowers. She was very insistent and told me the last poor lady who had died in office not only organized the flower rota but grew the flowers in her greenhouse and arranged them. Although the tears were streaming down my face I remained adamant that I had no intention of taking that task, I had no skill for it and no time as the week-ends would be needed for keeping my house in order, as I was going to work. Soon all was forgotten and forgiven. She became a friend and took the whole family to the Tattoo in Colchester and had us all occasionally to tea.

Len loved his two villages and we were near enough to the town for me to find part-time work. Eventually as the children became more independent I worked full-time as a hospital Social Service Worker, specialising in the care of single mothers and their babies. My main task for the church was to start a Youth Club with the aid of a Christian colleague and her husband.

Hannah joined when she was the right age and still in her late forties meets with the friends she made there on a regular basis. The other thing I took charge of was the Jumble Sales and having stalls at the Annual Fêtes. I was also a member of the PCC and had open house.

It was here that the gentlemen of the road caught up with us and we were frequently visited by tramps. One smelt so strongly when I opened the door that Woody standing beside me was overwhelmed and his fur stood on end all over his body.

Another time a young man came with no shoes on and told Len he had stolen his last pair and felt so guilty he had thrown them away. Kenneth our son bathed his sore feet and gave him some socks and a pair of his own shoes and we fed him and sent him on his way with the bus fare to reach the night hostel in Ipswich. When we heard later that a young vagrant had frozen to death under a caravan, I wondered if it was our young man and was troubled by drawing the line at taking him in and giving him a bed for the night but how could we do this with young daughters growing up?

The family all settled down quickly and made themselves at home. Hannah didn't sleep well at first. Our opposite neighbour had worked for the previous family in the house and her daughter told Hannah that my predecessor had died in her bedroom, so Hannah thought she might be visited by her ghost. I assured her that if she was, the ghost would be a good ghost, not a bad one, because I knew that she had been a lovely lady. This seemed to comfort Hannah.

We really settled down this time for the next twelve years. Our children were brought up to say grace before meals and to follow traditions attached to the church calendar. On Good Friday we all had only hot cross buns for tea and at Christmas Len insisted that the tree could not be put up and decorated until Christmas Eve and presents on the day were distributed after church and dinner and the Queen's speech. Of course they had stockings which Len took round after the Midnight Mass. Now when I visit my eldest son he still sticks to that routine and finds it gives meaning to the day.

Sometimes they were all in church but could choose to stay away when they wanted to. Both boys were bell ringers and Kenneth helped the Bell Master to change one of the bells when a new one had to be made and hung. He came home covered in ancient dust and very happy when the task was achieved.

As they grew up the children all made up their own minds about their attachment to church. On one occasion when a member of the congregation came with her four children she asked me why my lot weren't there; I assured her that if her children attended as often as mine had done they would come to no harm spiritually. They have all made their own choices but I am aware there is a code of practice ingrained in them, which I hope my grandchildren will also eventually follow in the so very different world they now grow up in.

After twelve years when Len was sixty-seven we retired to the town where I was still working with the two girls still living at home. Again we had trouble with one of the children.

Our youngest child Laura was sixteen and told us we were ruining her life by taking her away from all her friends. We tried to make her understand that we had to leave the Rectory and felt it was also advisable to leave the village. She however refused to join us and stayed on in the house all by herself as we moved out. She camped out there in sheer defiance for several weeks but in the end realised that the Rural Dean had come prowling around and was asking why the place was not entirely cleared. Laura moved in with us at last and decided it wasn't all that bad after all, much to our relief.

Now years later, when they are all settled and have families of their own and Len has been dead for many years, I am able to look back on a rich and fulfilling life dominated by the church calendar and festivals. A life in which I and my children were privileged to meet and get to know many lovely people of all classes and to gain an intimate knowledge of many different parts of the country.

Sometimes it has seemed sad to make yet another fresh start and leave hard won friends behind. It is not easy to make friends because of being in the public eye and so closely observed but in spite of that, relationships do develop and some are retained for life.

I suppose I've found it difficult to get used to the idea of women priests, simply because of the traditional way we lived and practised with women having their appointed roles, including myself, but I have of course attended services that reveal their energy and dedication. I don't know what to say about gay clerics. I've met and got to know many gay people of both sexes in my varied career and found them to be helpful and sensitive people with a lot to offer. However I can also understand why a position of authority in a church with ingrained doctrines on family and marriage causes such consternation amongst its members but I know we must go forward in faith and move with the times.

When we were married all those years ago the vicar during the ceremony asked us to follow him to the altar, so that the congregation could not hear and quietly said "I was visiting an old couple recently when the wife was taken ill and as she was taken off in the ambulance her husband called out 'please come back, you're all the world to me.' That is what I want for you two." Bless him! His wish for us was fulfilled.

When a clergy wife loses her husband she also loses her priest and even though Len had retired before he died, the time I often feel he is standing before me is when I'm in church. Sometimes it feels very peaceful to be there and sometimes it feels so very sad and painful but when the Blessing is given at the end of a service I know that I have been blessed indeed.

Stratford St. Mary church

CLAIRE LUNNEY

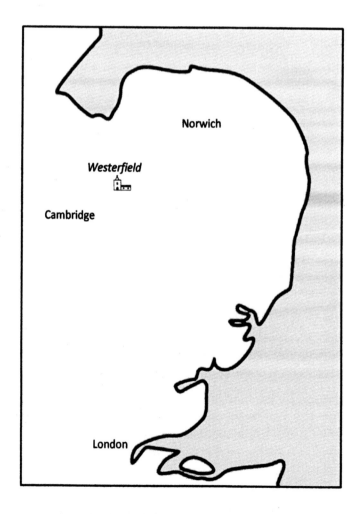

CLAIRE'S STORY

*'We gave ourselves to the people
and they gave themselves to us'*

My name is Claire Lunney and I live now at 6 Karen Close, Ipswich. My maiden name was Claire Cooper. I was an only child, born in Westcliff-on-Sea Southend in 1933. My maternal grandparents were Harry and Minnie Spence who had three children, Eva my mother, Alice my aunt and Edwin my uncle. My paternal grandparents took an active part in the life of the town. Grandpa was an Alderman and owned a very nice book shop and stationers in I believe, Hamlet Court Road. Grandpa and Grandma Cooper had two sons, Edgar my father, and Edwin my uncle.

I took my mother back there some years ago when searching roots and we met several people who remembered the Coopers. All I can remember about them was that, when I was taken by my parents into Grandpa Cooper's shop it was all mahogany fitments and very Victorian and I had to be on my best behaviour.

In 1939 I was evacuated up to Whaley Bridge near Manchester but the authorities might just as well have left us where we were because we virtually walked into the Manchester blitz. To this day I can see the flames reflected in the sky! My mother came with our party as a helper with the evacuees.

She lived with me in one or two billets and then we went to live with George and Lucy Turner and their daughter Margaret. They kept a grocery shop and George was the local baker. We were very well looked after by the Turner family. I remember spending many a long night huddled in the cupboard under the stairs during bombing raids but we were more fortunate than many because we had jars of sweets from the shop to sustain us. I kept in touch with Margaret for well over sixty years. She died in 2009.

In 1942 mother and I went to live in a little South Wales village called Pendine where my aunt, uncle and grandmother had been evacuated to, from Essex. My uncle worked for the Ministry of Defence Experimental Establishment and the influx of staff and families almost overwhelmed the tiny village. All the 'experimental people' as they were called were billeted with whoever would or could take them in.

*Me with my
mother in 1939*

*My father on
leave with me
in 1942*

It was in 1942 that my father came home on leave for the last time before he was killed and I remember walking very proudly round the village with this very handsome man in his Officer's uniform. He bought me a Brownie box camera, which I treasured for many years. I still have it. My uncle who was a Battle of Britain pilot was also killed, however all that is another story.

The village of Pendine has a vast stretch of firm sand, where they carried out record breaking car speeding attempts, which made it quite a famous little place. In September 1924 Malcolm Campbell had broken the then world land speed record. I soon made friends with girls in the village and went to a dear little village church, St. Margaret's, which I will always think of as 'my' church.

I literally grew up in that village. I went to the village primary school called Tremoilet and eventually I passed the Scholarship Exam as it was called in those days. I went to the Whitland Grammar School. When we first arrived in Pendine we were very fortunate because we went to live at Elm Cottage with my aunt, uncle and grandmother who had been taken in by an old man, Uncle John, as I called him. There was no lady of the house as the old man had just lost his wife and he and his son Griff were struggling to look after themselves.

We all moved into this tiny cottage with Uncle John and Griff, my mother, me, my aunt and uncle and my grandma, so there were seven of us. I remember having to sleep on a camp bed, a truckle as it was called in those days. I had to share my aunt and uncle's bedroom with just a curtain as a screen. Although we were cramped we all lived happily there for many years, we really did in spite of it being very primitive. There was no running water, gas or electricity, just candles and oil lamps. I well remember almost setting my bed on fire reading by the light of a candle!

Below: The village of Pendine   *Opposite: Our wedding*

My first task in the morning was to fetch the day's supply of water. This was from a spring of pure water which ran down the mountain beside The New Inn. I collected it in various containers. The drinking water had to go into earthenware crocks and the washing water into buckets and pails, until eventually the first communal tap arrived in the village; but this was still about a hundred yards down the lane. I also remember distinctly flicking on the first electric light switch when the electricity was laid on; that was amazing.

The loo was a story in itself. It was outside the back of the cottage, which meant running the entire length of the house under a covered way which was open at the far end, guided by a candle in the dark. I'd be in the one cosy living room doing homework or something, dying to go to the loo, and sit until I couldn't sit any longer. I would collect my candle and walk down this long passageway until I got to the bottom, where nine times out of ten, a puff of wind would blow it out. Ooh it was horrifying, it really was horrifying, especially for a young child. I well remember hurtling back to the warmth and comfort of that living room.

Despite all that and the fact that there was a war on, my school days and childhood in Pendine were in many ways idyllic. I was very happy in the village. I didn't leave there until I was sixteen, so that is why Pendine is home to me. I felt perfectly safe and enjoyed a great deal of freedom. During the school holidays I would join friends after breakfast and we would go off on our bikes and provided we were home by teatime and certainly before dark everyone

was happy. We cycled miles on our bikes and went for country walks, to say nothing of playing happily for hours on the beach and in the caves. How different from this day and age; all that would be impossible for safety reasons.

When I left Whitland Grammar School I went to college and did Business Studies and then in 1950 went to work in Barclays Bank where I met my husband. It was a blind date arranged through a mutual friend, John, who introduced us. We used to chat over the telephone, I worked at the local Head Office in Maidstone and Henry worked in various branches. If his manager wanted to talk to my local director, John would make sure that Henry got through to me first.

In those days it was 'not done' to use Christian names, it was always Miss Cooper and Mr Lunney. Then one day John said to me "Henry is going to meet you outside the back door after work, make sure you're there". "Humph, no way" said I, "I'm going out of the front door." However, I did go to the back, and here we are fifty-four years later in 2010.

Wherever Henry and I had lived we had always been involved in the church, I suppose one could say we had literally grown up in it. From about the age of seven I used to pump the organ for the Rector's daughter in the dear little church, St. Margaret's at Pendine. I possibly drifted away a little bit during the late 'teen years, as one does, being busy horse riding and playing tennis, dancing and all the things teenagers do and enjoy, but when we were married, which was in 1956, wherever we lived we both attended our local church. Our first home was in Gillingham in Kent where we had our first daughter, Yvette. Then from Gillingham we moved to Maidstone where we belonged to All Saints Church, where our son Ross was baptised. After that we moved to Whitstable and All Saints Church, where our youngest daughter Rachel was baptised and was their Christmas baby. Henry had been a choirboy there when he was a child, so we were going back home for him. We moved about quite a bit because every time Henry was promoted within the bank the policy was at that time to live locally, it is not so now. We were always in the Kent and Canterbury area but then we moved to Crowborough, just over the border into Sussex.

He was the youngest employee in the Maidstone and Canterbury District to be promoted as manager but God had other plans for him and called him to be ordained. He was happy and doing well in his job and had reached the age of forty-two. I'd always heard people talking about being 'called to the Ministry' and I thought "What a load of rubbish, nonsense, what poppycock." But of course, as we discovered, it does happen. Henry described it as being touched on the shoulder and so did I. By this time we had three children and I was also looking after my mother. I cared for her for many years. This 'call' happened when we were living in Crowborough, where I was helping run a large Young Wives' Group and Henry was on the Parochial Church Council and then he was elected Church Warden, so I became a church warden's wife. Between us we'd been involved in most of the jobs within the church, so we really knew 'the works'.

When he got the 'call' he went up to Wycliffe Hall in Oxford and I was left for two years at home with my mother and three children who were all at that time at three different schools. I had to find a job pretty quickly because obviously there was no salary coming in. Two years can go very quickly but conversely it can seem a very long time. I must pay tribute to the bank here because they were fantastic. Towards the end of every term a letter would arrive through the letter-box. *'Dear Mr. Lunney, We know that your term is coming to an end, we wondered whether you would be kind enough to help out at such and such a branch for your vacation.'* They knew darn well of course that we were absolutely relying on that money. This was our financial lifeline and happened religiously throughout the training period. I never felt resentment at the loss of salary but I do remember at one breakfast time cutting up one rasher of bacon into three, so that they could all have a taste.

We knew it was a joint calling; however, I needed a part-time job and I was very fortunate, because again the Lord was looking after me. I found a morning job with a civil engineering firm in Tunbridge Wells and they were fantastic, they really were. They knew what our circumstances were and the sort of thing that happened was I would come out at lunch-time to go home and find that they had filled up my car with petrol, that sort of thing. Marvellous! I stayed with them until we left Tunbridge Wells and Crowborough. I must pay tribute to my mother who looked after Rachel whilst I was at work in the mornings. We shall always be grateful to her.

Henry was ordained at St. Augustine's in Ipswich where he became a curate and that was interesting because he had several offers. One group of parishes in Norfolk begged us to go there and we would like to have gone but bear in mind the average size of curates' houses, two or three bedrooms and we were six people, a three generation family, so we had to turn that down. I looked after my mother until she died at ninety one, ever since the war really, which of course shattered her due to the break-up of the family and the loss of my father in 1942.

We were very much bound by where we could live and Henry was forty-four by this time, in middle life. We had to go where we could be accommodated but we were very squashed. We always gave my mother the second bedroom as a bed-sitting room, which meant the rest of us were pretty confined space-wise. I don't in all honesty think we could have endured another year in those conditions. Again we were very fortunate because Bishop Leslie Brown, who was a kind and understanding man, realised that it would be wrong to move the children from their schools having already uprooted them from Crowborough. By this time they were fourteen, twelve and six, just the wrong ages to change schools.

Leslie Brown said to Henry "You need your own parish" and thus it was that we came to Westerfield, which at that time was combined with Tuddenham St. Martin and subsequently with Witnesham. We lived in the old Rectory at Westerfield and were privileged to serve in such super parishes. Each one was different yet they formed one Christian family and we spent twenty happy years working with the folk there. In the country people don't like change. Had our parishioners been fed up with us we would have moved on but we were happy with them and they were happy with us. Country folk like their Rector to bury Grandma, marry the next generation and baptise the next. We were there for them, it was hard work. Everything was in triplicate because we always made a point of treating them exactly the same. It was costly too financially, supporting three Harvest Suppers, three village fêtes, three of everything but immensely rewarding.

I like to think of myself as a transitional village clergy wife. There were the old style wives who didn't go out to work because it was very much frowned upon and then there are the modern ones and I can think of several who come in this category, whose secular job is everything and they want nothing to do with the parishes. I suppose I was in the middle. Whilst Henry was in office I managed to work in the Health Service for over twenty years in pharmacy administration.

I was very fortunate and had three absolutely super bosses, one after the other. I was part-time at first and then I was full-time but again I was very fortunate in that I worked flexitime. If ever I wanted to attend a Mothers' Union meeting or go to a funeral or some such I was able to go. I was phenomenally busy. I can honestly say that when we were in the parishes we literally worked from half past six in the morning until midnight. The telephone hardly ever stopped. Several people have said "Oh, I wouldn't answer the phone, blow that." Some of these were clergy wives. Yet I can in all truth say that although we didn't have an answer 'phone in those days not once did that 'phone go unanswered. We absolutely gave ourselves to the parishes, we did. Since our retirement we have both been helping out, not of course in those parishes, but parishes round and about.

When we moved into the original old Rectory in Westerfield, that was an adventure in itself. The oldest part was dated from 1474 with umpteen rooms, beautiful but freezing cold. It had central heating after a fashion but it wasn't efficient. In the panelled bedroom, the major bedroom, there was a large walk-in airing cupboard and when you woke up in the winter icicles were hanging on the inside of the windows and we stepped inside the airing cupboard to get dressed. We lived in that house for almost three years and then the Diocese sold it off and built a new one at the bottom of the drive. It was a pleasant modern house but I must admit that I still preferred the old one. I do love old houses but I realise that they are costly to upkeep and are certainly beyond the means of a parish priest.

We had a lot to learn when we moved up to Suffolk. When we knew we were moving up here, friends down in Kent said "Oh you don't want to move up there, they don't like strangers up there." Oh dear, we wondered what we were coming to but after about a month we felt we had been there for ever. We were fortunate that Suffolk folk accepted us but we had a lot to learn. After we'd been in Hippo House, Fitzmaurice Road for a few days I thought 'I'd better go down to Ipswich and find my way around.' So I went to see a very kind neighbour up the road, Polly Taylor, a retired midwife living with a friend Sybil Nightingale, a retired missionary. They were a kindly couple who immediately took us under their wing. On the day we moved in they hoovered the house, arranged flowers and generally made us feel welcome. Polly told me where to go and wait for 'the tram'. I dutifully went down to The Haven Public House, which is now renamed The Crown, to wait for the tram, letting all the buses go past. After about half-an-hour I thought 'Wait a minute, there aren't any tram tracks.' I soon realised that Ipswich people were still calling the buses 'trams'. On another occasion I got talking to a lady at the bus stop and asked her if she was local or had come from elsewhere. "No, no, I'm not local," she said, "I come from Overstoke," at least two miles away. At first we laughed about this but I remember saying to Henry "We mustn't laugh, they are deadly serious, they are not local, they come from the other side of Ipswich." We did indeed have a lot to learn.

Tuddenham at that time was very much a feudal village. When looking back in the church registers, I remember being quite amazed that even in the nineteen thirties there were quite a few people signing their name with a cross. In the village lived a delightful couple who were really the 'Squirarchy' and they did a lot for the village in an unobtrusive way. They invited Henry to tea one afternoon and all of a sudden the lady of the house looks Henry up and down, as they do in Suffolk, sizing him up. "Of course, you realise you are on trial don't you?" So Henry said "Yes, yes, I'm well aware of that you know." A year later the situation was repeated and during the course of the afternoon tea she stated "You'll be pleased to know you have passed the test." It's good to know where one stands.

When we moved to Westerfield our son must have been about fourteen or fifteen, a difficult age for teenagers to move. He would come to church but because all the week he wore a neat shirt and tie to school, he would deliberately on a Sunday morning, put on his tatty frayed jeans very much the fashion in those days. One Sunday morning I overheard one of the elderly gentlemen in the congregation say, "Fancy them letting their son come to church dressed like that," to which I replied "Well, thank gosh he's here in God's house and not lying at home in bed." Now, approaching fifty years old, Ross is on the PCC at his church and acts as a sides person. His daughter Emma, our dearly loved grandchild, also plays a full part in the life of Henley church which is a source of great joy to us.

In 1986, we suffered a tremendous blow when our eldest dearly loved daughter Yvette died at the age of twenty-five. She was a solicitor and a delightful girl. That was and always will be a great heartache.

Our son Ross and his wife Pauline run their own freight forwarding business and work very hard. Their daughter Emma, now almost sixteen, has just completed her GCSE exams and will, all being well, be entering the sixth form for A levels. We are of course very proud of them all. Our younger daughter is married to a priest and they live in a village just outside Durham called Brancepeth. Rachel is a doctor. She lectured for some time to medical students at Newcastle University and is now a partner in a medical practice a few miles from Brancepeth, where she trains young doctors. Rick, her husband, was the vicar of Holy Trinity, a massive church in Newcastle, where they built the congregation up in a wonderfully Spirit-filled way and it was a joy to attend services there, I used to sit there with a tear trickling down. It was wonderful because they built it up from nothing, and it took your breath away.

Rick now has a diocesan post and works for the Bishop of Durham and the Bishop of Newcastle, covering an area from Berwick-on-Tweed right down to the North Yorkshire Moors. In view of this he has just one small village church again very Spirit-filled and lively. Rachel is in the choir at church and they put on plays and she joins in everything. Sometimes I find myself saying to her "Can't you ease up a bit?" She replies "You're a fine one to talk mother!" They are very similar to Henry and me when we worked in our parishes, in that they work hard and they play hard, which it is as it should be. All this energy is commitment really, isn't it!

Having truly given ourselves to God's people, now my dear Henry's health is failing. Following a mild stroke he had a nasty fall, which has exacerbated Parkinson's Disease, and is at present in a nursing home, where he needs a great deal of care. Very many people are praying for him and hoping he will return home but it looks as though we are in for a difficult time. We have always said that Henry "will die with his boots on, doing the Lord's work." I hope and pray that will also be able to be said of me.

Reverting to 'my' little church, St. Margaret's at Pendine, where I was evacuated to during the war, I owe it a great debt of gratitude. Initially it gave me a deeply founded faith and secondly, in old age, I owe it a great deal musically. When I first began attending on a regular basis the organist was Anne Williams, the Rector's daughter. Anne was only seven at the time but already an accomplished organist and pianist. I used to pump the organ for her and had to remember to keep on pumping! I had always wanted to learn to play the organ, such a beautiful instrument and when I reached the age of seventy I decided at last to do something about it before it was too late. It wasn't going to be easy to find a teacher willing to take on an old age pensioner but I was fortunate in finding John Harding, an elderly organist himself

Left: My 'Seventies' Challenge'

Opposite: Henry receiving the Maundy Money

at the United Reform Church in Ipswich. He took me under his wing for a couple of years. Very soon I was able to help out playing hymns for services in several of our local village churches and now I play regularly on three or four Sundays each month. I like to call this my 'Seventies' Challenge!'

I was asked my views on women priests. Being a traditionalist I must admit it took me a long time to come to terms with them but now I know the error of my ways, for I come into contact with many who are outstandingly caring and committed and for whom I have great admiration. I'm not too sure about the homosexual situation though.

To conclude this story of a 'traditional Clergy Wife' I must say what a tremendous privilege it has been to serve the Lord in so many ways over more than seventy years. Of course we have experienced lots of joys and also sorrows, the greatest of the latter being the loss of our dearly loved daughter. This was a tremendous blow and a real test of faith.

An outstandingly happy time was when Henry was made a Canon of Bury St. Edmund's Cathedral in March 1992, becoming a Canon Emeritus when he officially retired in 1997. Another Red Letter Day was in April 2009 when he received the Maundy Money from H M the Queen, when she visited the Cathedral. That really was a day to remember. We never fail to give thanks to God for allowing us to serve Him and His people. We gave ourselves to the people and they gave themselves to us.

ANN CRACKNELL

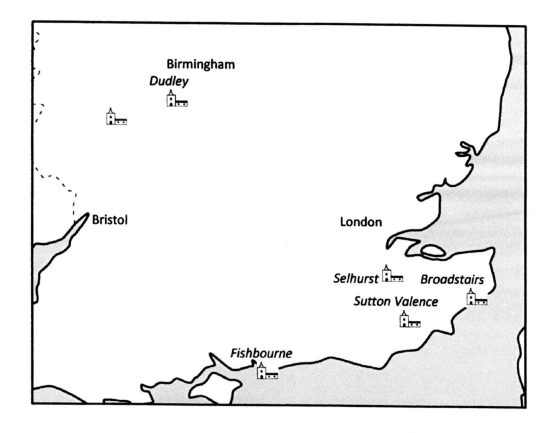

Ann's Story

'Curates' wives sit over there in that corner'

My name is Ann, my maiden name was Cracknell. I was born in Bromley in Kent; my mother was my father's second wife, his first wife died. They had a son by that marriage and I am the daughter of the second marriage, so I had a step brother. His name was Alan James but for some unknown reason I always called him Babu. He was fifteen years older than me so there was quite a gap but we were always very close. I didn't see a lot of him during the war years because in 1939 he left school and was immediately called up. He went to France and got caught up in Dunkirk, he came home and then did various things during the war and ended up D Day plus one in France but he survived. Sadly he died last year. He found it very difficult to settle down after the war and that was one of the reasons he emigrated to Canada, so I lost him twice in a way. I went to boarding school and he wrote every week, he never forgot.

We stayed at home during the war until the bombing got really bad and the school I was at was evacuated. My father wouldn't let me go, he said "Mother and daughter must stay together". My grandparents lived in Thetford in Norfolk, so we went and stayed with them for the majority of the war. My father stayed at home and slept in his office if he couldn't get home from London. He worked for an oil company that was eventually taken over by Mobil Oil. My mother and I came back home just before the end of the war.

In 1948 I was sent to boarding school for my secondary education at Chislehurst, which was a few miles down the road; I was a termly boarder because they didn't have weekly boarders but we had three exeat Saturdays during the term. Ours was a comfortable home and we never went short of things. My mother stayed there living in Bromley in the same house that she went to as a bride, until she died fifteen years ago. My parents were both Church of England, but latterly, although my mother never changed to United Reform she had a lot of friends who went there and she went with them. My father was always C of E, he didn't go every Sunday, so I wouldn't say they were regular attendees but I went to Sunday school every Sunday when I was young. I was very naughty. I was given sixpence to put in the collection and my friend and I put three-pence in the collection and bought an ice cream on the way home, my mother never knew. The boarding school I went to was a Methodist foundation, so there was Chapel every morning and every evening. I was happy there and I still keep in touch with some of the friends I made. I stayed there until I was eighteen and then went to Secretarial College. My first job was with a publishing company.

Me with my step-brother Alan James (Babu)

Below: Me with Michael when we were children

When I got engaged I wanted to work locally and I got a job in Beckenham with the Borough Welcome Institute; they researched medicine. I was on the veterinary side. The professor I worked for was researching cures for animals. My father and my husband's grandfather were friends up in the City, I don't know how they met or where but his grandparents would bring Michael over to my parents for days out and my parents would take me over there. So we've known each other virtually all our lives I suppose.

When I was twenty-one I had a party, I had more girls to invite than boys, so my mother said "Well, there's that Michael, why don't you invite him, he will be an extra boy?"

He was doing his National Service in the Army, the Royal Corps of Signals and he was on leave at the time. When he went back to Germany he wrote a nice letter, saying, *'Thank you very much for inviting me to your party, when I come home can I take you to the theatre one evening?'* That's when it all started. He already had a place waiting for him at theological college, so I knew right from the word 'go' that was what he was going to do. I knew it was his intention to become a priest. He went to King's College, University of London. He took his degree, then he did a post graduate year at Warminster and between those two we got married, so I went down to Warminster for the Post Graduate Year with him. We had to get permission from the Dean of the College to get married.

We had a flat on a corner in Warminster. I opened the curtains on our first morning and there I was staring into the top of a double-decker bus. It was a very rickety flat, riddled with woodworm. I don't think it would be allowed today because the toilet and the bathroom were just a partition off the kitchen. It was very primitive but cheap. There were just the two of us in our primitive top flat. It was ideal in one way because it was just round the corner from the college and I managed to get a job as a secretary with a firm of solicitors.

While we were at Warminster the college staff organized wives' and girlfriends' week-ends. We had various talks and discussions on being a clergy wife and some of the 'dos and 'don'ts'. One of the topics was dealing with calls from 'men on the road' who wanted money for all sorts of reasons, mainly drink. The advice was don't invite them into your home or give them money but do offer them a cup of tea and a sandwich or something else to eat.

Michael was ordained at Worcester Cathedral and then he was offered a curacy in Worcester but the curate's house was not okay. By this time we had a small baby, she was only a month old when we moved in.

*Our rickety flat
in Warminster*

Our curate's house in Worcester

It had a huge garden with the grass up to our knees and the house was in a terrible state. Nothing had been done to it by the previous curate who had lived there until a couple of months beforehand. We went into the kitchen and all that was in there was the kitchen sink, no draining board, no cupboard, no light bulbs, nothing. We had no furniture and there was no such thing as central heating; it was a struggle with a new baby. There was a second hand furniture shop in Worcester, so a lot of our things were five or ten shillings from there and that is how we got going. Jane my new baby was fine. She won a beauty competition, she was gorgeous.

The Rector and his wife were new as well; they'd only been there a few months when we arrived. The parishioners were difficult people to get to know, with the attitude "Well you're the curate's wife and you really don't stay very long, so there's not much point in being over-friendly." It was a bit lonely. I do remember one time shortly after I arrived, the Rector's wife said there was a coffee morning for clergy wives and would I go with her and I could bring Jane, my daughter. So we went along and the lady opened her front door and said "Oh you've brought a baby and you're a curate's wife." So we went into this typical Victorian Vicarage and she said, "Curates' wives sit over there in that corner and your baby had better be over there as well, she won't make a noise will she?" There I sat with another curate's wife, over in the corner, not allowed to speak and dreading the fact that my daughter might make a noise. I never went again. I didn't do anything in the parish really, I had made up my mind at quite an early stage that I wasn't going to be a Mrs. Vicar running things but I would put my family first. I did what I could but didn't want to be responsible for taking on anything except a supporting role really.

Then we moved over to Dudley. Michael was a Priest-in-Charge. It was a team Ministry but he worked in Dudley where we lived in the vicarage. He had his own church but he was part of a team. Dudley was a very industrial town of mixed race, very mixed. We had a rambling old Victorian vicarage again in not a very good condition. It had stone floors downstairs and huge rooms from ceiling down to floor. What furniture we had was very tiny in the big rooms. We lived next door to the Methodist Church and a few doors down from that was the Anglican Church. The Methodists had a very large mixed congregation.

It was fascinating on a Saturday to see all these West Indian ladies in their lovely coloured robes and gorgeous headwear turning up for weddings, it was really quite something to see. Then the next day you'd see them all turn up again for the Christening. This was in 1966 when the changes were taking place. It was an area of regeneration. The old back to back houses were being pulled down, creating a lot of look-alike bomb-sites really, while the new houses, but mainly flats, were being built.

The industry was steel and that sort of thing and the people mostly worked in factories. The foreign people were mainly getting jobs on the buses because it was a time when our English people wouldn't do a lot of the jobs that were needed in Dudley. They also worked in Birmingham, which was only a bus ride away and also in Wolverhampton. We were in the Black Country in the heart of England; Jane our daughter came away with quite an accent.

There I helped with the Guides, I had been a girl guide and one day the person running it asked if I would help, so I said "Yes". Then we discovered we ought to have a Brownie Pack, so I became Brown Owl and also helped with the guides. I enjoyed that and although the troop was connected with the church,

Our rambling old Victorian vicarage at Dudley

they were not really a denominational organisation, so anyone could join. I also worked as a part-time secretary, again in the local library, which I did until I gave birth to a son Paul. He was very poorly when he was first born, he suffered a lot with his chest. The doctor got quite concerned about him and when she heard we were moving to the Kent coast she said "Oh thank goodness you'll get some decent air."

We had quite a number of callers from the 'men of the road' whilst at these two parishes as our houses were on a main road. They were quite happy with a cup of tea and a bite to eat and would then go on their way. One particular gentleman said all he wanted was a better pair of shoes. I took one look at him and informed him that his shoes were in better shape than my husband's! He saw the funny side of that. Also during this time my father became very ill with cancer. We happened to be having a week's holiday down in Westbrook in Kent when we saw in the local paper that there would shortly be a vacancy for a curacy in Thanet. Michael applied and got that so we moved to Kent. Canterbury paid more than the North, so although we had another curacy it was level, it wasn't a boost but it wasn't less.

We were at a place called Reading Street, situated just outside of Broadstairs, that was a happy parish, we were very happy there. We had a much nicer house. It was relatively modern, an ordinary house that had been bought for the curate. It had four bedrooms with a room for a study downstairs and a nice big lounge-dining room and a downstairs toilet, it was a nice house. Michael had an aunt and uncle living near and we weren't far from either of our homes, so it was like coming home again and with my father being so ill I was able to visit him. After my son moved to the sea air he soon became stronger.

The time we were there were very happy years, we fitted in churchman wise with the vicar, he was very nice, but of course it wasn't all plain sailing. I helped in the Sunday school there and got very friendly with the doctor's wife. When we went there they didn't have a Sunday school and she was the one who said "I'd like to start one, would you help?" I said "Yes." She found one or two other people until there were about six of us and she was very 'go ahead', getting them to do all sorts of things, I enjoyed that. I joined the Young Wives' and I was secretary for that most of the time I was there. It was a church group which was supposed to feed the Mothers' Union.

Sometimes I went to the Mothers' Union as well and most of them were baby-sitters for us. I was on the PCC (Parochial Church Council) for the first time. I had to be on it really because they met in our house, so short of going upstairs there was nowhere else for me to go. We were there about four years and then we moved up to Croydon, to Holy Trinity Church, Selhurst.

There we had a big old rambling Vicarage but it had a bit of character and was rather nice. It had been empty for some time, so there was quite a bit in

the sequestration fund and they put in central heating for us. We had a lot of decorating and carpeting done for us as well, they worked really hard. On the day of Michael's induction, we invited Archbishop and Mrs. Ramsey to dinner beforehand. They were a lovely couple. The workmen were still in the house. My father had died by this time but my mother was with us and every room we wanted to go into, we couldn't, because there was a builder doing something. The only room we could be in was the kitchen and shortly before the guests were due to arrive the builder said "I'm afraid you wont be able to use the upstairs bathroom because most of the floorboards are up".

Then they left at half past five. We quickly did a dust round, laid the table and were all ready for the Archbishop and Mrs. Ramsey when my mother went to the downstairs toilet and it flooded. Fortunately the builder only lived opposite, so we ran across to him and he sent in one of his men to help. He was trying to get rid of all the mess in the downstairs toilet when the Ramseys arrived during all this kafuffle. Mrs. Ramsey roared with laughter when we told them the problem, they had quite a sense of humour. After dinner when they wanted to refresh themselves, we told them "You can use the upstairs bathroom but

Above:
Holy Trinity
Church, Selhurst

Right:
Our house at
Reading Street

there are not many floorboards, so do be careful." She said "So long as I can use the loo, I don't mind." They were so nice about it, we could laugh, so did they, they really saw the funny side of it. He was such a caring person. In spite of all the people he visited throughout the year he still knew who you were and who your family was. If we met him at an official function it was "Hello Ann, hello Paul, hello Jane," he would know us. He took that trouble wherever he went all over the world, I think his wife did a lot behind the scenes by informing him and we were very fond of him.

This house was right by the railway, it had a huge landing and a big window and every time a train went by our son Paul ran up to the big window to watch it go by. By this time the children were at school, so it was that much easier. I was on the PCC and this particular church had a Drama Group, so we both joined that as well and had a really happy time. We did mainly light comedy plays which were good fun. It was really the Youth Group which had outgrown itself but the members wanted to keep together, so that is what they did and we joined in. They didn't have a Mothers' Union but I did quite a bit with the Women's World Day of Prayer, which was very active, I preached on one occasion. We were happy there but the children were of an age when they needed to change schools, Jane was coming up to her O levels and we didn't really want to disturb her by moving too far away and Paul was approaching a move to Secondary, so we moved from one side of Croydon to the other, to Norbury, and they stayed at the same schools.

That again was a good move. We knew when we went to Norbury that there was a lot of reorganisation going on in Croydon. Some churches were doomed for closure and we knew that the one we left was one of those. We felt very guilty at leaving it. The one we went to was much more alive, the house there was very modern with central heating. Nothing much happened there. I was a member of the Mothers' Union. Our daughter got married there, to David, a man who was then Treasurer; he is thirteen years older than my daughter. He ran the Youth Group and she joined it when we moved in and she also joined the choir. David was also a Sidesman and a Server. When they got married they moved down to Hurst Green.

Here again the vicarage was on the main road, but by now the callers were becoming more aggressive wanting money for drugs, this was around the 1980s. We had one unpleasant experience in Norbury. This particular gentleman wanted a bed for the night, not at the hostel down the road but at the vicarage. When refused he left making all sorts of unpleasant threats. A few weeks later we had a break-in one night whilst we were asleep. He woke us up and Michael chased him out. When the police arrived they found that the burglar had tried to start a fire in a shed attached to the vicarage. Was it the same man who had threatened us earlier? We shall never know because the burglar was never caught.

*St. Mary's church,
Sutton Valence,
Maidstone*

After the second parish in Croydon we moved to Maidstone; at that time Croydon was being taken out of Canterbury Diocese and going into Southwark. My husband didn't want to move into Southwark, so we went to just outside Maidstone to a country parish where he had three churches, three villages, right across the weald of Kent. They were lovely, all different with three PCCs, organists, three churchyards and lots of administration. They were nice parishes; quite different, with a modern house, a good modern vicarage. I was on the PCC again and this time I was the Enrolling Member of the Mothers' Union with somebody else. We did it between us, it worked well until she and her husband moved away and then I took it on alone. I believe it is still flourishing. There was a Young Wives' Group as well and the three villages joined together for these groups, they had one meeting which met in a different parish each month. I also helped in the Sunday school and was on the flower rota. From an experience I had in our very first curacy, I had vowed and declared I would never do flowers again but it was quite different there at Maidstone. I was encouraged to help, so I did. They had a couple of Flower Festiivals whilst we were there and I helped with them.

Sometimes on the PCC I think I was a thorn in Michael's flesh, saying things that he felt the PCC need not know but I felt that they ought to know. Some times I said things that perhaps he felt he couldn't say from the Chair. There was never any argument after the meeting; when everyone had gone home we'd say "Well that wasn't, or was, a very good meeting," but there were no recriminations. We were there for seven years.

In every parish except the first I had a job outside of the parish and when I came home Michael said "Did you have a nice day today?" So I brought something else into the home, it wasn't all just churchy things, I mixed with people who were outside the church, some were very anti-church, some were sympathetic, they respected me for the job I was there to do, I was experienced at secretarial work and they accepted me as a person doing the job that I was paid to do. I was always part-time because I liked to be at home when the children were there and the money was very helpful. For the first few years we really did struggle but things did gradually improve, the stipends were beginning to be a bit more realistic too.

Neither of the children had any problems. At my daughter's school there were a number of other clergy children and my son went to Christ's Hospital School, so there were a lot of clergy children there as well. They were never bullied or anything, they were both quite well adjusted, so if they had been they would have been able to handle it. I wouldn't say they were models but we didn't have behavioural problems. Jane loved singing and joined the choir from a very early age and has always sung, still does. Paul wasn't so keen on church "Do I have to go?" Sometimes he came, sometimes he didn't, and we didn't say "Yes, you've got to go."

He liked it when we were in Norbury because that was more high church than where we had been before and on certain Sundays they had incense and a team of Servers and he enjoyed being on that team. They made him 'boat boy' one day when they were having incense and he thoroughly enjoyed that. I don't think he goes very often now, whereas my daughter goes and very seldom misses. We were very fortunate with both of them.

After Maidstone we moved to Fishbourne. Michael became Rector of Fishbourne and had Appledram as well. We were there for eleven very happy years, one of our longest. I worked in the library again part-time.

We had a very nice house, which has now been pulled down, which is sad. A new Rectory was built on a new estate for our successor. Jane was married by then with a family and Paul was married as well, so there was just the two of us. I started the Mothers' Union there and organised the flower rota and got a committee together and one year we had a Flower Festiival. I did quite a bit there, not Sunday school work because I felt by then I was getting a bit too old and they had plenty of young people to help. I organized various social events and was happy there.

When Michael retired we moved here to Barnham. Michael assists here, in the three parishes of Aldingbourne, Barnham and Eastergate; he just does services and I've settled happily into the parish as well. I belong to the Mothers' Union, I'm not anything official now, there are two groups, an afternoon and evening group, there's about fifteen in the afternoon and twenty in the evening. Both meet once a month and I also go to the local Clergy Wives' meeting here, in the Arun Deanery. The men had a Fraternal which packed up, the ladies try to keep themselves going but we are gradually getting less and less. Once a year we meet in the Bishop's Palace in Chichester and there are other meetings held elsewhere in this big diocese.

I meet once a month with some clergy wives, for a little prayer meeting and a chat, with a cup of tea and a biscuit. We all come from different denominations, United Reform, Methodists, and Baptists, everybody's there. We take it in turn to do the little prayer bit. The Baptists bring something from their denomination and the Methodists from theirs and we add something from the Anglican side, it widens your horizons a bit.

No way has it been a boring life, it's been very difficult at times, especially early on with a young family when we didn't have much money or furniture. Most of the stuff we had was bought for pence from charity shops or my mother knew somebody who was getting rid of something, like a friend who had a couple of wardrobes to get rid of, so we had them. I bought a chest of drawers for ten shillings for my son. When we moved here we couldn't get it through the front door, the removal man thought it might be worth a bit, so we went to an auctioneer who came out and said it was Edwardian and I got three hundred pounds for it. When Michael started his Ministry he had no desk, he had to work at the dining table. One day I passed an office furniture shop with a sale on and the man let me have a dirty, broken old desk for ten shillings. When he had delivered it he had cleaned it and mended it. Michael had it all the time until he retired when it eventually fell to pieces.

I feel I have had a privileged life. I didn't resent the poverty but found the later parishes easier than the first two. I found it quite easy to make friends because it helped that people knew who I was.

With regard to the changes in the church, over the past fifty years I have seen many changes in worship, from the Book of Common Prayer, Alternative Services 1, 2 and 3 and The Alternative Service Book to Common Worship. I suppose I am a traditionalist at heart. I am not a lover of what they call 'Happy Clappy' evangelical services, but tend to look more to the higher traditional Anglican form of worship and I like a mixture of old and modern hymns. I must say I find it hard to accept women priests and dread the day when we may have women bishops and dare I say, a woman archbishop.

MARGARET RIDDELSDELL

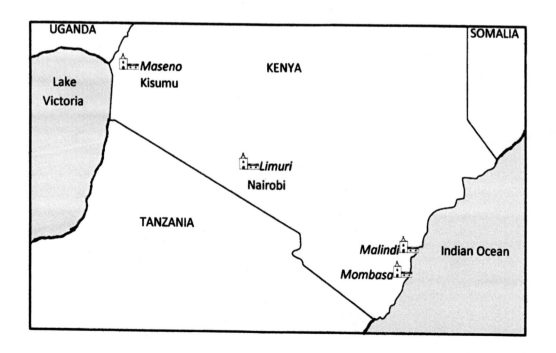

MARGARET'S STORY

' It's been an interesting life,
I am glad I married a missionary'

My name is Margaret Riddelsdell, my husband John and I live in Walton-on-the-Naze. I came from a middle class family, my father was a business man, he died when I was about fifteen. At that time we lived in a big house in Northwick Avenue, Kenton, Middlesex. My sister Kathleen was younger than me, we both went to North London Collegiate School in Edgeware, this is still the élite girls' independent school in the neighbourhood.

During the war when the air raids started we could have been evacuated but we preferred to stay at home. We slept under the dining room table for a while, then my father had a shelter built at the bottom of the garden. We slept there with my mother but our father wouldn't sleep there, he stayed in the house. We, in the shelter, worried about him and could not sleep because he was not safely with us. I had an aunt in Scotland and another in America, they wanted us to be sent across to America for the period of the war but our parents would not let us go.

My father continued to go up to London daily for his work until he fell ill and died in 1942. It was a very hard time for my mother, she had been left with an income from my father but our education was expensive.

Opposite: Me (centre) with my parents and sister

Below: Me (right) with my sister and the air raid shelter, 1940

We moved to a smaller house in a different area and then our father's company took on the responsibility of the school fees until we finally left school. The school had a religious Christian foundation; we had an assembly every morning with prayers and the Jewish children went to another room to have their own special prayers. My mother was very religious but my father never went to church, he was a Scottish Presbyterian, I think if we had been living in Scotland he might have gone. My aunt, my father's sister, always belonged to a church and her daughter was married to a clergyman. My mother was Church of England and took us to church every Sunday, if we didn't want to go we still had to go.

When I was about twelve my friend Mary took me to a Crusader Class where she had become a member and she wanted me to join it too. This was a Bible Class for girls who attended independent schools. They held summer camps and I went to one in Devon, this made a great difference to my commitment to Jesus as my Lord and Saviour. At some stage my friend Mary started to go to dancing classes, she had to find a partner to go with so she settled on Michael Riddelsdell. This was all during the war and when he was eighteen Michael was called into the Army and we heard then that Michael's elder brother John was an apprentice in the Merchant Navy. Two of the ships he had been on had been sunk by the enemy. In November 1940 John's ship the Port Hobart met the German pocket battleship the Admiral Scheer in the Atlantic, his ship was sunk and all the crew were taken prisoner. They were transferred to German supply ships, one to another, until they finally landed in Bordeaux. France was entirely occupied by the Germans. After some weeks they landed up in a prison camp for Merchant Sailors called Milag not very far from Hamburg. They remained there until the end of the war.

It was after that I first saw John on a Sunday morning in church. He was sitting near the front, Mary pointed him out to me and all I saw was the back of his head. It was later that he told us the story of the sinking of his ship, the Port Hobart. He said that he, as an apprentice, was on the bridge for the morning watch with the Third Mate who was in charge at the time. Suddenly the Third Mate shouted to him for a telescope, he realised that he was looking at a battleship coming in on them fast. He sounded the emergency signals at once and all the crew hurried to their danger stations.

The Port Hobart tried to run, every rivet on her hull rattling but it was no use, from about six miles away she dropped a heavy shell in the sea just alongside the bridge. The captain had the engines stopped immediately. The Third Mate told John to go and collect any valuables from his cabin now, with the few things he collected he saw a book of Bible Readings called Daily Light. All the crew, that night, were in the hold of the German battleship the Admiral Scheer.

John opened this little book at the evening reading of the 24th November. The reading was 'what doest thou here Elijah?' He laughed and showed it to his neighbour who laughed too. For the next five years he became more and more convinced that this question to Elijah was now directed at him, God was calling him to be a missionary, probably in Africa.

John said they were not threatened with violence in their particular camp. As long as they stayed inside the camp all was well. The Red Cross sent weekly food parcels most of the time but occasionally they ran out of these. Their guards were mostly sailors, many were quite elderly. There was one guard who would come into their barrack about lunchtime each day. He would take his loaded gun out of his belt, lay it on their table and stretch himself on one of their bunks and go to sleep, saying first "If you see an officer coming wake me quickly."

A picture of John was rummaged from the German camp after all the Germans had fled from the advancing British tanks in April 1945. Whilst he was a prisoner he was able to study to make up some of the learning he had not done at school. The Swiss Red Cross arranged for the examination papers to be sent from London University for any prisoners who wished to qualify for matriculation.

John took his exam in the camp and the papers were sent back to the Red Cross. Unfortunately they got lost and when he came home he had to mug up

Prisoner 90577 - John aged 17

as quickly as possible all the knowledge and sit the exam again that summer. He managed to get through and was accepted for Selwyn College Cambridge. He studied Geography for a couple of years to get his degree. He then went on to Ridley Hall where he did theology. Finally he was ordained in St. Paul's Cathedral in London.

I really met John whilst he was at Cambridge when he came back to Kenton for holidays. We got to know each other quite well and belonged to a group in our church known as 'The Senior Fellowship.' Most of the men had been in the Forces during the war. He asked me to marry him when I was only twenty. I knew that he believed he was called to become a missionary, I had wondered if that was a call for me also but I then turned down the idea as impossible. However if the calling came to us together that would be a different matter. It was something I had to face because it meant leaving my mother alone, my sister understood that it would be hard for my mother and Kathleen was very supportive of her. She didn't get married herself for six years after we went away during which time she lived at home, so my mother was well cared for. I trained as a teacher at Whitelands College in Putney and taught for two years in Harrow, not far from Kenton, during that time John was a curate in Kilburn. We got married in January 1950.

Then in September 1951 we went to the Church Missionary Society training college for men and couples, women were trained elsewhere in those days. We were told by some of the leaders in the CMS that it would be best if we did not start a family until we settled down in the country we were sent to. I accepted this advice but I was very anxious to have a baby and I was really upset when we first arrived there and met other couples with babies and young children. It soon became obvious to me however that they could not enter the training as fully as I was able to, so the advice I had been given was good even if it was a bit disappointing. The college was a big old house where we shared a room and had communal meals, so we didn't have to cook or do anything for ourselves. We learned a great deal which would help us in meeting and living with people of different cultures.

At the end of the training we went to Kenya sailing from Tilbury on 12th May 1952. The next day was my birthday, the most miserable birthday I have ever had. The journey took three weeks and two days to reach Mombasa, it was like reaching the moon, but we made many friends, especially David and Bea Milton-Thompson. They had recently been thrown out of China by the advancing Communists in power who were rejecting all Christian missionaries. They were to become our closest friends in Kenya.

We had expected from the CMS in London that we would go straight to the Kikuyu country but in Mombasa there was a letter to say we should take the train to Nairobi and our final destination would be decided. A very slow train left Mombasa at 6pm; we had a second class couch which provided us with two bunks to sleep the night. A meal was provided and the steam engine puffed us into Nairobi station at 8am. There was a wonderful reception from the Bishop of Kenya, the Secretary of the CMS and half a dozen long standing missionaries which included Peter Bostock. He introduced us to the growing church in different parts of the country. It was explained to us that we had arrived in Kenya at a time of unrest, when India had obtained its independence from British Rule.

Why not Kenya? The centre of this unrest was among the Kikuyu tribe. A number of these people had managed to acquire western education and had become leaders. Kenyetta was the outstanding man and dangerous to the future of Europeans living in Kenya. He was arrested, tried and sentenced to seven years in prison. The movement known as 'mau mau' was growing. It was thought by missionary leaders that we would be more useful at the Coast at this present time. When we had learnt some Swahili, the native language of the Coast and the lingua franca of East Africa, we would go back to Mombasa. Peter Mwang'ombe had just been made the rural Dean of the Coast, the first African to hold such a post. John could be a help to him if he asked for it. John would be called a 'Missionary Adviser' but would have no authority in the Church at the Coast.

While our Nairobi period continued Peter Bostock took John on a trip to Western Kenya to see what was happening in the church there. I have forgotten what it was all about, I begged off and remained in Nairobi. As soon as they got back I got John inside to tell him I was going to have a baby, I had seen a doctor and he had confirmed that I was pregnant. It was in October 1952 that we went back to Mombasa in that slow train in reverse, to live in an old house that had been the main Mombasa church before the Cathedral was built in 1905.

Right: Our house in Mombasa, the church before the cathedral was built

Opposite: Mombasa Cathedral built in 1905, the view from our bedroom window

In those waiting days we took a bus daily to the other end of the Mombasa Island to meet a Christian Arab for a session of Swahili conversation. Anne our first baby was born on January 31st 1953, a year marked by the coronation of Queen Elizabeth II and the conquest of Everest. She was baptised in Mombasa Cathedral in a Swahili service and among at least twelve African babies. The African babies were silent from one end to the other but Anne yelled her head off. Well, of course! If the African babies as much as murmured their mothers opened the front of their dresses and fed them. I was not as yet adjusted to another culture. I was however getting used to a new way of life. I had a cook who also did the housework but I never had an Ayah, a nanny, as other European mothers did. I always wanted to look after my own children. I enjoyed the heat but John found it quite tiring, 86°F in the hot season and 82°F in the cool season. I only looked after my own children as the family grew and did not do any parish work. John occasionally preached in the Cathedral in English. There was another church across the town with a Swahili-speaking congregation and he went to take the services there and sometimes to lead the worship. I was very happy there. Nothing was expected of me by the cathedral or the church or by the Church Missionary Society.

Although we were living on Cathedral ground John was primarily involved with churches and evangelism in the rural areas beyond the town. We always had to be careful financially, missionaries did not receive salaries, they were given allowances. The system of the CMS was worked out according to the size of their families and what the Society reckoned was the cost of living where they had been posted. An unmarried missionary living alone received a monthly allowance, a couple a little less than twice that of a single person. Allowances for children were given up to three in number. As we were expected to surrender our food vouchers when we left England our expectations were not very high.

I can't remember how much it was but John was very good at organising the money and keeping an eye on it. His father had been an accountant and his brother became an accountant too, so it was in the family. He gave me my housekeeping money and I could have a new dress if I needed it.

Our second daughter Elizabeth was born in 1956 while we were in England during our first leave. Tom came after we were back in Mombasa and only a month later we were moved from Mombasa to Malindi, an Arab town on the coast about eighty miles to the North. Accommodation for us wasn't ready and we moved house six times that year before we were finally settled.

There were three distinct communities in the town. There were the Muslim Arabs who had originally come from the Persian Gulf. They made their living as shopkeepers or by fishing. Every day they closed their work at the appropriate times for prayers in the mosque. While we were there they built a magnificent new mosque, we understood that the funds came from South Arabia. The next most numerous were Giryama Africans from the villages along the coast and inland. They were looking for work. Many of them were Christians and members of our church. The third group was of course Europeans; most of them were British settlers who had come to Kenya to farm in the highlands. Some had retired in Malindi, others had holiday homes there and appeared and disappeared. Some of these people wanted a service once a month. Christmas was the major occasion, John was the vicar for them and said they were regular church-goers annually on Christmas Eve.

There was no school for English children, in fact there were very few such children. Anne had started school in Mombasa but it was too far for her to attend and there were just three others, boys of her age. The wife of a hunter who took tourists on safari wanted to have something to do, so she volunteered to teach these children until they were old enough to go to a boarding school in Nairobi.

The four years we spent in Malindi were noted for their problems and accidents. Before we moved into the house that was being built for us John went down with jaundice, a nasty disease, not only for the patient but for those around him. 1960 was the year which marked our furlough. CMS wanted us in England and John wanted to learn some Arabic. We decided we would go by sea; it was still cheaper to travel by sea than air in those days, so bookings were made for two adults and three children. It was very pleasant; the Red Sea was not too hot at that time of the year. The ship was the Braemar Castle. We came through the Mediterranean to Gibraltar and anchored in Gibraltar Bay. A gale was blowing from the Atlantic. The following morning we found that the ship had dragged her anchor during the night and gone aground, some ugly rocks poked up out of the water about fifty yards away from us. We had to wait for high tide and then it took two tugs to pull us into deeper water; we then went into dock while a diver examined the bottom. Finally we were told we could continue our voyage. May I say that the Bay of Biscay was not very comfortable either?

When we were in England Anne went to Walton school for two terms which was her first experience of a proper school; she enjoyed it and coming home each day. After our return to Malindi, Anne had reached the age of seven and would have to go to the Primary Boarding School in Nairobi. This was the most traumatic event in our lives so far. We were advised that it would be best for her to join the school party which went up by the evening train. If she went with the school party she would be leaving us, if we took her to the school ourselves we would be leaving her. At least this is how the argument went. We drove her to Mombasa and on the station she joined the escort. We still have the photos of her now, in the train, staring out of the window at us on the platform and looking utterly bewildered. We were making every effort to hide our tears as the train went off.

I could continue to recount many events, good and bad but it would be wrong to give the impression that our stay in Malindi was unhappy. The children loved living there, the beach was only one hundred yards from our house. They were there almost every day as the afternoon got cooler. Of course I went with them. Elizabeth, aged four, made friends with our gardener's wife who lived nearby. We knew that this woman could not speak a word of English but Elizabeth came back and told us everything she had said to her. I wouldn't say that Elizabeth could speak Swahili but she could certainly understand much of what was said to her in that language.

John and Nathanial Mweri had become involved with a major village to the north called Fundisa. The people there had declared that they wanted to become Christians and needed quite a lot of instruction before they could be baptised. All this was very exciting. Then the floods came. Kenya had been going through a dry period for several years, the floods changed things all over the country. The area of Mount Kenya was particularly struck. It was also the source of the longest river in the country, called the Athi River there, further along its four hundred miles it became the Galana River. When it met us at the coast it was the Sabaki. Unfortunately I had to go into hospital in Nairobi. We took Elizabeth and Tom to Bea Milton-Thompson at Kaloleni, she was only too pleased to have them and they knew her.

John was much involved with Fundisa. Anne of course was at school. We heard that the four hundred miles of river had overflowed its banks, where it became the Sabaki it carried the bridge just north of Malindi out to sea. Then the rains themselves caught up with Malindi and the town was completely isolated, no vehicles could come in or out. John told me afterwards that they had thirteen inches of rain in fifteen hours; the whole of our garden was just a lake.

The people in the villages inland were cut off and had no food but the RAF came to our aid and carried bags of maize and dropped them where they were needed. Malindi was not isolated for very long and I got home after my operation and collected my children from Bea on the way.

Then a very strange letter came from the Bishop in Nairobi. He had agreed with the CMS Secretary that we would leave Malindi and go to St. Peter's Bible School in Maseno in Western Kenya. The Principal had left to go to a job in England. Someone was needed who could teach in Swahili. Nathanial Mweri was quite able to continue to organise all that was needed in Fundisa, which was quite true. Would we please go to Maseno as soon as we could? It was two or three weeks before Christmas, Anne was just about to come home. We certainly would not leave Malindi until she had returned to school but we started to make all our plans to travel the six hundred miles as soon as she was gone.

Anne went back to school about the middle of January, a week later we set out for Maseno, John myself and two little children. There were signs of the floods almost the whole way. It took two days as we spent a night in the Nairobi Guest House. We had to make several long diversions to avoid routes which were impassable. Finally as the night came on, we found the Bible School and the nice little thatched house that was to be our home for the next few years.

It was strange to us and very different to living in Malindi. There was no electricity; our lights, cooker and refrigerator were all operated with paraffin. The main part of the house was a living room, a bedroom large enough for a double bed and two very small bedrooms, more like cupboards. Then on the other side of the courtyard was another building, which held a kitchen for all the cooking and a bathroom-cum-toilet. Outside was a brick erection with an old oil drum on it and a space for a wood fire below, which was how we got our hot water.

Right: Our first house in Maseno

Opposite: Anne with her bosom friend in Mombasa

There had been changes since Bishop Beecher had been appointed. Kenya had been a single diocese prior to 1953 and it was known as the Diocese of Mombasa. Shortly before we arrived it had been divided into three. We were now in the Diocese of Maseno and the bishop there was the Rt. Revd. Festo Olang. He was living in the large house in the Bible School grounds in order to be accessible to visitors.

There were a growing number of churches and very few clergy. Each padre had the care of about twenty churches. John's task was to double the number of clergy as quickly as possible. There was a theological college in Limuru but they would only accept men who had completed secondary school, there were not enough of them available. The men who would be trained in Maseno would be older, with proven gifts of leadership, but with only primary education. We started with eight students. They had to leave their families and live in dormitory accommodation in the Bible School. We had to feed them of course, so we had to hire a cook who lived locally, we had a grant from the Diocesan Office but it was not very large. Their diet was some maize with beans and green vegetables, there was a little meat twice a week.

It became my task to measure the daily rations to the cook. I became the mother of the student family. I took their temperatures and issued anti-malarial drugs; a bad case I would send to the hospital which was about a mile away. Before long the local mothers would bring their babies if they had pushed maize beans up their noses or something like that. Many children caught scabies because they were not kept clean. They called it 'twist'. With the help of a nurse from the hospital I set up a 'twist' clinic with a lecture from me on how to avoid it.

Me advising parents how to avoid Scabies and children waiting to be treated

Maseno is right on the Equator, there is a notice on each side of the road to indicate the line where the traveller crossed it. The Bible School and the Police Station are on one side, the Secondary School and the Hospital are on the other. Kisumu, on Lake Victoria, is seventeen miles from Maseno and was the main shopping area in our day. The road from one to the other was horrific but I understand it is not like that today. Maseno has developed and is the site of the University of Western Kenya. The Bible School now calls itself St. Phillip's Theological College and is hardly recognisable.

I continued looking after my children and they had to face going to boarding school. Elizabeth went when she was seven. I cut her long locks the day before she left me as it would be easier for her to handle. We all went by car and took Anne to her dormitory first. Then we went with Elizabeth to the new children's department. As we left her Elizabeth howled at the top of her voice. Someone told us that the moment we were out of sight she stopped and went off to see what would happen next, we always said she was born with no sound control. Two more years and it was Tom's turn. We always knew that he was the most sensitive member of our family, things so often went wrong for him. He found his first term very difficult. John was taking the children by car and we had agreed that if Tom appeared too upset to bring him home. He took him in and had a word with the House Master who said "No, don't take him away. If he goes away now he has to go through it all again."

Our fourth child was born in Victoria Hospital in Kisumu. It was in the middle of the rainy season when I woke John at about 3am. He went down the garden to wake our neighbour Pat, so she could come and sleep in our bed to look after our other children in the morning. The roads were very muddy and slippery. When we reached Kisumu I said to John "Don't go to the hospital yet, let's go and look at the lake." We did for about two hours. When we finally went into the hospital the nurse said "You're not in labour yet but you cannot go home this weather." The operator of the telephone in Maseno was not on duty from midday on Sundays until Monday morning. The Chief-of-Police in Kisumu, a friend, had said "If the child is born at the week-end call me and I will get the news through by our radio system." At about 2pm on Sunday two burly policemen came into the Bible School demanding to see Mr. Riddelsdell. When they were finally sure they had the right man they said "You have a son." Pat came running over "What's his name?" "Mark."

Bishop Festo was living in the old missionary house called 'Sunrise.' It had been built by the first missionary to arrive in Maseno, every new student who came there added a bit to it and it looked like that. It had six rooms and several outhouses. Then a new road was built that would allow Festo to take his car to his own house a few miles away. That was just what we wanted. He could live there and be available. It was just what we wanted too with our growing family - his house. At the same time our children were making friends with some of the local boys. These children had no toys other than things they made for themselves. I restricted my children to having no more than two Dinky cars each. If they appeared to be much richer than their friends, visitors just came round to see what they could get. There were a few, rather older than ours, who came to exercise their conversation in English. These also protected them from the others.

Elizabeth (centre) at her farewell party before going to school in England

Our second house in Maseno

While we were in Maseno a new branch of the Mothers' Union was opened. I became a member and another missionary was leading it. It grew quickly but many of the husbands disapproved of it. We understood it was on account of the word 'union' and its association with the right to strike. That would destroy the unity of the family and the authority of the husband. When we went back to Kenya thirty years later I was very impressed by some of these groups. In Mombasa a Mothers' Union was busy building a hostel for girls who had come into the town to find work and found it very difficult to get accommodation.

There were several European teachers in the Secondary School with young children in Maseno. They all had the problem of how to teach their children before they went to boarding school. Some took them to Kisumu each day. Our friends Paddy and Roy had four, two girls and two boys about the same age as ours. Another had three. It was Paddy's idea I think to start an infant school in her own home. She invited any of the teachers, African or European, to send their children if they were the right age. She also asked me to join her teaching staff. All our children except Anne had their earliest schooling at Paddy's. Every day Paddy came to collect me in her car, this is what encouraged me to learn to drive and take the necessary test.

After Independence in 1963 the African Government took measures to see that all State Secondary Schools were open to African children. It was uncertain what would happen to Missionary children. The headmistress of Limuru Girls' School wrote to warn the parents of European girls that she may not be allowed to admit their children next year, if they were wise they would arrange places for them in schools in England. This would affect Anne. Elizabeth had already gone to King Edward's School at Whitley in Surrey and settled down well. Tom was finding it difficult to understand the accent of the African teachers and they tended to use corporal punishment more than his earlier teachers had. He was just eleven and that was the age at which he could go to King Edward's.

I found it very difficult to see three of my children for only two holidays a year. There were a number of private schools which were allowed to continue. They had their own fees and no grants. The CMS decided that they would cover the fees for missionary children, so that is where Mark went to board when he was seven. He was only one hundred miles away from us. We could visit for school events and bring him home for half term.

At this time I was pregnant again and had another little boy who we named Peter, he was born in England when we were on leave. The most recent group of ordinands had just been made priests, so we took the opportunity to visit Jerusalem on the way. We had Tom and Mark with us and walked them so much that Mark stopped as we walked down one of the narrow streets and said "I thought God lived here?" This was all in March and Peter was born in Colchester Hospital the following October.

Our next move was to St. Paul's United Theological College at Limuru, near Nairobi. Men from the Anglican, Presbyterian, Methodist and the Dutch Reform Church had joined together to train their future clergy. Each church had some tutors on the staff. Some students were studying for a Makerere University Diploma but the majority for the Limuru Certificate. Most of them came with their wives and children. There were more than one hundred living there. There were about ten teachers on the staff but none of them were Africans. When John joined the staff the Principal was an American Presbyterian. About a year later he retired and went back to America. Then, to everybody's joy a Kenyan, Samuel Kibicho, who had been in America doing a PhD came back and was immediately appointed Principal. At the same time an Anglican who had been studying in England was appointed the Vice-Principal. The students thought this was a great advance, unfortunately it did not last.

*Students training
for ordination
and (top left)
Bishop Festo of
Western Kenya*

Within a year Sam Kibicho was offered a post on the staff of Nairobi University, obviously it was advancement and he accepted it. At the same time Horace Etimeci also resigned to take up another job in Nairobi. The College was left without any African tutors. The day after this was announced, Sam Kibucho came to talk to John in our house. The College Council had had a meeting and wanted to know if he would be acting Principal until it was possible to find another African Principal. After talking this over with me and praying about it he said "Yes."

Our children continued with the same schooling arrangements. Mark was still at Turi, the older ones were in England at King Edward's in Whitley, Surrey, all at the same school. They all had to be away but they all came home for the holidays. While John was teaching at the College, Peter our youngest was still under school age. There was a nursery for the students' children and I took Peter to join them. They put him in a group according to his age, which was largely playing with clay. He was not allowed to learn to read because in their view he was too young. He was bored and refused to go so I gave him some teaching at home. By the time he was old enough to go to St. Andrew's School at Turi, his sister Elizabeth had left school and come home to Kenya. It was to be a gap year before she decided what her future should be. She applied for and got a job as an assistant in the little boy's dormitory at Turi School. Although Peter was only six it was too good an opportunity to start at boarding school and be tucked up by his sister at bedtime. Elizabeth found it difficult to keep a straight face when he addressed her as "Miss Riddelsdell."

John was faced with a lot of problems when he became Acting Head. There was resentment among some of the students that the Principal was a European again when Kenya was now an independent country. The country had just introduced decimalisation, pints became litres. It had become the custom that to students who had wives and children living in the College with them, the College gave to each child under a certain age a pint of milk daily. Just before Sam Kibicho left the senior students had obtained his agreement that children who had a pint of milk would receive a litre.

At the end of John's first month he had a letter from the Church Commissioners in Nairobi, who sent the support grant for the number of African students regularly, to ask why the cost of milk had just been doubled. John had to explain that money was very short and each child would receive half a litre daily. They were very angry and threatened to strike if they were not given a litre per child. Leaders from the College Council came and addressed the whole College. If there was any more talk about a strike the College would be closed and all the students sent home. Only those who signed an agreement would be allowed back. It quietened down after a while but the dislike of having a European Principal once more was there for the whole of the two years we remained there.

We moved from our house in the College to what was regarded as the Principal house, chiefly because it had a larger office. I lost my garden which I had attended to carefully and that was a disappointment. John's work was now more administrative than teaching and he spent long hours at his desk late into the night. He wanted to get the College accounts right before a new Principal took control. I hardly saw him except for meals. During this period two African tutors joined the staff. One of them left quickly in search of a higher salary. The other was John Nyesi. He was a Luo and we had known him when he was a boy at Maseno School. He had been a student at Limuru but had no degree. At the end of two terms his future for this office would be considered by the Council. They tried to find a suitable man to be a Bursar, to carry the administration, the first was not competent and the second not honest.

One evening before Christmas John collapsed. The doctor thought it was a heart attack and put him in a car to take him to Nairobi hospital. I went with him and stayed there all night while he was in Special Care. The next day however the doctor said his heart was sound, but he needed a holiday. So we looked for a place we had not been to before. We packed all our camping equipment in or on our Peugeot 405 and I drove all the way because the doctor said John should not do so. We found a place to camp in Samburu. We enjoyed exploring an area and a people we had not seen before and got back to Limuru in time for a new term. The College Council met again and appointed John Nyesi as Principal from the end of the current term. We had to decide whether John stayed in a teaching capacity at Limuru or asked to be moved elsewhere. We thought that John Nyesi would have greater freedom if we were not there. John wrote to Festo Olang, who by this time was the Archbishop of the Province of Kenya and living in Nairobi, he replied by appointing him Principal of Trinity College, situated in the more crowded side of Nairobi. Just what courses were to be held there was not clear.

John's father had had a very serious stroke. He asked if he could have a month's leave to go and see him at his own expense. This was granted. I was often left on my own by John in Africa but that never worried me because I could by then speak the language and talk to people and had plenty of friends. Some of them were local friends. Now there was to be a final change. After John came back he received a letter from CMS in London. The Society's Representative in Nairobi was going on leave to England, so would John stand in his place for six months? This seemed to be God's purpose for the immediate period. What would be beyond that would become clear. Anne was in England in a teacher training college in Clacton. Elizabeth was studying catering but not certain that would be what she wanted to do lifelong. Tom had left school and come home to live with us. He was attending classes to try to get an extra 'A' level. Mark was at King Edward's and excelling at cricket. Peter was still in Turi and very happy there. We had no idea of what we had to face.

In Uganda Amin, at the head of the Army, was ruling with extraordinary violence. Christian leaders were just vanishing without reason. Missionaries were advised to leave and take refuge in Kenya. Telephone communication between Uganda and England was cut off but the line was still open between Uganda and Kenya. Communication between the Church in Uganda and CMS London was through our house in both directions. Amin had it in his mind that the Church was planning an uprising against his rule. He had Archbishop Lewum's house searched for weapons but found nothing. Amin summoned Lewum to come and talk to him. The Archbishop went with some other bishops and church leaders. He was called from the waiting room to see Amin by himself. That was the last time the bishops saw him alive. The following day it was officially announced that the Archbishop had died in a car accident. It soon became clear that he had been shot.

The day of his funeral was appointed and his body handed over in a coffin, only a limited number of people were allowed to attend. No one was allowed to enter for the funeral. To overcome this, a service was held in Nairobi Cathedral. A previous Archbishop of Uganda, Bishop Brown and the CMS Africa Secretary, Jesse Hillman flew in for the service.

While all this was going on a car drew up outside our CMS Guest House. A man wearing a purple shirt and a dog collar, obviously a bishop, asked where Bishop Brown's room was. When he found no one there he went in, sat down and waited. When Bishop Brown and Jesse Hillman came back they gasped to see Yona Okoth, the Bishop of Bekedi. Many people were afraid he was under arrest or worse.

Jesse had heard that Nairobi was full of Amin's spies and realised that Yona's public arrival would put him in considerable danger. He found that I was the only person there and asked to borrow a plain shirt. I gave him one of John's dullest. He went back, removed his regalia and put this shirt on him, then they spirited him out the back way, over the lawn to our house. Remarkably no one saw them go. A servant said they had seen a bishop come in but not seen him since. He must have gone. I hid him in our spare bedroom. We did not breathe a word of his presence to anybody.

After about a week, Mrs. Okoth was smuggled over the border from Uganda and also brought into our house. They stayed with us until the General Secretary of the National Christian Council of Kenya, who was a Liberian, made arrangements for both of them to be put on a flight to Liberia. They remained there until Amin's fall and flight to Saudi Arabia. Later Yona Ocoth was elected Archbishop of the church in Uganda.

The Carey's were due back in May, so we had to find another job. The Guest House in Nairobi was being handed over to the Kenya Church and would be known as the CPK Guest House in future (Church of the Province of Kenya).

The new body planned to open a branch in Mombasa. I was asked if I would run it for two or three years before handing it over to an African warden. John would be the bookkeeper and carer of the building generally. But we had at this stage made our decision because of the needs of our family. Anne had already finished her higher education without a home behind her. The grandparents had helped us but now my mother had died. John's father had had a stroke and was now in a nursing home in Dover, near John's brother Peter. Also John was now fifty four. If he was to find a job that was worthwhile he needed to start while he had some energy.

Reluctantly we decided the time had come to leave Kenya. We had been in Africa for twenty five years. During this time we came back to England for six to eight months, every three to four years. We rented a house and the children would go to local schools while they were still at the primary stage. They had a varied education. I wasn't really pleased to come back, we all regarded Kenya as home but it was the obvious thing to do, so we had to do it. I missed Africa very much, especially the climate. When we came back John became the vicar of St. Andrew's, Ilford in the Chelmsford Diocese and worked there for eleven years before retiring.

We lived in the vicarage there and I enjoyed that. I used to help in a Play Group from nine in the morning to twelve in the church hall and I headed up the Mothers' Union for a short time. It was a very nice house with gas heating. When we moved there we had no furniture or anything, we had left it all behind. The houses we had lived in had always been furnished. When we mentioned this, furniture came tumbling through our front door, it seemed that half the people of Ilford had more than they wanted. I did things in Ilford like sitting with people who needed continuous attention and earned a bit of pocket money but we never had lacked anything we needed. Our daughter Elizabeth married a Canadian while we were there. When she had her first baby I worked at some odd jobs to raise enough money to pay the fare to go to see her and our first grandchild and to help Elizabeth of course. Very few clergy wives in those days did not have a full-time job. They were either teaching or doing some other job but not many stayed at home.

All my children haven't actually stayed within the worshipping community of the church. When we got to Ilford Anne was teaching, Elizabeth was nursing and Tom was at college. The two younger ones did join in church activities. Peter was in the choir. Mark was in the Youth Group for a while, but the latter disbanded because there was no adult leader. In the end there were too many members and not enough leaders, so it all collapsed, he then joined the local sports club. By this time Mark had left King Edward's School because the Council of Essex would not give a grant once his father had ceased working overseas. They said he must now go to a local school. It was easier for Peter because he did all his schooling in Ilford.

Before we left Kenya there were complaints from pupils at secondary schools, where teaching was in English, because they could not understand the language of the Prayer Books used in the school chapels. The Synod appointed a group to translate the Book of Common Prayer into simple modern English for use in schools. John was involved in this work and it was published by the Church Publishing Centre. Although it was not produced for this purpose the Provost of Nairobi Cathedral used it in their major services. It began a movement to produce African Christian Liturgies.

Right:
St. Andrew's
Ilford in the snow

Opposite:
Me outside
the vicarage at
Ilford with
my daughter

When we arrived at St. Andrew's Ilford, we found that the Church of England was experimenting with new services for Holy Communion and Evening Prayer to replace the language which was five hundred years old. A book was produced called The Alternative Services Book 1980; the Parish Council agreed that we should buy a supply of them. Many of the older people did not like it. They didn't like the kiss of peace in Holy Communion; the teenagers thought it was wonderful. This led on to more changes starting with the removal of some of the pews at the back of the church for people to meet and have a cup of coffee after the service. Later a new Communion Table was placed just under the chancel arch so that Holy Communion could be celebrated much nearer to the congregation. There was also a longer Communion Rail for people to receive the bread and wine nearer to the congregation. The Bishop gave permission to certain lay women and lay men to distribute the elements. All these changes took place over eleven years. It did not finish after we retired. More recently St. Andrew's has accepted a woman vicar. This was a goal I strongly approved of.

We retired to Walton-on-the-Naze. John's family had lived in Walton for two hundred years. My mother had gone to live there before she died. John's father had died; his mother was ninety two. She was living in the smaller of two bungalows. We went to the one next door. I looked after her for eight years and we had all our meals with her. She lived to be one hundred and received the Queen's greeting card. When she was shown it she said "Oh, she should not have been bothered." Mother died just two months later.

The following year we went back to Kenya for a holiday. It was twenty years since we had left. We met so many of our friends who now have died. We saw Archbishop Festo, Bishop Peter Mwang'ombe and his wife Mariamu our daughter's Godmother, and Gilbert Supai, the evangelist John worked with in Mombasa. We met Susan, Anne's bosom friend in the earliest days; she took us to see her parents. We were not interested in animals. We left that to the tourists.

Back in Walton I became a church warden, an office which the Riddelsdells have occupied at various times in the previous one hundred and sixty years. It has been a very interesting life. I am glad I married a missionary.

HILARY SMITH

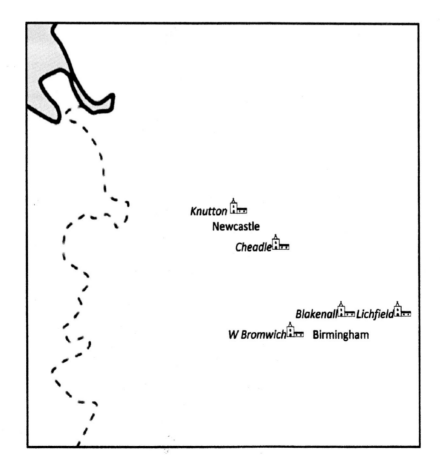

Hilary's Story

' I'd rather work in the background'

My name is Hilary Smith and I live in West Bromwich. Our last parish was in West Bromwich but we moved into a different parish when Derek retired. My maiden name was Poxon. My grandmother lived with us when I was a child and she was the churchgoer, my parents weren't, apart from odd occasions. My grandmother had quite an influence on me because my mother had to work during the war so I was left with my grandmother. I started to learn the piano and I can remember her paying me sixpence to play certain hymns that she liked. I went to a Methodist Sunday school until I was ten and then a friend from school asked whether I would like to go to church with her, so I asked Mum and she said "Yes, that's fine so long as you go somewhere."

I went to the church Sunday school with this girl and that was the last time she went. It was strange really and as though she'd got to get me there somehow. I continued to go and quite enjoyed the Sunday school and later on I became a teacher, I preferred it to the Methodist. It just sort of clicked with me I suppose and parents wanted you to go in those days.

I had one sister who was four years younger than me. I was born in 1934 but I can't remember my sister being born at all. My mother worked in a shop during the war and my father was just over the age limit and every time the call up letters came they were pleased because he hadn't got to go, so we weren't really affected, except that I can remember the bombing. I was terrified in bed when I heard the sirens and hearing the planes come over and staying awake until the 'All Clear' went. We had a couple of bombs in the village but they were ones that didn't blow up. I can remember Coventry being bombed, seeing the glow.

We weren't well off but we weren't poor either and I never remember going without anything. Both my mother and father worked in shops so the food situation didn't worry us. They worked in different shops but both for the same firm, both food shops. It was how they met because originally they did both work together until my father got promotion and my mum stayed at the same one she'd always worked for. We were living in a village called Heath Hayes near Cannock in Staffordshire.

I met my husband through the church. We were both Sunday school teachers. There was a group of us at the time and we used to go to each other's houses and do things in groups and then we paired off. Derek worked for the Coal Board at that time.

First of all he worked in the office for two or three years and then he went underground. He trained as a mechanic, a fitter. He had to mend the conveyer belts and the machinery underground. When we got married he was studying with the Coal Board to get promotion and he enjoyed his work very much. I knew before we were married that when he was about fourteen he'd explored something about the priesthood and our priest at the time went into it and just said "You're studying the wrong sort of subjects, so it's no use" and it was dismissed.

After we'd been married about a year he was restless. We were living with my mother because housing was not easy to get and we were saving up at that point to get a house of our own and we just talked things over. He'd got this feeling that he'd got to explore the Ministry again. Our church was a daughter church of Cannock and we'd got a Priest-in-Charge but the priest who had married us had moved soon after. I said to Derek "Let's go and talk to Father Dodd," as we knew him at that point and so we did and he suggested that Derek should get in touch with the vicar of Cannock, which he did and he explored things with the church authorities as to what needed to be done.

Of course Derek hadn't got any O levels at this point, all the certificates that he had were not academic if you like, so first of all they said that he had to get at least five O levels and he may have to do A levels. What he did was a correspondence course to get his O levels which took him almost three years. The first year I think he got three and then re-sat the next year, so it took him the three years. He was working full-time, so he had to do all the work in the evenings and at the week-ends.

We had in our dioceses then a Guild of St. Stephen which has now gone unfortunately. It was for people who felt they had a calling so Derek joined that and it was the then Bishop of Stafford who took Derek under his wing and when he had achieved four O levels and re-sat two he said it was time he went to the selection board. He did that and fortunately got through and they said he would have to do one year pre-theological training as they called it. For that he went to Bernard Gilpin College in Durham which isn't going any longer. It was a general course where he did all sorts of things like philosophy and that type of thing and after that he went for three years to Chichester.

Whilst he was at Gilpin I was working up in Heath Hayes at a school in a non-teaching position, earning some money. I was called a Welfare Assistant but it was like a classroom assistant really. By this time we'd moved into one of my mother's houses. She owned a couple. My sister had moved into it first when they got married but when they wanted to move on to a bigger one it just dropped right for us. We were renting the house but my mum didn't charge us much rent really, we only had my wage to live on whilst all this was taking place. The plan was to stay there until Derek had finished his training but the year that he was in Durham was 1963, a year of absolutely dreadful weather in January. I had frozen pipes and if it hadn't been for a father of a friend of mine I don't know what I would have done because I was terrified of floods in the house. It was only heated by coal fires in those days with no heating upstairs and all this put a doubt in my mind 'Can I stand this for another three years?'

Derek wrote to Chichester while he was still at Durham to see if it was possible for us to move down there and live out whilst he was at college. They were just starting with this married man's business because beforehand it had been mostly single men. The Principal wrote back and wanted to see us. I remember going down at Easter Time and he interviewed both of us and said "You can live out but you have to do two terms in college first."

So we moved down to Chichester, the both of us, in New Year '64. We stayed there for the rest of Derek's training and Nicola our eldest was born down there. We had to find our own accommodation. Derek found a little bungalow. We'd been saving really since we were married but we didn't have any grants at all. In those days they didn't provide anything. We had to live on our savings, both our families were very good and we rented this bungalow which was a couple of miles from the college. Derek had got a little three wheeler Reliant car so he was able to travel and that worked out very well. Our daughter was born in the bungalow while we were down there so we called her our Sussexian.

When he'd finished his training we came back to the diocese and he was ordained at Lichfield Cathedral in June 1966. He had started on this road in 1959 so it had taken him seven years. We were already married a year before he started on this course. We had always both been very much part of the church so I encouraged him. It just seemed natural really. While he was at Chichester a sister of one of the tutors used to invite the wives round because there were more married men coming forward and she explained some of the problems of being a clergy wife. After his ordination he became curate at Cheadle in North Staffordshire and we had a tiny two bedroomed house on a new estate. It was a curate's house but adequate and we were there almost four years. It should have been initially three but the Rector, who was very good, asked him if he would stay on another year. Chichester had been quite high in churchmanship, but that one and most of the parishes we had been in were more middle-of-the-road I would say.

We then moved to a second curacy at Blakenall Heath in the Walsall Deanery. It was a very large parish with three churches, mostly working class. There were a lot of factories around there. It was a change for us because Cheadle was a country town if you like and more middle class I would say, so it was a good experience to have the two different types of parish.

The house we moved into was absolutely dreadful. We went to see the vicar in the house before we moved and in the dining room there was all black damp all over the walls. By this time we had two children. Our second baby had been born at Cheadle. The vicar said "Oh I don't know whether we can do anything about that." But I think he gathered from the way we were reacting that we wouldn't come if he didn't do something. We couldn't go into a house like that with our babies. Anyway, he did do something about the damp but there was no heating as such. There was a gas fire in the living room but nothing else at all, anywhere. The kitchen was bare bricks and it was a semi-detached house with three bedrooms. We moved there and were all right but I never felt happy there. I think it was the house that got me down a bit. You went in the front door and the rooms just stretched back one room to the other sort of thing and as I say it was freezing cold.

While we were there a vicar in a neighbouring parish was having some sort of central heating put in through the diocese I suppose and he had some old fashioned storage heaters and he said we could have those if we could get them up to the house which was about three miles away. Derek and the other curate went down to fetch them in the car thinking they could just lift them in but found they were full of bricks. He did manage to get two so we had one in the hallway and one in the study. The hallway one managed to send a bit of heat upstairs but some mornings you'd come down and there was no heat because they were very temperamental. We were there for two and a half years. I hadn't done any outside work since we moved to Chichester because of having the children and I didn't do anything in the church during this time while Derek was a curate because of the children. While we were in Blakenall we'd decided to adopt because I'd had problems when Alison was born, our second one.

At that time adoption was easy so we went to the Church Adoption Society and we had Andrew. He was ten weeks old when we had him, it was like having a new born baby but he'd passed the worst of things by then. So we had three children when Derrick moved to his first parish. By then Andrew was almost two, Alison four and Nicola seven,

We moved to Knutton in Newcastle-Under-Lyme, Staffordshire. We had a beautiful modern house in its own grounds with a lovely garden with raspberries, gooseberries and blackcurrants. It had central heating even in the four bedrooms. Andrew had his own room, the girls preferred to share and we had a room for my mother when she came to stay, so everything worked out. My father had died when he was only fifty, so that was before I was married. My mother went to live with my sister, so she wasn't on her own but often came to stay.

*Our beautiful
modern house
at Knutton*

When we arrived in Knutton the church warden's first remark was "The vicar's wife has always done the flowers." To which I replied "Not this one." I'd never been a flower arranger but I did start a Ladies' Fellowship group because the Mothers' Union had just literally folded and the parish was very run down when we first went there. The previous vicar had been there years. I got this group together for any age after calling a general meeting to see if there was any interest. There was, so I became the Chairman and we elected a Treasurer and Secretary. That meeting was held in our house but Fellowship meetings were held at our church school. There was a lot of interaction between the church school and the church. The headmaster became a Parish Reader and came a lot to our church. Derek and he got on very well. It went very well while we were there and for a long time afterwards. I never wanted to be on the Parochial Church Council because there might be problems with differences of opinion.

We'd only been at Knutton three and a half years, thinking we were going to stay for about seven years, which was the normal sort of span, when the Bishop of Lichfield wrote to Derek and said he knew we'd only been there a little while but would we consider going back to Blakenall Heath where he'd done his first curacy to set up a team Ministry. All the parishes that Derek has had the bishop had instigated. You didn't apply for parishes in those days, certainly not in our diocese.

The offer was made by the bishop and then you went and met their representatives. We did that after talking it over and then of course we went back to Blakenall Heath. We were a little bit sad because we had got to know a lot of the people and the children had as well. Nicola had just passed the Eleven Plus which fortunately they accepted at Blakenall and she went to the Grammar School there but first she had one term still to do in the juniors so she went back to the same children that she had known before we left.

Alison, aged seven, was still in primary school but Andrew was affected the most because he had only just started school and when we went to Blakenall they had this Initial Teaching Alphabet system, so he was really confused for a while. He'd started off with ordinary reading but now he was in this classroom where everything on the walls was in this ITA. The teacher said he need not use it but of course he was quite confused for a while until he got sorted out and I think the move affected Andrew more than the girls. The girls were going back to their original school. The vicarage was a nice modern house. We've been lucky to have all modern houses because I wouldn't have liked a big old ramshackle house.

When we went there Derek was the only staff. There should have been other staff but there wasn't. The vicar that had been there when we were there before had moved and they'd had quite an unsettling time. They'd had a person who after a few months went over to The Greek Orthodox, so it had been very unsettling.

For the first four months Derek was completely working on his own and then another team vicar came and a few months after that we had a lady parish worker. Then another team vicar came within the first year, so we had two team vicars and one parish worker who worked with Derek at the main church. Someone obviously thought that Derek was good at building things up and after a while it became a very successful team Ministry. It was two years before it was all sorted and he became Rector after that. That first group got on really well together and the wives. When the parish worker left we had a curate in her place that went to live in that horrible house. It had heating in by then but still was not a very good curate's house and has since been sold.

After five years the team vicars moved because their contract was for five years and Derek's was for seven after the setting up of the team. We went over the seven and were there for ten years which was nice for the children and I

Derek as Mayor's Chaplain while Rector of Blakenall Heath

did a bit of secretarial work but only in the parish for Derek. I taught myself to type and used to do the marriage registers. I became the PCC secretary but I only took the notes. I did that for several years. A few of us started a little singing group and we used to sing at some of the services. We called ourselves The Christones because it was Christ Church, so we were the Christ Ones. They'd got a church choir as well but at special services we used to sing and we went out to Old People's Homes and anywhere where they wanted someone to sing and had heard of us by word of mouth.

I also played the organ a little bit, not for Sunday services but if they were stuck for a funeral. I had learned the piano as a child and I only played the organ as a piano. I couldn't do the pedals or anything. I did get a little fee for playing the organ and doing the registers, so I got a bit extra. We didn't have loads of money but I never felt hard-up and the children were not deprived. I suppose I'd got used to having so little to live on whilst Derek was training that I'd been broken in. We hadn't got a lot to spare but we managed. I never worked in an outside job and that was okay for me. We did have holidays. There was a clergy holiday place at Wells-next-the-Sea and we went there for several years with the children because it was cheap. Eventually we bought a touring caravan and we used to go off in that.

At the end of our stay at Blakenall Heath we got a call from the Dean of Lichfield to say would we be interested in a parish in Lichfield, so we went over to see him and St. Michael's with St. Mary's, two parish churches in the centre of Lichfield and off we go over there. It was very different there because Blakenall Heath was very working class and Lichfield very different, very middle class. After we'd been there about a year he was asked to take on another parish as well but he did have a deaconess.

At Lichfield there was a little singing group that sang once a month at the Family Service, so I was part of that and I always helped with anything that was going on such as social events but I don't think anything was expected of me. I used to run the Sunday morning coffees in church but didn't have a specific role. We were there for twelve years and were happy. Samuel Johnson had lived in Lichfield and the Samuel Johnson Society always had a week of celebrations in September with a Service in the Market Square on a Saturday. The choir from St. Michael's were always invited to go and sing and Derek used to take the Service there.

Upper: Derek with the Deaconess Hazel
on the left and me on the right at Lichfield

Centre: Derek as Mayor's Chaplain at Lichfield

Lower: Derek taking the Samuel Johnson Society
Service in the Market Square at Lichfield

As well as the happy times we had some sad ones because two of our children were married there and both got divorced. One was married for four years and the other only two. My husband wanted to marry both of them but when our middle daughter Alison got married it was strange how it worked out. Derek didn't marry her because Paul's father was very ill with cancer and not expected to live, so they were married at a Registry Office in Coventry thinking he'd be able to come to the wedding service but in fact he was too ill to come and they just had to go and visit him in hospital. They decided they would have a Blessing a month later and that was held at St. Andrew's, so Derek took that service.

They are still married but it is our eldest daughter Nicola and son Andrew whose marriages have failed. Andrew had a son who stayed with his mother but we still see him; he is now seventeen. Andrew went into the forces and unfortunately had to have a kidney out after he joined so he came out and he does security work. He's been all over, the Caribbean, Ireland and the Continent and working in Kurdistan. He's remarried now and lives in Monmouth.

Both of the girls were in the choir and always joined in everything and did bell-ringing as well. They went to the Brownies and Guides and were always part of it. Andrew did come to church but more under sufferance as they say. He did go to the Cubs and Scouts and to church until he was fifteen and he'd been a Server as well. But at the age of fifteen he got himself a job in catering where he was working Sunday lunchtime, so that worked out all right for him, didn't it! The girls were always happy to have Derek as their father and vicar, Andrew less so. I can remember him getting down in the car if Derek was dropping him off at school, he didn't want his friends to know and Derek was Chairman of the Governors of his school for a long time and that didn't go down very well either. I can remember him saying to Derek one day "Why haven't you got a proper job?" He didn't think being a vicar was a proper job, but it was all right most of the time.

Our last parish was St. Andrew's in West Bromwich. I think Derek felt he wanted to finish off in the urban area. He's an urban priest not a country priest and we had been in Lichfield for twelve years. We were offered West Bromwich and that was very different again, a much smaller congregation of course and only one church, after three. We were supposed to have a curate but there wasn't one. They did appoint a half post soon after we came and the person did half a diocesan post and half a post with Derek at St. Andrew's. It was a more working class area than Lichfield but I think we just adapt really to where we are. By this time Alison was nursing at Wolverhampton and would come and see us on her days off, so she was the one who spent most time with us at West Bromwich. The other two had moved out so we were really just living alone in the vicarage. Derek was sixty-four when he retired and that was on the grounds of ill-health. The stress was building up and the doctors were saying "Have you got to be working?" So he did retire a year early. That was all right because we knew it was going to happen and he told the parish about nine months before.

While we were at St. Andrew's at West Bromwich there was an unofficial joining up of Methodists and Anglicans. They signed all the agreements on our last day of Derek's retirement which was quite nice because it kind of finished everything off. The Methodists had joined with St. Andrew's because their Chapel had closed down, so they became part of St. Andrew's but they had all their own finances. The Methodist minister came to take part in the service once a month. So strangely enough my life in the church started with the Methodists and at the end of my husband's Ministry uniting with them.

We had found this retirement house two years before. It is not very far away, only in the next parish, so Derek was able to come down and check that things were all right here. This is a Pensions Board house which means we have put in a certain amount of money and own a part of it. You can choose where to live as long as it isn't in the parish where you've been working. He helped out when he first retired doing funerals for a while but then found they were getting too much.

The funeral directors were for ever after him when they couldn't get somebody else, so he decided he couldn't do that. He did help out at All Saints' for a while. That's our parish church here, but not for the last three years. He has done some mentoring for people on a course but he stopped doing services because he found that due to his health problems he was letting people down and couldn't do that any more.

Looking back I wouldn't have wanted life any other way. I did feel privileged a lot of the time to be a clergy wife but on the odd occasion I felt the hours were too long for my husband and all of us. It affected our family life because he had to do things at the week-ends and evenings, so I felt a little bit resentful at times, I think.

It was also difficult to make friends because of my position and it could be lonely. We do have friends now from the parishes we've been in which is strange because they aren't always the people we felt closest to when we were in the parish. We have friends from Cheadle, Knutton, Blakenall and Lichfield who have kept in touch, but it can be a lonely life because you can't make special friends with someone. We'd got other friends from outside the church and from younger days like school friends that I've kept in touch with and we were lucky to work in our original home areas.

In the modern church with regard to gay bishops, I feel the church does accept gay priests as long as they are celibate, so I feel the natural progression is to accept gay bishops under the same conditions really or you are preventing them from preferment. The women are no problem for me or Derek because he has had women curates working with him.

I've never felt obligated to do things in the parish. If I was asked to do something and didn't want to I would just say "Oh, that's not me." When we went back to Blakenall, someone asked me to open a fair, I said "No, no, that's not me I don't do any public speaking." I haven't done anything publicly; I'd rather work in the background.

JUNE

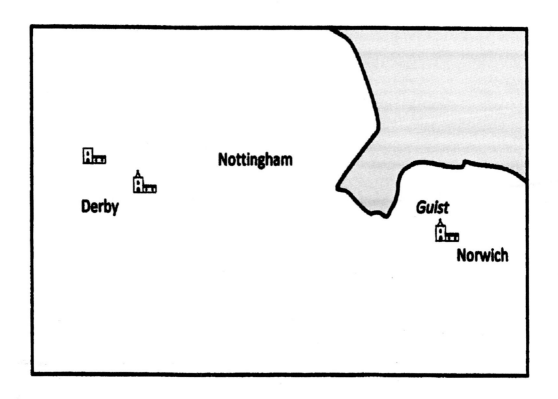

JUNE'S STORY

'I adapted to being a clergy wife quite easily'

My name is June, I live in Lincolnshire and I was born in Charlton in London. My mother and father weren't religious, but I'm sure they believed because my father used to quote the Bible to me when I had done something wrong. My twin sisters were older than me. I had a happy childhood. The war started when I was four. It didn't concern me at all because my parents protected me from what was going on. I heard the news but I didn't really understand it, but as I got older I began to realise that my mother was frightened and hated leaving us in the house.

We had some bombing but lots of bombs used to go astray and not hit their target. My father was a fire-watcher and told us most of the bombs went in the Thames. One or two landed near the house but didn't explode, so we had to leave our houses while they cleared the bombs and walk the streets for an hour or so before we were allowed back in. Sometimes we had no water and had to use the stand-pipes but that was our life, I didn't know any different.

It wasn't until I was about nine when the doodlebugs started that I began to realise it was frightening, because when they were overhead and the noise stopped you knew they were going to come down. At one end of our street one wiped out the station but there were no houses on that side. Then a little later the rockets started and they were more scary because you didn't hear them, you just heard the crash but had no idea when it was coming and one wiped out the other end of the street and two or three of our friends were killed. When the doodlebug dropped my sisters and I were down in the shelter. My parents were at work and when we looked out, there was dust everywhere but the house was still standing, so as far as we were concerned that was all right.

When I hear what happened during the war from people who write stories and make films, I think 'Were they there?' My experience wasn't being hard up, well, we were hard up but we had food to eat, we didn't go hungry. My mother was a good manager. We had decent food to eat but didn't have many clothes mind you, we had only our school clothes but that was because we weren't very rich, but everyone was in the same state who lived in the same area. My father was a fork-lift truck driver, what they called semi-skilled, and earned a low wage.

I was appalled when I started work at age sixteen to find I was earning exactly the same as him and he worked six and a half days a week. My mother didn't work to begin with until the war and then she did war work in a factory; she sewed up bags for animal feed for farmers. She didn't like the swearing that went on and complained, so they stopped swearing when she was on duty, but she must have learned the swear words without realising it because when she began to get senile she was in a Home and we were told what dreadful language she had. She didn't even like 'damn' and 'blast' and we got ticked off if we said them. We said "But she doesn't swear; it must be unconscious." I don't know what she said in the Home; we didn't ask.

I had a happy childhood, my parents weren't religious, they didn't go to church but my sisters, the twins, and I did. They were four years older than me. We had all the usual squabbles but now we are as thick as thieves and meet regularly. So yes, my childhood was happy.

We slept in the air raid shelter during the blitz, the Anderson shelter, which I rather liked. It was quite exciting being down there together. My mother didn't like it, my father wasn't there - he was fire-watching. We were evacuated for three months during the war but it wasn't very nice at all, not a nice experience. We went to Tunbridge Wells. My mother came with me because I was only four. The twins were split up and the lady where my mother and I were wasn't very nice. She didn't really want us but had no option, poor soul. She wasn't rude or nasty but she made rules. "Out of the house by half past eight in the morning and don't come back until tea-time." So we were out of the house all day long, my mother and I used to play Pooh Sticks to keep me happy.

My sisters could only go to school for half a day. The locals went in the morning and evacuees in the afternoon and the education at the school was a much lower standard than ours. My mother didn't like it, so she said "We'll all go back and die together in London". We went back to London to face the blitz; I was much happier, I must admit.

Our family was a huge extended family. There were lots of cousins in the Forces, about eight or nine, one of whom was in the Atlantic convoys but not one single one was hurt or killed. When they came home on leave we had parties, grand parties, I used to like them. We had 'Knees up Mother Brown' and singing and everyone stayed overnight. The children slept in one room, the women in another and the men in another, all on the floor and I really enjoyed those parties, so on the whole my childhood was very happy. I went to church regularly and even though my mum and dad didn't go they always made sure that I could do what I wanted with regard to going to church. They would delay going out until I had been to church. I went to Sunday school until I was about fourteen. My sisters came with me to church and lasted until they were about eighteen going regularly.

I liked Evensong. It seems strange that a six year old girl would like to go to Evensong but I liked it because people spoke to me. In those days children should be 'seen and not heard'. My grandmother used to say "Keep quiet and speak when you are spoken to," but in church I could speak. I rather liked that and they were interested in me, I think that is why I came to church. They were very modern towards children and also you were allowed to express yourself. They didn't query "Why are you doing this? I don't want you doing that." You could talk to the vicar and he would talk to you. On one occasion he said "You should go to confession," and we said "We don't want to go to confession." It was a high church and he said "Well, you ought to." So my friend and I said "Where does it say so? There's nothing in the Bible or the Prayer Book that says you've got to go to confession." He gave in and we did not go to confession. He was Anglo Catholic. I still am, I still prefer the Anglo Catholic services but I've got used to the other ones as well.

I went to work when I was sixteen, to begin with to work for an insurance company doing calculations. I used to be good at maths. I was working on premiums and for that I earned twelve pounds a month. To begin with my mother had the whole lot and gave me pocket money but after a couple of months I said "Can I give you some of it, so that I actually have my own money?" I then used to pay my own lunches at work, buy my own clothes and give her about ten shillings a week, which wasn't very much.

Later I changed my job and went to France as an au pair. It was lovely, I had an ordinary working class family. I had O level French and German, so I could write French and speak it haltingly but I couldn't understand when it was spoken. Because I had written to them in French they thought I was a good speaker and I obviously wasn't. But it didn't take me long, I went in September and before Christmas I was speaking fairly fluently. They were a nice family, the parents worked for the French railway. They had three children, but looking after three children was nothing because I used to take the kindergarten class at Sunday school. My mother said when she knew I was going "You get rid of them after Sunday school but not when you are looking after them, you have them the whole time," but I enjoyed looking after them. I was there for six months but then both my sisters had their first children and I wanted to get home and see the babies. I went back to my parents and lived at home until I got married when I was thirty one.

My mother had looked up a job before I went, working for the old fashioned GPO on the Continental telephone exchange thinking I wouldn't go, but I asked her to "Keep the advert and when I come back I'll apply." In those days you couldn't dial direct, you went through the operator, so I went in as a French speaker and worked with the foreign operators which meant booking calls with them. By this time I was quite fluent and used to converse in French with the other operators and there were people speaking French all round me. It was based in London, opposite St. Paul's in Faraday Street. I went there purely as a stop gap until I could find something decent to do with my French but I liked it and it was a very good career structure, as you went on you worked in every single field and they trained you everywhere, so in time you were experienced in all sections. I went to the training section in the end. Then we had degree students coming in to be trained for management, not as operators. They were trained on the board and then went into the traffic control centre. I stayed there until I got married.

My husband-to-be came to our church. We had a hostel for students who had left school and were preparing to go to college for the Ministry but had a gap in their education. Alan had left school at sixteen and went into an apprenticeship. He used to repair TV and radio sets and what have you, so when he wanted to go to college at twenty one he'd had that gap. Students like him were sent to our church and other places, where they studied to get their A levels, working part-time to pay their way. Actually, he failed his A level Religious Knowledge. Our daughter got A grade in hers and she used to boast about it when bishops and others came to our house that she had done better than her father; she still does! He never did get it and went up to Durham for another pre-university course and then went to St. David's in Wales. He could not take a degree course because he hadn't got his A levels but gained a Diploma in Theology, with two distinctions in Greek. All that took five years.

When he finished his training we got married. We got engaged at Christmas just before he finished his training and married in July. The Bishop said we should not get married straight away because he thought it would be too much of a strain for Alan to get married and do all the things he had to do

before being ordained, we should get married at the next Christmas. I disagreed; I wanted to get married in July not in the winter. I was rather 'stroppy'! So we got married in July and Alan was ordained in Derby Cathedral in September and we had a curacy in Derbyshire. My mother didn't mind me marrying a cleric but she wasn't so keen on me going so far away from home, although I had put my name down to emigrate to New Zealand, I just wanted to go there to do something different. Meeting Alan changed my mind.

Our wedding in 1966

Our first curacy was in mid-Derbyshire. It was a small village but whilst we were there it grew and became a suburb of Derby. It wasn't joined up but we were not far away. We had a three bedroomed house. One was a box room, but no central heating, it was freezing cold but we had a gas fire in the sitting room. It was so cold that when Alan was out in the evening I used to take my coat into the sitting room and put it on when I left the room to go to the kitchen to make a drink. But Alan sorted it. When I was expecting our first child he bought a small night storage heater and put it at the bottom of the stairs and it kept the hallway and stairs not warm but it took the chill off. He also secondary glazed two windows in the hallway. I don't think we had any unhappy occasions there, our vicar was lovely and gave Alan a good practical training in how to be a parish priest, but towards the end he became ill and was given a small parish so that he could recuperate in peace.

For some months Alan ran the parish until a new vicar was appointed. The new vicar was most peculiar. He wasn't nasty he was just totally uninterested in us. The first thing he did was to tell my husband we couldn't have the holiday we had booked because that was when he wanted his holiday. His wife seemed to think she could tell me what to do and I'm afraid that didn't go down well with me. By then I had two children and she sent a message round 'Please come round and see me.' So I said "Why can't she come round and see me?"

But I dressed the children up and went round and she said "I have decided to start a Young Wives' Group and you will run it." So I said "I don't know anything about Young Wives', what are they?" "It is the precursor to going into the Mothers' Union they attend for a year and then go into the Mothers' Union." "But I'm not a member, I don't go to the Mothers' Union, I don't intend to." So she said "Well why don't you join?" I said "Because you don't let Associate members vote and I think everyone should vote whether they are married, divorced or whatever they are. If they are a mother and they come why can't they vote?" I didn't join the Mothers' Union and I've never joined it since although I now think it is a very good movement actually and they do a lot of good. On that occasion I wasn't going to be in the MU so I didn't see why I should run the Young Wives' but she had taken it for granted that I would. "Well I've already put it in the magazine that you will be holding the meeting in the hall." So what could I do? I could have put in the magazine that I'm not going to do this but that isn't very nice so I went along with it and thoroughly enjoyed it and didn't worry at all because they were a nice group. We had our first meeting and I made lots of friends through it and I was quite happy there. After a year when they were supposed to go to the Mothers' Union they wouldn't go. I said "Apparently the Young Wives' is leading up to going into the Mothers' Union which takes a year, how do you feel?" "We're not going, we're staying here." None of them went and nothing was said. What they do now I really don't know. That was a long while ago.

*Our first year
with our two
children, 1972*

This new vicar wanted to organise you to do things but not show any interest in you and his wife seemed to think I was her curate! When the old vicar was there, who was lovely, my husband and I ran a Boys' Club and a Girls' Club. I did the Girls' Club because I wanted to. I also took a Guide Company. It wasn't a church one, it was a general one. He never expected me to do anything except what I wanted to join in with and I joined the drama group too, which I quite enjoyed. I have always enjoyed church life.

Our son was born a year after we were married and our daughter eighteen months later. I loved having the children and used to take them with me when they could be taken anywhere. I used to take them to Guides and when our son got too big to get into the carry cot any more and I was expecting again he went into a bed, so that he wouldn't feel pushed out when the baby came along. The Guides volunteered to baby-sit. I let them do it two at a time. The older ones, fourteen plus, used to come along and I was only about two minutes along the road, so when anything went wrong one could shoot along and get me. We weren't really happy about it but it seemed the best way. Then it all went wrong because an American Guide came along who was very self assured and she baby-sat because she was mature in every way.

When I got back our son was sleeping peacefully, she hadn't done any harm to him but "The baby cried" she said "He wanted something to eat." So I said "What? You are supposed to call me." "Well we didn't want to disturb you so we found something in the fridge." "What did you do with it?" "Oh we just took it out and fed him." Apparently that shut him up straight away. She'd changed his nappy efficiently but that made me very uneasy, so I sent a note round to the parents saying I would have to leave Guides unless better arrangements could be made. She was about the third or fourth Guide that had sat for me, so it didn't go on for very long and nothing happened to our baby, he was perfectly okay and she was very efficient but it made me very uneasy, so that was it. In the end the parents baby-sat.

We were there for three-and-a-half years, it should have been only three years but that was something else the new vicar did, but we didn't find out for a long time. He was asked if Alan would like to move on to a second curacy but he didn't tell Alan, he just declined the offer on Alan's behalf and we didn't know anything about it until three or four years later. It felt he wanted to control you which I didn't think was a good idea. We got on with them, sort of, and moved on to the next curacy in about three-and-a-half years. We went to a place in mid-Derbyshire between Nottingham and Derby. It was a coal mining and steel town which was interesting. When my husband did a funeral and went to the Wake, the miners always had ham sandwiches and beer. The vicar got whisky!

One of the miners' wives told me she would go to the butchers and buy steak for her husband and mince for herself and the children. Her husband gave her two hundred pounds a week to spend on food. I was absolutely staggered, I used to spend about six pounds but the miners had to be strong and needed the meat. We didn't live in the parish because they only had one curate's house and that was already occupied. We lived in a vicarage in a nearby parish, and when the other curate went we still stayed where we were and that I think made me not part of the church. I went to the church each week but I only had one person I befriended. Also the vicar's wife said when we came, quite rightly I suppose, "You are not to do anything because you've got two small children and you've got to look after them." But it cut me off completely, I never felt part of that church.

Alan got on quite well there, it's just that I didn't feel part of it, I felt isolated. When I went to church people sort of said "Hello," but I only made friends with one person who one day when it was pouring with rain said "Get in the car, you can't take the children home in this down that long hill." So she took me home and I got very friendly with her. She helped me through depression because after I'd had my second baby post natal depression hit me about two months later. I went to the doctor who said "This is minor." I thought 'Well if this is minor I wouldn't like it to be major!' When I first had it I used to sit at the table and I couldn't get up and start the day. Alan used to help me get up and once I was up I could look after the children. That was no problem, I could always look after the children but it was very hard to do anything else. I shouldn't have been lonely because I had this friend from church and eventually became friendly with another mother nearby. We took our children to school together. The depression lasted quite a while until our son started school at four and a half and I met people and felt much better then.

I did feel rather isolated. Curiously with depression, you feel you are not part of the world, you are watching it go by, that is how it affected me. I went to the doctor and she was very good, she gave me nothing to take, no tablets. She said "Each time you feel bad come and see me." We would just sit and talk and knowing she was there, I got through it with her help and with the help of my friend. She used to come along on Friday and bring fish and chips and say "Come on, no cooking," and we'd sit and eat the fish and chips. I used to go to her house for tea and she got me through it, she was marvellous. I still went to church but it was at the church where I felt cut off, I had no reactions, I did everything automatically. When we went to the next parish, Alan was the vicar. That was in North Derbyshire. During our first year there I got over the depression completely.

I got involved with the Guides and the Youth Movement and didn't bother to go anywhere about the depression. No, that was it. I used my good friends, not drugs. They were mainly outside church; it gave me a sense of freedom, I don't know why. Some people said that I was far more friendly with Methodists in this first incumbency than I was with the Church of England people. I had one friend who was a very strong Methodist and that was because we had children that grew up together. Why not! I find on looking back that that comment was a bit unkind because I did a fantastic amount for the church. I did Sunday school, Guides and I was Chairman of the Women's Fellowship, so looking back I thought that was a bit unfair really; I just didn't do flower arranging and needlework! I heard that comment after I'd left but I think if I had realised while I was there what they thought, I'd have been hurt but I enjoyed being involved.

In Derbyshire we had a huge vicarage with seven bedrooms. We had heating but we couldn't afford to run it and we used to put it at fifty degrees. There were radiators everywhere, in all the bedrooms and one in the bathroom which we left on. It was oil central heating and soon after we got there in the early seventies, the cost shot sky high so our brief month or so of being able to turn it on and have a warm house vanished completely and my children said the house was freezing cold which it was. Then they changed us to gas half way through. That was better but we still couldn't really afford to use it properly.

I just accepted this relative poverty but I found it very hard when the children came home from school and said there was a school outing. My heart used to sink because I couldn't work out how to find the two or three pounds each. I've found out since that there were grants, but I was never offered any. When our son went to Secondary School my sister had a friend who worked for a church charity that offered grants for clergy children, so I applied for one for his school uniform and I got the full grant. That was fair enough but when our daughter went the year after and I applied again I was told you can't reapply within two years. I thought 'Well for heaven's sake she's going to school now,' but I didn't get anything. When I told my sister that I couldn't apply she said "That is ridiculous, they've got hoards of money that they are not giving out." That really shook me because her friend was secretary of that charity, so she must have known. I was really shaken that they would do that; they must have known the clergy were hard up and didn't get paid very well and I thought it was a bit unkind.

Alan had a car but he was never there and if I wanted to visit somebody I couldn't go because we were right in the middle of Derbyshire. If the car was sitting in the garage I thought 'This is ridiculous, the car is sitting there, I ought to learn to drive.' So I got a job as a Home Help to pay for the driving lessons. I went to three houses in the village, which got me six pounds a week, which was very good and I learnt to drive in my forties. I loved it and had no problems at all, I really liked it. My first experience of going into town was when a nun came to speak at the Women's Fellowship, someone said "You are the only one with a car and she needs a lift back to Sheffield." I'd never driven to Sheffield but I could hardly say no. I got in the car and drove to Sheffield at about four o'clock with no problem at all but when I came back it was full rush hour. At the first roundabout I hesitated and got blared at and hooted, the second was a bit better but when I got to the fourth I was sailing round. I'd only passed my test for a week and I was terrified.

I liked the parish and did Guiding there and all sorts of things. There were two ladies who were lovely and had a working party for making things to sell on garden party stalls. I don't sew, I hate sewing, I can do it but I just don't enjoy it, but one said "Would you take over?" I said "But I don't sew." She said "That's okay, all you have to do is look at the work and if it is okay you accept it." "I can't tell people they can't work very well." "That's okay, that's what we want, the present one tells people how badly they do it and hands their work back to them but she doesn't come any more." So I did what they asked, I didn't sew, I just received the work and passed it on to the organizers, they looked after that side of it. I think the previous person didn't like me because she felt I had usurped her position, but I hadn't because she had already left. On the whole nothing much happened but she had a quarrel with someone in the Fellowship and it did make it awkward, and I was told I ought to sort it out. So I had to go round and see them both and get them to talk to each other, which I actually succeeded in doing. I was President at the time and later Secretary and then Treasurer; we did run it very diplomatically. There was one person who was the leading light and a couple of devoted workers who made it all worthwhile.

The car made a difference to my life. I could take the children swimming which was forty minutes drive away and take them to fencing and dancing lessons. We stayed there for thirteen years. Alan said "Unless you stay in a parish for a long time you don't get to know people." Towards the end he was happy but I thought there was an undercurrent and I couldn't work out what it was. Although I loved it there and had lots of friends, many of them through Guiding, there was something not quite right. I still don't know what it was. I have a feeling it was something against Alan but he can't remember it. He didn't feel it at all but I had this feeling there was something wrong somewhere. He was a very good parish priest. When he had a chance to move on I was hesitant because our son had just started his A levels. But he came to me and said "Mum, let Dad go, I'll manage," but I still don't know whether by doing that we messed up his chances because he only got two As at the new school and he'd had very good marks at his previous place.

Looking back I think there were a lot of things that I now wouldn't accept. Not so much what I did, because I quite enjoyed doing it, but I conformed to being a clergy wife quite easily and didn't break out and become independent. I have a feeling that I conformed too easily in order not to upset things for Alan in the parish. I didn't want to do things that the parish would object to.

I started work when the children were about ten and my husband would be at home when they came in from school. I started off doing Home Help for a while then I got a job as Security Personnel on the gate at the local factory. Apart from paying for driving lessons, it enabled me to buy my own car and so gave me more independence.

When I started as a Home Help some in the parish didn't like it. One lady said "You are not going to clean my floor." I said "I'm going to do precisely that." Anyway she used to give me lovely cakes and things and she got used to it after a while. Once a month her sister used to come round and be very active and clean the house thoroughly before I came and when I turned up she said "You don't need to do a thing, sit down and talk." So I did; all my ladies were lovely, I enjoyed working with them. At the factory when I was on the gate, I had to write down the car numbers and their names and business before I opened the gate. There was nothing to it really. It was a nuclear engineering factory.

On one occasion we had a murder in the next village and the policeman came in to see me and was so pleased to look at my little book. "That is brilliant" he said, "I know exactly who's come through this gate." The only trouble was, there was a back gate which lots of people used and which I couldn't see, he was devastated. I was part-time and didn't get much money but it helped.

After thirteen years there we went to Guist in Norfolk. Alan had had a sabbatical in Norfolk studying the working of clergy teams and groups of rural parishes which he thoroughly enjoyed, then forgot about. Quite a while later someone approached him and asked him if he would like to come and take over a group of parishes in Norfolk, someone had remembered him! That was one of the best, they were so friendly. Derbyshire was friendly but because everyone had their families round them they didn't know what it was like to have no family around you. I didn't feel particularly bad but once, when I had an operation, no-one came to ask if they could help me because they all had their aunts and uncles and cousins around who could help them, so weren't aware that I had no-one. My parents were a long way off and my sisters had children and were not nearby, I managed all right but I did feel a bit neglected then, but I enjoyed the work I did.

Right:
St. Andrew's,
Guist

Opposite:
Garden party at
Guist, 1989
(me centre)

We had a huge garden in our first parish and the Guides could camp in it and I used to take them away to camp as well. We did have holidays. We booked cheap little cottages, which my daughter said prepared her for the digs at University! In Norfolk we had five bedrooms and two so-called dressing rooms, one we used as a workroom for Alan and one as a store room.

We had central heating that we could now afford to use because I was working and part way through they double-glazed every single window for us. It was a group of parishes; Alan had six churches, all separate, all villages but he used to manage and enjoy it. The actual parishioners were exceptionally friendly.

In Norfolk we used to have coffee sessions in our house and a pancake party on Pancake Day and garden parties and all sorts of meetings and events. I did a part-time job, a job share, and then my colleague was very ill for about two years, so then I did a full-time job and went back to part-time when she came

Right: The
rectory at Guist

Opposite:
Alan and me with
the Guist Church
Millennium
Tapestry

back. I was a dental receptionist and would relieve the nurse if necessary but after a while I wasn't allowed to do that because you had to be qualified. Before that I did a job in a care home, we had to get some money because the children went to school just outside Norwich and we were on a main road and one bus came at seven and another at about ten, so it cost us a fortune to take them to school. Luckily the school secretary, who lived close by, came along and offered to take them.

I like meeting people, I'm a people person. Alan was not a 'people person,' he was rather shy at first, but he was very good at visiting and got over his shyness. I loved people coming to the rectory but in our Derbyshire parish they would come to the back door which was our living quarters and they would go through to the Parish Room which was right opposite our stairs, so I had to make sure I was dressed all the time. I couldn't relax and wander round in my dressing gown. In Norfolk they were more discreet and always knocked and we had a big hall with all the doors going off.

Alan with Dr. Barnardo on the site of Watt's Naval Training School in Norfolk, which trained Barnardo's boys for life at sea, on the centenary of its foundation by his ancestor. July 2003

We had a burglary at the Norfolk house and when the policeman came in and looked at the study "Good grief!" he said "Look what they've done here." I said "No, they haven't been in there, it's always like that, my husband is very untidy and I don't clear up after him." The dog was in there so I knew they hadn't been in there. I lost everything that was gold, including two gold watches, one of them my mother's but luckily I had my engagement ring and my grandmother's ring on. In the bedroom all my other jewellery was strewn all over the floor, luckily my cross and pearls had fallen under the dressing table. But I never got depressed in Norfolk; I was too busy with work and parish work.

We started a Sunday school at the parents' request and I was involved in an Explorers' Group which met once a month to get to know the children. We took them out and had teaching sessions between myself and three very good leaders. One of them couldn't read and write when she left school but taught herself and became a church warden and Deanery Secretary and read regularly in church. We were in Guist for twenty years. At the beginning it was five parishes but then they added a sixth and towards the end they tried to add a seventh but Alan wasn't wearing that. I tended to go to church where Alan was going, all round the Group. It was confusing at first because some people went round all the churches and you couldn't remember where you had seen them. It took me about a year to get to know where people came from and who they were.

When we got to Guist the children were both in the sixth form at the same school. They conformed with coming to Sunday school and church and were confirmed. Then when they were teenagers and got part-time jobs which involved working at week-ends they drifted away.

Our son couldn't have cared less about being the son of a clergyman but my daughter was teased. She had lots of friends but at the senior school she used to get gibes about her clothes. She didn't have fashionable clothes and she had sensible shoes and there were comments made. She really was upset about what they said. The effect was that they both found friends outside the village.

I used to be Anglo Catholic and deep down I still am, but women priests don't worry me at all, I don't see how you can be a priest and not accepted as a bishop. They can't have one without the other. A bishop is a priest after all.

We had a so-called gay vicar when I was a teenager. One of the church wardens said "This man is a homosexual and he's got students in the house, he shouldn't have students." He was really angry. He was sure he was gay, but then the vicar ran off with someone's wife, so I said "Now, what do you say about that?" The vicar just disappeared.

He wasn't a very good priest and he didn't like women. When we had a church parade for the Guides and one of my guides took the flag up he ignored her, so she looked at me and I pointed to the altar. One of the servers came up and took the flag. I went to see him about it and he said "Well there's no point in discussing it now June, I intend closing the company down, some of your guides don't come to church." I explained that it was an open group and some of them were Methodists and he couldn't close it down because it was an open unit "Well I can stop you using the church hall." "You can't do that either," I said "because the PCC control the hall." So he just left us alone after that.

Gay priests don't worry me. I've worked with a lot of gay people and on the whole they are marvellous. I couldn't care less about them becoming bishops. If a gay can be a priest he can be a bishop. I think people should stop talking about it and leave them alone because we've always had them, but no one realised and everything worked okay. You can tell quite often by the way they talk and mainly about the way they feel, they really are brilliant people. The ones I've worked with were nurses at the Home where I worked. They worked mainly on nights when they got no hassle from the patients and no one else could get at them. They were caring, they were intelligent and witty and very nice to work with. They can't have one without the other. A bishop is a priest after all.

Only one I've worked with admitted it; he was the assistant matron. The rest didn't say anything but I had a feeling that they were. The one that told us when I was having coffee with a friend said "There's something I want to tell you." We said "We know what it is, you are homosexual." He said "How did you know, I didn't want to go on deceiving you?" I said "It's the way you behave, it's obvious."

I enjoy church life, I never resented it at all, I accepted it. Alan had to spend lots of time away from home and we didn't see much of him, but now we have retired if he does too much I tell him. I don't mind him doing it, but even so

I resent it and I don't know why. He could stop but he doesn't want to. I've given up now because I mentioned that he was doing too much and he got quite upset. All our life we couldn't go away at certain times. We couldn't go at week-ends and I worked in the week. So I used to go away by myself to see my parents and my sisters with the children, but it would have been nice to have Alan with me. Now he can and he does come.

There is no parish priest here, so he is filling in with two other retired clergy. I've extracted a promise from him that if we need to go away he will tell them he's not available, and he has accepted that. He takes some funerals in the parish and odd weddings. At one stage he was doing them all and two services a Sunday and may as well have been 'in harness' again. He takes services very well, they are friendly services conducted in a serious way. I find now lots of clergy make things too jolly and friendly and they put me off completely because I don't think people want entertaining, they just want to worship. Alan is appreciated here, they like him taking services. He takes one service most Sundays and a midweek Communion, but if we want to go away they find someone else. We both go to a Bible Study where he helps on the same basis.

One thing I want to say about poverty. I couldn't believe when we first got married that I had been earning in a week double what he earned in a month. We did have big houses that I and the children loved but we couldn't afford to keep them warm; but I've had a very happy life. I really enjoyed working for the church.

One anecdote illustrates Alan's problem. A consultant told him he needed a multiple heart bypass urgently - he reached for his diary to see if he could fit it in. I grabbed the phone and said "He'll be there."

HAZEL TREADGOLD

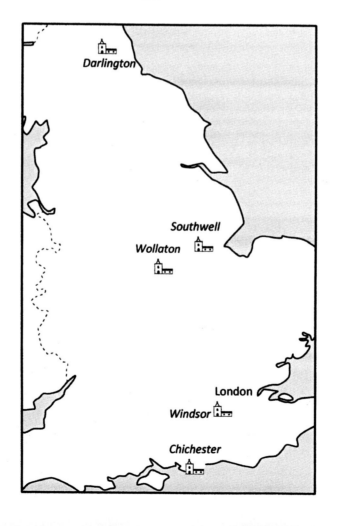

HAZEL'S STORY

*' I was determined never to look like
the conventional clergy wife'*

My name is Hazel Treadgold and I live in Boxgrove near Chichester in West Sussex. I am an only child and I suppose I am middle class. My mother came from Somerset and my father from the Thames Valley. He was in the insurance world and they very soon moved up to Nottinghamshire, which is where I grew up. The war started when I was three years old. Very sadly my mother died when I was ten, she had been ill for a very long time but she was a remarkable woman and a wonderful mother. I also had a wonderful stepmother. When my mother was dying she suggested to my father whom he should marry, which was typical of her. My mother was very clever, had a great sense of humour and was exceptionally brave because she suffered from very bad health.

She had a strong influence on me and I still remember many of the things she taught me. My father was on his own for a year after my mother died. It was a difficult year; we had housekeepers. I missed my mother so much but when I went back to school I felt a bit of a star really because I was the girl whose mother had died.

*Me with
my mother*

*On holiday with
my stepmother
1947*

My stepmother was very smart, always well turned out, well dressed, a good cook and a brilliant housekeeper, very different from my mother, but they both had a tremendous influence on me. My father was more difficult and although he had a temper I remember when I was ill with whooping cough he made a theatre on the bed and made me laugh and laugh. There was a big drama at Christmas because it was during the war and you always had to make Christmas lights work every year and it was a great performance. He was not a handy man. I remember being taken down in a blue dressing gown to see the lights and he had actually got them working.

So, it was a happy childhood.... well up to being ten, we went to church. My mother had been very involved in her village in Somerset and with my father went to church once a month to Communion and weekly to Matins and that was a large part of their life. We moved from Brighton to Nottingham when I was three during the war and I was taken by my mother to see bombed out houses. I was evacuated later to my grandmother in Somerset, but only for a term, and went to the village school. I wondered what a 'mixed infant' was. I told somebody "I'm not a girl, I'm not a boy. I'm a mixed infant." It was quite an interesting experience as the village children were quite suspicious of me. They were very much village children in the depth of Somerset in those days. I was put on a train in Nottingham in charge of the guard and met by my grandmother in a pony and trap at Evercreech Junction. On one occasion there was a village fête and I had to arrange wild flowers, which I'd always been quite good at, and I won but they swapped the tickets over, I was then second. I adored my grandmother who had a great sense of humour and I had a cousin nearby, so that was fun. My grandmother was not like her generation at all and still madly in love with my grandfather who was passionate about cricket and earlier hunting.

I never minded being an only one, just occasionally I thought it would be nice to have a brother or sister but I don't mind being on my own although I enjoy people. I like meeting people, seeing people and being with people and that was how my mother was, absolutely. We certainly weren't a clerical family but were connected with the church. I went to a Methodist Sunday school because my friend went and it had brightly coloured chairs; we all fought for the red chairs. I went in my blue coat, white gloves and a poke bonnet during the war.

I was very good at English history. My history mistress wanted me to go to Oxford but perhaps as a result of my mother's death, I developed a very bad stammer. It was sad really but I was determined to get rid of it. It held me back at school a lot, not in written work but orally. Also my father didn't really believe it was necessary for girls to go to university. So that is a sadness but you get on with life and move on to the next thing.

I did get rid of the stammer. I was hypnotised. I'm not sure how it worked but it did. If I'm tired it still comes back and occasionally when I'm on the phone. My father was a disciplinarian and he did shout at me at times. When I was eighteen I had a frock that I thought was 'the bees' knees'. He said "You are not going out in that trying to look like Marilyn Monroe" so I didn't go out that night. You knew where you were in the fifties, I didn't mind growing up then. My father said "If you come home pregnant you will be out." We lived simpler lives. I think we knew where we were because we had the boundaries, it was easier, we were disciplined but it could be hard.

My father was determined, because I was the only one, that I should not be spoiled. He was an excellent tennis player and wanted to turn me into a county class tennis player. I was good at tennis but not quite up to his standard. I can't remember him praising me but there were expectations of me. I probably didn't live up to them either in the sporting field or academically. I was very good at history and biology but hopeless at maths, totally non-numerate. He was not an easy man. I think on reflection, as I realised from my stepmother after he died, that he had had a very tough life before he married my mother, with whom he was blissfully happy. That had a bearing on him and looking back I wish I had understood him more. When you're young you don't appreciate the difficulties that your parents have been through.

I went to a very good secretarial college and worked for a very remarkable man in Nottingham who was a bit of a womaniser, but not with me. He was very clever and expected you to be confident and he taught me to have confidence, to get on and do things, use my initiative, be able to meet people and that was a huge education in a way which perhaps I might not have got at university. He didn't expect me to stutter and stammer and I jolly well didn't. I owe a lot to him and worked for him for about four or five years and then I went to London and worked for an MP. That was a revelation. We were then living in Surrey.

St. Giles' Youth Fellowship,
(I am seated seventh from the left with John behind me on the back row)

In the fifties you didn't leave home in the way people do today. My family and my husband's family were friends and he lost his father when he was eleven. We were members of an incredible Church Fellowship; it was much more than a Youth Club. Seven of the boys in that fellowship went on to be ordained. We had a really old type gentleman rector who was lovely, one who went out to tea with the grand old ladies of the parish.

He had this great friend who taught Classics at Nottingham University who was also the leader of the Youth Fellowship. You wouldn't think of her as a typical youth leader. She wore a tweed suit and black shoes, had grey hair in a bun and florid cheeks and bulging eyes, Molly Wittacker, but she was the most remarkable person who ran this Fellowship. We had great debates with people from Nottingham University, I became the secretary of it and Molly saw that we had stimulating speakers. We played tennis and we were all very middle class and people I suppose with ambition but we went to church, that was the great thing and she guided and directed us.

That was where I got to know my husband. He was doing National Service but felt the call to be ordained. He'd been in the choir and his mother went to church in the conventional way for those days. I was five years younger than him and he thought I was too young, so we broke up and he went off to University to read Theology and then he went to Wells Theological College for his ordination training.

We got back together again and were engaged for quite a long time because at theological college he was told that he could not marry for two years. In those days you accepted the discipline unquestionably. In the end though, because he was an older student, we were allowed to marry during the last six months he was at Wells, as a privilege. That was a marvellous time. We went and lived in

*Wedding day
June 1959
with Rector
of St. Giles*

*Opposite:
Our children,
Marcus, Simon
and Joanna, 1970*

a flat in a funny little semi-detached house in Wells with a real Somerset lady who said "I bain't having them there 'theologicals' going up my stairs because they bain't be any better than anybody else. This be a respectable house." So we used to creep up the stairs. It was a wonderful year, 1959, and we were blissfully happy. I was working full-time and we lived on my eight pounds a week but it paid the rent and we ate.

A friend said "What a waste going and marrying a clergyman, you'll never have any money." My father liked my husband immensely and thought he was a nice safe pair of hands. My stepmother was lovely about it. John was titled to Southwell Minster in Nottinghamshire as Vicar Choral. That was a great turning point in our life because we both learnt a huge amount there. We went to look at another parish, then the Bishop said "We want a new Vicar Choral at Southwell Minster," which is the Cathedral Church of Nottinghamshire and it's a parish church cathedral, the most beautiful Norman building you've ever seen. "If you can get on with the Provost, H C L Heywood, Hydrochloric he's known as, you can go there but don't come running to me in a year if you don't get on with him." So we went into this damp Georgian house which I loved. There was no central heating but they put a sink in the kitchen. John was Curate and also sang the services at the Minster, he had a very good voice. This Hugh Heywood was a tremendous man. John learned so much from him, what to do and what not to do!

There have been times when we were hard up, when we moved up to Southwell and of course when the children were young. I can remember getting very fraught at times. Marcus was born when we were in Southwell in this Georgian very pretty house which we decorated ourselves. We have a lovely picture of Marcus's Christening cake in front of the patched wallpaper. He was born in hospital in 1961 after a very hard, traumatic labour but I had wonderful care. Two and a half years later I had Simon in 1964 and then we moved when he was a few months old to Wollaton. We had been in Southwell for five and

a half years and were very happy there. The Provost had been Dean of Caius College Cambridge for eighteen years before he went to be Provost of Southwell and was an academic. John had to submit his sermons to him before he preached but that was very good training and there were no microphones, which most churches now have.

We moved to Wollaton, a suburb of Nottingham, where we had two curates and well over thirty thousand people in the parish, a nineteen thirties rectory and were jolly hard up. It was hard work and what I did find trying was my husband being responsible for the marriages and preparation, and the curates for the baptisms and preparation for two new housing estates. I'd be running up and down stairs to answer the door while I was trying to read the children stories. I'd had another child whilst we were there, Joanna, a little girl in 1968. In the end my husband stopped these people knocking on the door like that and he made appointments to see them in church.

We had a mediaeval church with large congregations and the church had to be enlarged. My husband was a young man and full of 'get up and go' and introduced all sorts of what were then modern ideas, modern liturgy, all that sort of thing. It was a very exciting and a very exhausting time. When I was first there a parishioner came round, the baby was yelling upstairs, Marcus was grizzling and the washing machine which was not automatic in those days was overflowing and the breakfast things were still on the kitchen table, this woman said "Oh Mrs. Giles, the previous rector's wife was always out of the house by nine o'clock in the morning, all made up with her hat on." I collapsed into tears when she went.

There were two Young Wives' Groups, I ran one and the curate's wife ran the other. Then I ran, reluctantly to begin with, the Mothers' Union and a Women's Fellowship. I took the children to Worship With Mother and they joined the Cubs. There was a lot of school carting about because the boys went to the High School Prep Department in Nottingham. One of the things I was very grateful for there was we always had friends outside the parish which I feel is very necessary. There were Clergy Wives' meetings, which I didn't feel I wanted to go to, but my husband said "Well it's not necessarily what you get out of it but it's what you give," and that was a great lesson. I talked to one wife there and she hadn't got a car; they'd been missionaries and had come back to a very deprived, very tough parish and she'd never been out anywhere. When we asked her to supper she said "I don't know whether I'll even be able to hold a knife and fork properly," and that was a great lesson to me. It's not always what you can get out of things it's what you can give to people.

I thought how lucky we were because we had lots of friends, quite a good social life but we both worked very hard. We had the children and we had bonfire parties at the rectory, an old tennis court that had gone to pot in the war and the parish fête in the garden. The children loved it, they had great fun there. There were lots of children running in and out because we'd got the biggest garden.

It was very, very hard work and there were times when one was exhausted and frustrated and perhaps a bit tearful but on the whole it was a happy time, very interesting and full of things happening. We were there for ten years. Then we were phoned by Lord Barnard who lived in County Durham and he offered John a Living in a parish in the town centre of Darlington.

That was a very different experience indeed. Darlington is the only middle class place in the whole of County Durham, it is the only one that sometimes has a Conservative MP. It is a prosperous little town actually, but very inward looking. Again we met friends from outside the parish. It had all that was good in a small town and all that isn't so good. St. Cuthbert's was a big town centre church with two daughter churches. We had three houses there. They sold the vicarage which we were quite keen to keep because we like old houses but the Diocese was determined to sell it. Whilst they were finding a new vicarage we were in a semi-detached house for six months.

Then we moved into a very smart area into a big 1920s house, it had six bedrooms and three bathrooms with a lovely garden. The Diocese then decided that it was too big and we had a modern vicarage for a year. There were two boilers that had to be stoked in the second house, one for the hot water and one for the heating, which was only downstairs because in Durham Diocese they didn't believe in having central heating in the bedrooms. We were there for about seven and a half years. It was a very different way of life, very different indeed to the first parish. It was a large town centre church, one of the daughter churches was quite smart and the other was in a poor parish. John Hapgood was our Bishop and a quite remarkable man. I worked in Darlington for an accountant three days a week and I had lodgers. Our life up to then had been pretty conventional.

Then one day a voice came on the phone and said "Oh, it's the Dean of Windsor here, is your husband in?" I said "No." So when John came in I said "The Dean of Windsor has been on the phone", and he said "I expect they want to know something about somebody for a Living because he's a patron."

Me with H M Queen Elizabeth (the Queen Mother), centre,
at the 1985 Windsor Great Park Flower and Produce Show

Anyway to cut a long story short he rang again and it was to offer John the job of being a Canon of Windsor and also to be the Chaplain in the Great Park, where there is a private chapel of All Saints belonging to the Queen, in the grounds of Queen Elizabeth's house. That was completely out of the blue, we'd had nothing to do with the Royal Family, they were 'beings apart' as far as we were concerned and we don't know to this day why John was selected. We went down for the long process of interviewing, including being interviewed by the Queen and Queen Elizabeth and he was eventually appointed a Canon of St. George's Windsor (a Royal Peculiar) and Chaplain in The Great Park.

At the wish of the Queen Mother we had the Chaplain's house in the Great Park and two rooms in the Castle. The house was big. Princess Margaret called it 'That incongruous house' stuck in the middle of the Park with a great lawn in front of it. It was an Edwardian Villa. We had a drawing room, a sitting room, a dining room, a study and a big kitchen downstairs, with six bedrooms upstairs and three bathrooms.

It had an attic which was converted into a flat. My stepmother was living with us, but too blind to go to the flat, so she actually had a bed-sitting room with us for the time we were there. The Queen was exceedingly kind and said "Have you got enough furniture?" We were given some furniture from the overflow of Windsor Castle. That was a very different life.

Coinciding with that when we were in Wollaton, screaming and kicking, I had become the Enrolling Member of the Mothers' Union. I was never going to join but we had a very persuasive Diocesan President who came to me and said "Look, I know you don't agree with the attitude of the Mothers' Union, with the anti-divorce business, but we want to change it." The MU in Canada and New Zealand had more severe rules than the Canons of their respective churches on that particular issue. Since the 1969 Divorce Act things had changed and people could be divorced against their will and the MU was hurting lots of people with its rigid unbending attitude. I was asked to take the vows on for myself and help change it. So then I became what is now called a Branch Member and was then Enrolling Member. Eventually I became Central Chairman of The Young Families Department, which meant I was going up to London a lot. Whilst we were still in Darlington I became a Central Vice President of the World Wide Society. We were still in the Diocese of Durham and I was popping up and down to London. Yes, we had changed it. I'd been until that time a pretty conventional clergy wife. There was an MU in Darlington but no form of it when we went to Windsor. After a while all sorts of things came together. While we were still in Darlington I was asked to put my name forward with others to become the Central President. It's now called World Wide President to make the job clearer but I said "No, I'm too far away and my daughter is still quite young, I couldn't possibly do it and all the travelling."

When we went to Windsor I was freed up to become the Central President of the MU but the Dean said "You will have to write to the Queen because you are now part of the Royal Household; it must be in your very best handwriting!" I had a reply from the Queen saying she would be very honoured if I let my name go forward as long as it wasn't too much for me. The Queen is a patron and she came to the opening of the refurbished Mary Sumner House and always took a keen interest in the well-being of the Society.

My letter from the Queen

There were expectations of us at Windsor, we had to do a lot of entertaining. For instance, we were asked to give a dinner party for Prince Edward's twenty-first birthday. We were probably better off there than anywhere else. We had a big garden and after the war King George VI, who was a great gardener, went round the Chaplain's Lodge garden which was in a terrible state and said "The Chaplain must have a gardener." So Crown Estates paid for a gardener and we had a full-time gardener. I was given money for entertaining and domestic help which came in a brown envelope each month.

I had my stepmother living with us and looking back now I don't know how I did it but the gardener's wife, who had been in service, came every morning and kept an eye on my stepmother and gave her lunch every day although I often got up at six o'clock to prepare it. I was away an awful lot. I went round the world twice and then at home there would be big things like Garter Service in April. I could be one week at the Garter Service, another in the Third World getting bitten to death by bugs in a bed in Africa and then the next week we'd be going for drinks in the Royal Lodge with Queen Elizabeth. It was a world of great contrasts and not the typical clergy wife's lot. That way I've had a much more interesting life than I ever envisaged. I did most of the cooking for the entertaining but I was fifty whilst we lived at Windsor, so I was quite young and had a lot of natural energy.

I was brought up to feel that you always support your husband, and although I had quite an independent life in some ways doing these other things, I did try and support him by going to St. George's whenever I could and that sort of thing. Every year there was a service of nine lessons and carols in the Great Park Chapel and afterwards The Queen, the Queen Mother and other members of the family always came for drinks, so that was quite a challenge. It was an immense privilege and Queen Elizabeth had wonderful house parties, political ones where we met Lord Hailsham and Lord Carrington. At another house party we would meet her 'horsy' friends including Monsieur Hennessy who was there for the Hennessy Gold Cup. He said to my husband "You must come and see us in France." He said "Where do you live?" "I live in Cognac of course!" We also met her artistic friends like Sir Frederick Ashton and John Piper.

It was a wide spectrum. I was also seeing lots of bishops and people within the church through the MU. I travelled round Great Britain; I travelled round the world to Madagascar, the Seychelles and Africa. I went four times to Australia, tourist class, on my own. I was met and looked after by the MU wherever I arrived. I believe rightly the Presidents now go club class. I was the first Central President to go to Burma and was nearly shot in Uganda just after all the troubles there. I'd been sent in 1972 to open a Children's Home in Nigeria just after the Civil War there. That was a great eye opener, I hadn't seen the developing world before, I'd never seen such poverty in my life. That was in the '70s and '80s and sadly I don't think it's got much better. The Mothers' Union tries to help these women through its over three hundred workers around the world. In the old days they were white women, who felt called to go out and help, but nowadays they are indigenous people who have been trained and they go in and help with hygiene, nutrition and baby care and now of course they talk about Aids, birth control and those things. These workers are at the sharp end. The MU does a huge amount of caring, it has a huge literacy programme in Burundi, Rwanda and Ethiopia where it does tremendous work. It aims to make women self-sufficient.

Right:
Wash, wash in
Papua New
Guinea, 1986

Below: the
Provincial President
of the MU Burma
welcoming me, 1987

In the pulpit of St. Paul's Cathedral Melbourne Australia

My biggest tour in 1987 took about six weeks; I was shattered at the end of it. I went to Burma for about ten days, then flew to Perth in Australia and went to the far North-West into all the big cities and the Outback. I spoke three or four times a day and I remember sometimes throwing a couple of suits into the cleaners early in the morning and picking them up at lunchtime as I left the town. I needed to get up at five in the morning to look immaculate; they work you hard in Australia. Then I flew to Tonga and Fiji. I came home straight back into family life - "What's for lunch?"

During my last year as Central President of the MU, now the World Wide President, two very significant events took place as far as I am concerned. 1988 was the last time the MU held a World Wide Conference and over three hundred members attended from around the world. I chaired the Conference which took place at Swanwick in Derbyshire. It took an immense amount of preparation. Many members arrived early to visit their link dioceses, they all had to be met, welcomed, cared for and transported to and from the venue.

At the World Wide Conference 1988

Me (left) with Mary Haggart at the Bishops' Wives' Conference at Kent University in August 1988

The Agenda had to fit the needs of such a diverse group of women so that all felt their voice could be articulated and heard. The services had to be both meaningful but imaginative. At that time the MU was very constrained by its constitution and small but significant steps were taken to smooth the way for the changes that were needed for it to progress and for larger scale changes to be undertaken. This Conference was a very expensive and complicated undertaking, especially for the members in this country and it was the last MU World Wide Conference to be held on such a scale. This was all done before we had computers to help us, but I did introduce them at Mary Sumner House.

The other significant event occurred in August 1988. I had been preparing for it as early as 1985 with Rosalind Runcie, the wife of the then Archbishop of Canterbury. She asked to see me and explained that the Lambeth Conference for Bishops was to be held in '88 for three weeks and would I undertake to chair a Conference for the bishops' wives assisted by Mary Haggart, the wife of the recently retired Primus of Scotland? He was to be the Chaplain to the Conference. I accepted this challenge and Mary and I shared a small table in my office at Mary Sumner House and had the help of the Central Secretary and of her secretary when they could spare the time. As Lady Runcie said when it was all over "It was done on two and a half wheels and a piece of string." To say it was a mammoth undertaking is an understatement and it was all going on whilst being Central President, preparations for the WW Council which followed it and life in Windsor. The bishops' wives rightly wanted to own the Conference and there had to be equal input worldwide. Well over four hundred and fifty wives attended from very diverse backgrounds, some very highly educated and some hardly literate and some speaking many languages.

I chaired an International Committee of Bishops' Wives, a small British Committee, attended the Bishops' Conference planning meetings in Canterbury in Kent University where the conferences were to be held and I flew to the USA to meet American Bishops' Wives. All these meetings were held to plan a programme to cover a vast range of interests, get speakers, organise prayer groups, translators, outings and visits, find warm clothing for some and meet dietary requirements. We also planned to provide afternoon tea every afternoon in cups and 'keep fit' every morning. Rosalind Runcie was on the front page of the Daily Express in shorts doing Keep Fit. Eventually the last meeting of the wives ended on a positive note with wives from around the world sharing signs of hope, while Rosalind Runcie released white doves of peace, which were actually pigeons. I could go on and on, I've only really scratched the surface. I suppose these two conferences were real high points in my life. Before I embarked on this great task I hadn't known Mary Haggart but we never had a cross word and she is still a great friend. I am a broad brush person and she is an 'I' dotter and a 'T' crosser, so we got on perfectly and I owe her a great debt of gratitude. Also I could not have done it without the unfailing support of my husband, he was a real star.

It was all an amazing experience and there was all that at St. George's going on. Whilst I was in New Zealand I remember seeing my husband on television at the Duchess of Windsor's funeral and saying "Oh, that's my husband on television!" When we were separated we wrote letters and phoned, there were no mobile phones. My stepmother was living with us and was blind. She used to save cornflake packets to collect messages from Mary Sumner House in her big black writing. She loved it. People were very kind to her. She was very thrilled one day when the Queen came up to look at her bed-sitting room.

I was six years as World Wide President of the MU. It was hard to give it up, like giving up your baby but then I thought 'Right, I'll enjoy the cushy life at Windsor.' But then God doesn't allow you a cushy life does He? No! John was invited to become Dean of Chichester. That again was an immensely busy period, not always easy. The Dean is in charge of the running of the Cathedral and the then Bishop the diocese. It's a huge diocese. We lived in Chichester and it is ninety miles to Camber Sands which is still in the diocese. We had a house that I simply adored; it was the most lovely Georgian house in The Close.

We've always known people outside 'the patch' which was one's salvation because I think you can get what I call 'very parish-bound'. I had seen and met everybody in the '80s at the top of the church and at the top of the country, Prime Ministers, Kings, Queens and that was not your average clergy wife's experience; a very wide spectrum and quite unexpected and a great privilege. We've still got friends from all our previous parishes. We were in Chichester for twelve years.

Deanery Garden
Flower Festival
1996, Chichester

We've always had an open house, we've had huge numbers of people through the house, all sorts of people, and I think that is terribly important. I have loved that but I can understand that there are people who do not like it. We've always lived in very nice houses and had big gardens. I've felt that you are only there by virtue of the job and you can be overwhelmed by it, really overwhelmed, but having said that I think people matter and need to know that you are caring for them and are concerned about them and that, I suppose, is my philosophy of life. I've been allowed to carry it out in some very lovely places.

Whoever you are, you need to be cared for and listened to. I was a magistrate, not at Windsor because I couldn't cope with it then. I've been a governor of an excellent Church of England Comprehensive school in Chichester, in charge of the Cathedral Flowers and I ran the Cathedral Fellowship and did a large amount of entertaining. There was the Cathedral Trust which raises money for the Cathedral and I used to entertain people for the Trust. We had a lot of meetings in the Deanery and would go off to East Sussex quite a lot. You have to entertain the Great and the Good and that sort of thing.

There is a strong parish feeling in the Cathedral and we enjoyed taking an interest in Cathedral life and the huge number of volunteers that keep the show on the road. My husband started the Cathedral Flower Festival in 1996, which is now held every two years and makes a hundred and twenty thousand pounds. That is a huge undertaking. There were endless things happening in the house and garden but we had a gardener for one and a half days a week.

The children were coming home regularly and funnily enough they didn't rebel. Joanna is the one who still goes to church, our eldest son Marcus came and lived in Chichester when his marriage broke up and then lived with us here while he got himself sorted. He made friends with the lay vicars and would go and have a drink with them. I think they've been very proud of their father because things haven't come easily and we've both worked extremely hard. Sometimes I know I caused them to be hassled a bit when they were young with the moves, and leaving Nottingham was quite traumatic for Marcus, the eldest.

We were paid as a Suffragan Bishop at Windsor but were hard up in Nottingham and Darlington, but we survived. I worked to buy them tennis rackets and give money for school trips and things the children needed but we never took them abroad. That is something I do regret, I'd love to have done that. However, they say they saw a lot of England that other children didn't. Their experience has made them good with people and they can talk to anybody. Sometimes I wish I had been able to spend more time with them because childhood is very fleeting, isn't it?

My husband and I do accept women priests, but that, being in Chichester made a lot of difficulties for him in the Chapter and in the diocese. In the end because he's good with people and perhaps I am, we overcame those difficulties but there were times when it was pretty painful actually. That's the sacrifice isn't it, not the exhorted sacrifice but a sacrifice. You're so involved with what your husband is doing, not the confidential side of it, but the downs as well as the ups and that can be very draining and cause worry and concern. A lot of what I did was to support him and most of it was very enjoyable. During our last year at Chichester we had a new bishop and all that that involved. What I want to say is, do things for yourself that are not involved with the church; it's terribly important to have a wider perspective on life and do it from a Christian viewpoint as part of your Christian commitment. Being a magistrate was part of a whole new world.

You have asked me for my attitude towards homosexuality within the church. With regard to gays, John and I have always had quite a large number of dearly loved and respected gay friends, priests and bishops among them. I think they often make particularly good priests because they have a feminine side which is compassionate and caring. In the Chichester Diocese which is strongly Anglo-Catholic, there is a relatively large number of gay priests. As a product of the forties and fifties what I do find distasteful is the idea nowadays that it is almost 'fashionable' to be gay and also the lack of dignity and discretion that can surround the whole subject.

There are many wonderful homosexual and lesbian Christians. They are all made in the image of God and have been made to suffer dreadfully over the years. I am all for them being able to be themselves but it is when they flaunt it that I don't find it edifying. I am in total agreement with Civil Partnerships for people in long term relationships who wish to make a commitment to each other but I do not believe you can call it marriage. Marriage is between a man and a woman for love, procreation and companionship.

Over twenty years ago, when the subject of homosexuality was not talked about the way it is now, the Mothers' Union was increasingly concerned for parents who thought their children were homosexual and frankly did not know how to deal with it. It seemed a bewildering matter for many Christian parents. The MU published a pamphlet for parents entitled 'Understanding Homosexuality.' This was very 'avant-garde' in the late seventies and early eighties and we were the first organisation within the Church of England to look at any aspect of this subject. Because the MU is a broad church organisation it does not have an official view on homosexuality. The pamphlet was designed specially to be helpful to parents. This was misunderstood by some people and as Central President I had some awful letters from 'so called' Christians.

When I married I suppose I had a romantic view of being a clergy wife and I've had my ups and downs but never regretted it. I was asked to give a talk on the subject of clergy wives at St. George's House Windsor, a very prestigious Conference Centre set up by the Duke of Edinburgh and Dean Robin Woods.

I did a lot of research on the subject, helped by Ruth Hook, the wife of the Bishop at Lambeth at the time. I felt that as a committed Christian I would be expected to do things in the parish and she made the point that Christianity is a sacrificial religion and I should expect to make sacrifices. However, there is, especially for clergy wives, and I quote what Ruth Hook called 'the exhorted sacrifice' which can be exacted by virtue of the fact that you are a clergy wife which some have experienced and found very hard. I am sure that attitudes have changed in the past twenty years but they still linger. I have to say that it has never worried me to have women coming to see my husband, confiding in him and coming into my house, although I know from experience that some wives find this difficult. I would not respect my husband if he betrayed people's confidences to me. An MU friend of mine who is a consultant's wife reminded me that clergy wives are not unique in this way, but sometimes they think they are!

However, I would like to pay tribute to the many clergy wives I have known over the years who were women of commitment and faith, often with a great sense of humour, who have triumphed and survived th ups and downs of life in a vicarage life quite remarkably. Splendid women! On the whole I have loved the life, sometimes felt pulled apart by it, but always viewed it as an immense privilege. My great joy now is my grandchildren and having more time to enjoy them.

My 70th Birthday

SUSAN HOWDEN

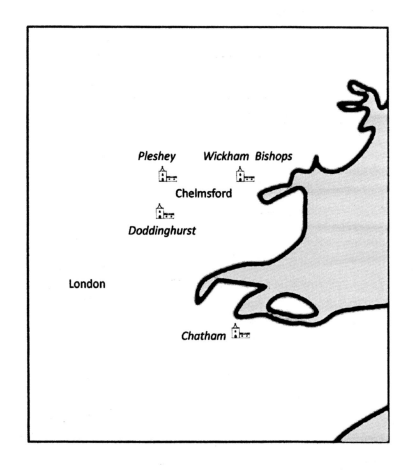

SUSAN'S STORY

'God, what do you want me to do here?'

I'm Susan Howden and I live at 12a Back Road, Writtle, near Chelmsford in Essex. My maiden name was Susan Spencer-Payne. I was born in London in Harley Street in 1940 and my father owned the whole building. He was a dental surgeon and we had a flat at the top of the house. As well as my father's surgery many of the rooms were let to other medical practitioners. Because he was worried about the effects of the war, my father bought a farm cottage in Radwinter near Saffron Walden, where my mother and I lived whilst my father stayed in London and came home at week-ends.

My mother was my father's second wife. He had three children by his first marriage, two girls and a boy. After my parents married they had me and then two years later she gave birth to a little boy but they were both very ill, the baby died but mummy survived. It was a very extraordinary situation because the gynaecologist who was dealing with her said "I have another baby boy here. The mother doesn't want him, why don't you take this one home?" So that's what they did! It was done legally, but it wouldn't happen these days. I was only two and a half and didn't remember anything about that and I didn't know until I was twenty-four that my brother was actually adopted and he didn't know until after that.

We lived in Radwinter until after the war and then we moved to Rye in Sussex to Church Square, to a house called 'St. Anthony' which is a well known Tudor house on all the postcards of Rye. We were there from '45 to '48 and then we emigrated to South Africa where I had a lovely time. We lived in Somerset West, which is now a very big town, but then a small village twenty eight miles from Cape Town. Lots of British people were emigrating to South Africa in 1947, '48 and '49. I grew up in a bungalow in a two-and-a-half-acre-plot from the age of eight until I was sixteen. I was sent to various schools, one was a Catholic boarding school called Springfield Convent in Wynberg.

While I was there my half-brother, who was in the Merchant Navy, came to see me and looked very smart in his uniform. He had docked at Cape Town Docks. Afterwards one of the nuns said "Is that your brother?" So I said "Yes." She said "Is he your real brother?" "No he's my half-brother!" "Oh I see, your father was married before, so you're a bastard." So I said "Yes." In Catholic eyes my father couldn't marry again. There was another girl who was in a similar situation and she used to cry at night because she thought she could never go to heaven.

*Me with my parents
and adopted brother*

My parents were Anglican and we went to church regularly. My father was a Sides-person in Somerset West and he did a lot for the coloured people. They set up a Birth Control clinic for the Coloureds. When we arrived in South Africa it was just when the Apartheid was developing. My mother was a ballet teacher and before the war had a ballet school in Baker Street so when we went to South Africa she started again. I learnt dancing and went to the Eisteddfods in Cape Town. I did ballet and drama at school and then I dropped the ballet and kept the drama. While I was still at school, aged thirteen, I played Wendy at the Hofmeyr Theatre in Cape Town. At the age of fifteen I was in a play with Joss Ackland called 'The Book of the Month'.

Then the idea came that I should return to England, so when I was sixteen I came back with my mother in the early part of the summer and had auditions for the Central School of Speech and Drama and the Royal Academy of Dramatic Art. I didn't get into Central School but RADA accepted me. My mother was with me for a few months and we drove all round England. I got a learner's licence and she taught me to drive. We went to Wales, visiting relations and so on. She found me accommodation in an LCC hostel in London in Eaton Square, where there were lots of nurses and students. Then I went to RADA and mummy went back to Africa. I was seventeen when I started at RADA. I didn't stay in the hostel the whole time; I was there for part of the time then I lodged with an aunt and uncle. He was Dr. Gordon Sears, Superintendent of the Mile End hospital. They had two daughters, Heather and Ann Sears, who were both in theatre and had made films. From RADA I started to work in the theatre.

In 1964 during a summer season in Newquay I met my husband John who was the scenic designer. We did weekly Rep and I was there as an actress by this time having done quite a lot of work as an assistant stage manager and stage manager in other places.

John was trained as an architect but after completing his training he decided he didn't want to do roofs and drains and be an architect but to work in the theatre, so he started at the New Theatre in Bromley which is where he lived. His father and his uncle were priests. He comes from a family of priests. He was born in Iran where his father was a missionary. John's father was born in China again of missionary parents.

After the summer season in Newquay he went to Barrow-in-Furness and I went up to Tyne Tees Television in Newcastle, where I was a Continuity Announcer and John was across the mountains on the other side of England. I was the one with the car and could drive and he couldn't so I used to go over and see him and then our relationship fizzled out and we got involved with different people. This was in 1964. I was at Tyne Tees TV for a year and then I left. Actually I got the sack because I wasn't really very good and made mistakes. On the night when Richard Dimbleby died, I was on duty. On air I said "Sir Richard Dimbleby has died" and transmission control buzzed down to me and said "Did you say Sir?" So I said "Yes, wasn't he?" They didn't know and they 'phoned ITN who also didn't know and they had to look it up. Apparently he'd got an OBE or an MBE or something but he hadn't been knighted. We were going to make a tributary programme to him. What I said was the final straw that broke the camel's back. I was still 'on air' and my boss came into the studio and said "This will be your last transmission, you're dismissed." I said do you want me to make this next announcement?" He said "Yes". Of course it was in the papers in Newcastle but actually it didn't really matter because this was in December I think, just before Christmas and John by now was working in Colchester in the theatre there. My mother had been ill with cancer, so it meant that I could go back home where they were now living in Tunbridge Wells. So I went home to help my father look after my mum. She died in the February.

John and I got back together again, that was in 1966 and we got married on the first of October. By this time John had decided that he wanted to go into the church. He had already been to see the Bishop of Tonbridge, the Rochester Diocesan Director of Ordinands. This was all the more surprising because when he was fourteen John said to his father "I don't want any more to do with your God and your church". His father said "Okay you go away and find out for yourself," which I think for 1954, in those days was a very wise thing to say. But whilst John had been working in the theatre in Colchester, he realised that God was calling him.

He decided to talk to somebody, so he went to see his uncle Gordon Hewitt who happened to be a Canon of Chelmsford Cathedral. They had a long talk on a walk along the river into Chelmsford and out again and at the end of it Uncle Gordon said "Well I think you should go and see your bishop because I think it's right for you." John said "I don't know who my bishop is!" He went to a selection conference in February 1966 and was accepted for training.

John started training for ordination at Salisbury Theological College, in October 1966, a couple of weeks after we got married and had returned from our honeymoon in Newquay. One curiosity of the start to our married life was the way the Bishop dealt with the news that John had become engaged. At the time of his application he was a bachelor, so he was given a bachelor's grant. Then he went back to the Bishop and said "I'm going to get married". The Bishop of Tonbridge said "Well you can't do that and go to college. You either get married and then you go to college after two years, or you go to college now and don't get married until after your training." John contacted the Principal of Salisbury Theological College, one Canon Harold Wilson. He was a lovely man and a lovely priest, a blunt Yorkshire man who said "I will speak to him, I want you and I want your money, you are coming," or words to that effect!

So we got married and he went to college on a bachelor's allowance. We lived in Salisbury in a little house we rented in Sydney Street by the gasometer. Opposite us lived a teenager who came to us for advice about going into the theatre. We spent some time talking to him and he baby-sat for us. He went on to a very successful career in theatre, TV and film, including playing the baker in the film version of 'Joseph' and winning 'I'm a Celebrity get me out of here.'

His name? Christopher Biggins, and we still watch his career with pleasure. Later we moved into a flat in Castle Street. I worked in a shop just outside the main gate of the Cathedral Close, a sort of gift and kitchen shop, John Daveys. I also did house-work for somebody and looked after children, amongst other jobs.

Above: John and I get married

Left: Our curate's house at Wigmore

Our daughter, Sarah, was born in 1968 and was the first baby to be baptised in the college chapel. Some friends of ours were the first couple to be married in the college chapel. We had a wonderful time in Salisbury.

John was ordained in Rochester Cathedral at Michaelmas in 1969 and his title post was in Wigmore which is part of the Medway towns near Chatham. We had a new house on a new housing estate, the largest private estate in Europe at the time. We were lucky; it was a lovely detached house, with four bedrooms, one of which became John's office. We had some super neighbours with young children and our son was born while we were there. During our time at Wigmore, BBC Radio Medway started up in Chatham and John got involved. He was asked to do 'Thought for the Day' and started helping with the religious programmes.

It was a good time in Wigmore, plenty going on in the church. We stood to receive communion and had the modern service. The church was a sort of theatre in the round if you like, with seating on three sides of the altar. The parish priest was an expatriate German with some very progressive ideas. We were there for three years and then we moved to Oxfordshire for John's second curacy as part of the Banbury Team Ministry, living on another new estate.

John as a radio broadcaster

Here John got involved with BBC Radio Oxford, presenting the weekly church magazine programmes. In 1972 when we'd been there about fifteen months John went to see the Bishop of Oxford. He told him he would like to leave parish Ministry to work with the BBC doing religious broadcasting, and could the Bishop give a house for duty. The Bishop didn't take too kindly to this and said "No, get back to your paid job, or just leave now." When John came back to the house our vicar wanted us to leave more or less straight away because he wanted to get another curate to put in the house. John said "I can't go yet, I haven't got a job." He tried everywhere to get a job in religious broadcasting and eventually got one up in Hull for Radio Humberside doing sports and art. He hoped that eventually the religious side would come in. John started looking for a house in Hull. The whole thing with the parish in Banbury got rather nasty. John said "You can't turn us out of the house; I've got a wife and two young children." Eventually we bought a house up in Hull and moved. The whole episode put us off the church and we didn't go to church for quite a while actually. The neighbours over the road, who went to church, kept on coming over and saying, "Let us take your children to Sunday school," and we said "No thank you." Eventually we did go back to church. It was interesting because the church authorities didn't know really what to do with John; non-stipendiary Ministry was really a new concept.

John was licensed by the Archbishop of York in the chapel at Bishopthorpe. At the refreshments afterwards upon being told that John worked full-time for BBC Radio Humberside, the Archbishop said, "Ah, Ministry at the edge!'" He was right but he had no idea how to deal with extra-parochial Ministry. John worked at Radio Humberside for eight years. He soon stopped being a sports journalist and produced music, arts, and outside broadcast programmes. He started on-air brass band competitions and also presented the breakfast programme, the flagship current affairs show for the station. When the Queen visited the region for her Jubilee in 1977, John produced all the station's output for the visit and followed three feet behind the Queen in all her walkabouts.

During this time we were going to church and he was officiating. He was licensed as Honorary Curate to the parish that contained the University of Hull. The incumbent was Michael Vickers, who was to become the Bishop of Colchester. But much of the time we went to church in the parish in which we lived, Kirk Ella. I was heavily involved with the British Heart Foundation. I was chairman of the Committee. During my time we put on a fantastic fund-raising event with Marks & Spencer's Fashion Show in the Hull City Hall. As a result of the funds raised, over ten thousand pounds, my name was put forward for invitation to a Garden Party at Buckingham Palace and John went as my escort. I also worked as an auxiliary nurse at the De-La-Pole-Hospital in Hull. I was on duty two nights a week, which worked out well but sometimes John had to take the children into the radio station because he was on the early morning radio show. He would have to be there at about four or five in the morning.

John started to look after the daughter church of Kirk Ella parish and took the services there. Whilst we were up in Hull he also did various attachments with the BBC in London. He was one of the male producers on Woman's Hour. He also worked for Topical Tapes on the BBC World Service in Bush House making programmes that were sold all over the world. Typically an attachment lasted for six months. While he was doing this of course we were on our own up in Hull and he came back every week-end.

Eventually he got a job in the Local Radio Training Unit in London, training people in the art of radio broadcasting, and in 1981 we then moved down into Essex. We lived in a village called Stock which is near Chelmsford and he commuted from Billericay for five years to London. His office was in The Langham, opposite Broadcasting House. The building was once, in the early years of the last century, a very smart hotel. Today it is once again one of London's leading hotels. Here they taught people to be broadcasters. Many of the famous names you see on television today were taught by John.

While we were in Stock, John was licensed as a Non-Stipendiary Minister. I worked part-time looking after a lady who was house-bound and had lost her mind. There was a team of people that went in to help look after this lady. Our children were at day school in Billericay.

We lived in Stock for five years during which time I became church warden. I was also on the committee of the Horticultural Society. I got involved with fund-raising for the church and everything else as one does. John was trying to further his career with the BBC and he wanted to be manager of a local radio station but every time he had interviews he was pipped at the post, so he realised that God was saying "That's the end of that, come back full-time to the church."

Doddinghurst Rectory

At about this time there was an interregnum in Doddinghurst and the Bishop of Bradwell said "Could you fill in?" which John did. The parish said "Ooh we'd like you to come and be our parish priest". But John admitted that he was not interested at that point. It was then filled by an American and he became unwell and there was a second interregnum at Doddinghurst and John filled in again with the result that they asked him if he was interested this time. John and the Bishop agreed it was a good idea and he became their parish priest.

This was actually sooner than we had intended because our daughter was just finishing her sixth form to go to university, so we thought we'll wait before going back into parish life because it would mean a huge cut in salary. However God had other ideas and we moved to Doddinghurst Rectory on the day that Sarah sat her final A level exam. Our son, Ben, was at the end of his GCSEs and was then going to go on to A level, so he continued at the same school, The Mayflower School in Billericay. We spent five lovely years in Doddinghust. We had a five bedroomed house – amazing! It had a huge hallway and a study for John and a huge sitting room.

The windows were those metal ones so they weren't particularly good for keeping the draft out but it was centrally heated. We had a very big garden which had not been attended to for quite a few years. I spent a long time digging and getting mushroom compost from a farm nearby to break up the clay soil. We had a big party for all the people in Stock to come and see us, it was a lovely day. We really enjoyed living in Doddinghurst. We did lots of fund-raising and I helped John and got involved in the parish. I've never had anything to do with the Mothers' Union. There'd been no Mothers' Union in any of the churches I've been in. We formed prayer groups. In Doddinghurst the Methodist Church shared our church building and had a service after us. With Methodists and the Roman Catholics, John set up a Local Ecumenical Project and a covenant was signed. We had a huge barbeque once a year that was held in the rectory garden and was a big fund raiser.

I had become a traditional clergy wife! All through my life I had been involved in the church and even in South Africa, when I wasn't at boarding school I helped with fund-raising and had a little jewellery stall with stuff we had made and I had attended church every Sunday for years. So being the Rector's wife was nothing new, in a way! When we were in Newquay for the season where I first met John I went to church there on a Sunday and the only way John could get to see me was to go to church with me. That started the rot, he began to come back to church.

I wasn't a leading light in anything, I was just always around and helping with fund-raising things and enjoyed it. Our children came to church and our son was confirmed in Stock church on Easter Sunday eve and our daughter was confirmed in Kirk Ella. The two of them went to a Youth Club in Billericay, where they had an excellent curate and that is really where they found their faith. Sarah went to university in Lancaster and was away from home a lot but she has always been to church. She now worships in Witham at the URC where she preaches regularly. Ben has not been as involved as Sarah but he is a prayerful person. He is a Christian and he and his wife take their children to church, but not every Sunday.

After five years in Doddinghurst the Bishop of Chelmsford asked John to be the warden of the Retreat House in Pleshey and also be the parish priest there. The Retreat House is over a hundred years old and John has made a film about it.

I didn't want to go, I cried all the way there, I had been very happy at Doddinghurst and didn't want to leave but anyway we went. Pleshey is a very small village with a population of under three hundred people. It did have a post office then but doesn't now. John's office was in the Retreat House of course, so the phone never rang in the vicarage and it was very quiet. The house was very old. It had four bedrooms with lots of small rooms. The sitting room was bigger and it had some weeds growing up through the floor which we never managed to stop. It was between the Retreat House and the church.

When I first got there I went to post a letter in the village and as I was walking back up the street I said "God, what do you want me to do here?" because there was nothing. As I went on walking up the road I called in at a group called Pleshey Circle which is for elderly people and I was welcomed by the Chairman who said "We haven't had a vicar's wife here for years." So I thought 'Oh thank you God, right.' In fact, in the end I was chairman of the Pleshey Circle for quite a few years. I also ran a pram service for the mums and toddlers and worked in the garden of the Retreat House and was paid as the gardener. There were

*Pleshey
afternoon teas*

*Opposite:
The church
at Pleshey*

two of us and I still keep in touch with the person who does it now. Also soon after we arrived in Pleshey two ladies came up to me and said "You will do the Vicarage Teas won't you?" So I said "What are they then?"

It involved having tea in the churchyard, but I said we would do it in the vicarage garden, so all through the summer we had a quick lunch and put the urn on in our kitchen and rigged up our open ended barn, which is where they served the teas. We used to have queues of people every Sunday afternoon because Pleshey is an attractive village with old houses and it's still laid out in a mediaeval way with a Motte and Bailey Castle. It has an interesting history and lots of tourists, visitors and cyclists. There are lovely walks with footpaths, cowslips, violets and primroses everywhere, so we had many people for our teas. It was quite a commitment over nine years. We had a rota of people signing up to do the teas and bake lovely cakes but we always had to be there as it was at our house.

Running the Retreat House, a guest house with twenty-two beds, was hard work with lots of administration. John had a staff of seventeen, a deputy warden, kitchen and bedroom staff, a PA and gardeners. In fact John was really a religious hotelier. In addition he was the parish priest. As I have said, the parish was very small but it still had its expectations with regular services, occasional offices and the usual fund-raising necessary to keep the church open.

John was also in charge of Spiritual Direction for the Diocese and when people needed a Spiritual Director he fixed them up with one. Because of his experiences with the BBC he was good at management. It was quite a job. An annual programme of retreats involving everything from parish week-ends, through activity retreats such as painting and prayer and twice yearly walking retreats, to eight-day individually guided retreats was a constant drain on resources. We were at Pleshey for nine years which was the longest we'd been anywhere. The pressure got to John and in the year 2000 he had a breakdown, and we left Pleshey.

Our final job was at Wickham Bishops, a lovely hilltop village. We were there for just over four years. They were very welcoming people, we did lots of fund-raising and we had a lovely time there. They looked after John and then he began to look after them. We had a beautiful house, built in the 1920s, with five bedrooms and again loads of land, so I worked in the garden trying to get some things done, creating a vegetable area and so on.

Our garden was the perfect venue for the annual parish barbecue and for teas during the church summer fête. Although we had left Pleshey, John still ran a couple of Walking Retreats at the Retreat House. We also ran some in Worcestershire at the Retreat House in Cropthorne. They were always great fun.

In 2003 while we were away on holiday we were burgled. Our daughter Sarah phoned us to tell us she had discovered the break in and went to find the church warden. A lot of antique furniture had been taken, an antique bureau, mirrors, tables and all of my mother's jewellery, silver, pewter and Lalique glass. They broke down doors to certain rooms which I had locked. It was a terrible moment.

Above: John was made a Canon of Chelmsford Cathedral in 1997

Right: Our house at Wickham Bishops

Opposite: The whole family at our Ruby Wedding in 2006

After that the diocese decided to put a burglar alarm on the house. The house was isolated next door to the churchyard, with huge trees all around. At the same time John, who had had two hernia operations, contracted prostate cancer. This was successfully treated, in Leeds, with Brachytherapy but John decided to retire slightly early. He was sixty four when he retired in 2005 and we bought this house in Writtle. One good thing about the burglary was that it helped us to downsize. We were never badly off, and we have been hugely supported by the family. We've also been very lucky because John's work with the BBC for thirteen years gives us a pension that is as good as the church pension, which was also for many more years of work and in fact when we retired we found we received more than we did when we were working!

I think it's good to have women priests and I think we should have women bishops and gay bishops. I don't think we should judge. If God is calling these people you can't say no to God, they have been through rigorous training. They have had all the interviews and things like that and if they are suitable and their faith is strong, you can't say no. God has made us in all these different ways and none of us are perfect.

John paints; he is a water colour artist and makes films, a skill that he learned at the BBC. He also produced plays in some of the churches. Everything you've done in your life, you find, looking back, there was a reason for it and it has equipped you for the next stage in your life. I feel so fulfilled and I wouldn't change anything, I think it's been a good life and continues to be so. We feel very blessed.

GILL'S STORY

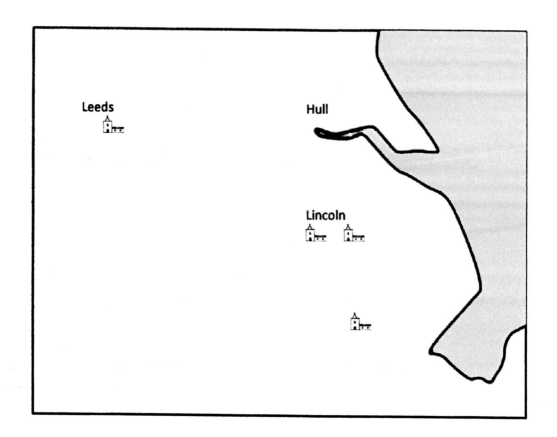

GILL'S STORY

*' I certainly didn't feel privileged
at being a clergy wife'*

My name is Gill. My mother was a Methodist and we went to the Methodist Church, my father was not a church-goer. My father was a railway signalman, he died when I was thirteen in 1955 and after that we were really quite poor. My mother went to work after he died. She went to work in a shop, for a stationer in Peterborough. We went to the Methodist Church and I went to the Methodist Sunday school and was made a member of the Methodist Church when I was about fifteen. I had one sister who was two and a half years younger than me.

We weren't affected at all as a family by the Second World War. With my father being a signalman he was exempt but he was in the Home Guard. My mother always said we were lucky to be living out in the country. We were living in a village near Peterborough. I don't remember the war at all.

When my father died our lives changed quite a bit because my mother had to go to work and of course we were very poor really because she only had a small widow's pension and there was no pension from my father. We thought we would have to move out of the house but we didn't because the next man that came to do my father's job was an unmarried man and didn't require the house, he was living in lodgings in the village. We were allowed to stay on and had to pay rent but in fact in the end they sold the house to my mother. She lived there until she was in her seventies I think and then went to live in an old people's bungalow in the village.

I went to the local Secondary School and my sister went to the Grammar School. I was an Eleven Plus failure in those days. I was quite happy there and did quite well. Then I went on to the Tech. College and did a Secretarial course and from there became a secretary. I was happy at the school but I didn't feel we were taught what we should have been. I left school at fifteen and then went on to the Tech. until I was eighteen. Then I went to work at the local paper mill as an office junior and worked up from there. I left there to work for the East Midland Allied Press in Peterborough as secretary to one of the directors and that's when I got married.

I met Terry at an old time dance. He was with a group of friends and I was with my friends. My sister was at Teacher Training College by this time. Terry and I went on a trip together. We became engaged and then the church thing came up. He was an Anglican and very loyal to his church. He was working at an engineering firm in the buying section, chasing up orders and that sort of thing. He didn't go to theological college until he was thirty.

I worked until we got married and then we moved up to Leeds. We lived in a village, suburb really, just outside Leeds. That is where he was a curate. In 1966 he went on a diocesan trip to the Holy Land and that was when his vocation was confirmed. We were engaged when he went to college. Terry went to King's School in Peterborough, the Grammar school but had to leave at fifteen because his parents could not afford to keep him on. It was one of those things, he should have stayed on but there were no grants in those days. He was very good at music, playing the piano and he got his LLCM and went into the Army before I knew him, doing his National Service but as a regular. He wasn't called up; he was deferred because he was doing exams. Eventually he decided he would go and get it over with and went in as a regular for three years, rather than in National Service for two years, in the Parachute Regiment Band playing the French horn. He stayed in this country much to his regret because it was the time of the Suez Crisis and he said as far as they got was guard duty at Aldershot!

*Our wedding
in June 1969*

When I met him I didn't know if he went to church. It was during the time I knew him that he decided to be ordained but I can't say I thought a lot of that, it didn't bother me. I would have married him whatever his job was, love is blind isn't it, you don't think about these things. In 1967 he went to Bishop Hostel College in Lincoln for two years to study theology. We were married in June 1969 and he was ordained in September of 1969. We actually got married by the warden at the college in the college chapel.

After we were married he had to go back to college for a term. So although we were married I didn't move to Lincoln, I lived at home and stayed on at my job. He also lived at home during that summer because he didn't go back to college until the September. After that final term we moved up to a parish near Leeds for his first curacy. He was ordained Deacon at Ripon Cathedral. My sister was married a year before us and was living in Bury St. Edmunds. We were getting on with our lives but we've talked a lot about this since and we've said "Poor Mum, we were married within a year of each other and she was used to having me at home, it must have been very lonely for her." She was very unselfish and would not have made it an issue, she used to come and see us a lot by train. With my father being on the railway she had free and reduced travel, so that was one advantage.

We had a council house on an estate in Leeds. It was opposite the pub. It was a complete culture shock to me because I'd never lived in the town. We laughed about a chap that came out of the pub one night and banged his head against the lamp post when he was obviously drunk. It was a massive parish, there were two other curates beside us and it was ecumenical, supposedly working with the Methodists. It was just after the time of the discussion of the union between the Methodists and the Anglicans that was rejected by the Anglican Church. Now they have a covenant more recently.

Although we were supposed to be working with the Methodists at the time, I was not allowed to receive communion in the Anglican Church, so I started going to the Methodist Church. It was a good Methodist Church there, lively and very well attended. In fact I was the treasurer of the play group. I used to go to the morning service there and to Anglican Evensong in the evening. I thought by doing that I was being fair. But I was told I had to make up my mind what church I belonged to. I couldn't just go to Evensong, it wasn't acceptable. From then on I just went to the Chapel, I was so hurt, I really was upset. It was so difficult because it was supposed to be an ecumenical parish. Without the Methodist minister I don't know what I would have done, he was a real comfort, a fantastic person and very supportive. He told me "You mustn't be pulled between the two." He was seeing what it was doing to me. Anyway I just didn't try any more and went to the Methodist Church for the rest of the time there.

Me (left) at a church fête with a parishioner, early 1990s

I got to know the other curate and his wife who were the closest to us, they got married in the same year. They lived a couple of miles away in the same parish. They were very friendly and we are still friends. They live in Cambridge now they have retired. She was good to talk to. The other curate was older than us and in his second curacy. We joined a flower arranging class together and went to organ recitals in Leeds Parish Church. She used to come to the chapel with me at times as well. We were there for three years and I loved the people, they were so friendly and very kind. There was one couple who used to invite me round every Friday evening as she knew I spent a lot of my time alone. I did in the end get some work whilst we were in Leeds. I couldn't have a full-time job but instead joined an agency and was sent to various firms on a temporary basis doing secretarial work. Another thing was that we didn't have a telephone, so if I wanted to ring my mother or my sister up I had to go down the road to the call box.

Expectations of parish work had never been explained to me. I suppose I didn't realise how the parish would come first most of the time, before our private life, having to take on other people's problems etc. I don't remember the first task I took on, except perhaps helping with functions at the big Parish Centre with one of the other curates' wives, when we discussed over whisking the dream topping how we would do our own thing and not be told – rebels! But I didn't mind helping out with parish fêtes and things.

After three years we moved to the South Lincolnshire countryside. We were only there for about eighteen months because it didn't really work out. My husband thought by going there it would be a complete change from being

Terry in his robes 1996

Opposite: Our lovely vicarage in the snow

in the city. The people were nice there. I got a job working in the local Estate office and I went to church and nobody questioned it. There we lived in a Police House, which wasn't bad, not bad at all.

Eventually the Bishop offered him a parish closer to Lincoln. Terry was Priest-in-Charge of the daughter church and we were both very happy there. We were only there for three years but I think it was the happiest I've been, everybody was friendly. There wasn't a Mothers' Union, I've never been a member of the MU but I have been to Young Wives'.

After three years Terry was offered the Living of a large parish of private and council estates where we lived in a purpose-built vicarage. We felt the problem there was that we lived amongst all the little council homes in this beautiful vicarage with four bedrooms. Consequently it was difficult for people to relate to the church and we felt as though we were stuck up there and people looked upon us as having a lot of money. One girl came to the door one day and she said to me "Do you have servants?" We had a lot of problems there with vandals both with the church and the house. We were broken into five times and there were always young people breaking into the church and trying to set fire to it. The church people were fine and most of the people were okay. Terry was very happy there, he liked the job, it was a challenge.

I was quite happy there too. I typed the magazine every month, then checked it through and duplicated it and put it together, quite a big job, and then I would help with the flowers and was on the readers and prayer rotas. I was also on the Women's World Day of Prayer Organising Committee and led it on several occasions. They had a Methodist Church there and we used to get on quite well with them and have joint services for things like Remembrance Sunday and Good Friday held alternately in our church and theirs.

Ever since Leeds I've attended the Anglican Church. I think I like the Liturgy more although I think the Methodist Church has a lot to offer too and I still have a great loyalty to them. In fact I worked at the Methodist Youth Office in Lincoln for the Youth Officer. I went to the Induction of the local Methodist Minister and afterwards at the refreshments a chap came up and introduced himself to say he and I shared an aunt. I'd never met him before but his aunt was married to my uncle, so by marriage we were related in a way. He had just come to Lincoln to work as the Methodist Youth Officer and he wanted a secretary and was looking for somebody. So I went to work there for about three days a week, and stayed until 1998. He left and someone else came and I stayed on. He was the officer for the whole district and visited all Methodist Youth Clubs in the Lincolnshire district. That was my contact with the Methodist Church there.

I didn't feel we were that poor because we hadn't got children to bring up, I suppose that would have made the difference. We weren't extravagant really but we did have holidays and went abroad. Our house wasn't used by everybody in that parish, they had a hall as well, and I think the vicar now has an office in the church. We had plenty of people coming to the door though including tramps. In the end I was finding it quite difficult. I couldn't cope with being broken into, people messing about, throwing stones at windows, coming over the fence and pinching all the apples, all that sort of thing, it was just a general nuisance really. We had a very good relationship with the police.

So we came to a group of villages five miles away and that was totally different again. We had been trying to move for about ten years or more. It was a place to give us a rest really. Each place was separate with its own PCC, garden fêtes and harvest festivals. I just used to attend the church where Terry was going.

We had a big Georgian vicarage there, old fashioned with five bedrooms, servants' quarters and goodness knows what, we only used two rooms upstairs. It wasn't warm, it had storage heaters but they put in central heating for us while we were there, it was very damp. It was interesting to live in a place like that but it was too big to keep warm.

I was quite happy and carried on going to work in Lincoln. Eventually the Youth Officer left and they didn't replace him. Like the church they made it into areas more centralised in the East Midlands. As our office was at the YMCA in Lincoln I'd got to know the people there. I thought I'd finish and not get another job but one day the secretary of the YMCA rang me up and said "How about doing a bit of typing to help me out?" So I got this job and stayed there until I retired two years ago doing just general office work. I enjoyed my work because the jobs were all things that were good to be involved with. I was okay in that parish.

We went there in 1994 and left in 2000, we then retired and bought this house. My mother had died in 2000 just before we left our last parish, she had moved to a residential place in Peterborough. She was nearly ninety-one when she died and had been widowed since 1955. We live not far from our last parish. The reason we came here was because of the trains, it is so convenient and it is lovely now as I have no car and am able to get the train to Lincoln and Peterborough. We have buses every hour and it really is convenient. We have a doctor, a library and a Co-op in the village. I've got lots of friends from work and friends in the village as well.

My husband died nine years after retiring in 2000. He had been taking the services at a village nearby. Their vicar had to leave because of ill-health. I still go there because I got to know everyone and have friends there. Terry was working until three weeks before he died; I couldn't believe how many friends I'd got, people were so kind. One friend kept coming to see me every week for a whole year and just let me talk.

Terry and me the day after our retirement in October 2000, with friend Hugh (centre)

Opposite: Terry with Harry Secombe at a Songs of Praise recording

When I married Terry I had no training and I didn't have any idea about the Church of England. I'm not a traditionalist and women priests are fine by me. Terry requested a lady priest to take his funeral, and a lady chaplain at the hospital came to see him who was kind and helpful. We had been married for forty years.

I certainly didn't feel privileged at being a clergy wife and sometimes there were feelings of resentment at always having to be available for phone calls at two in the morning etc. and never knowing who was going to be at the door when I answered it. It was very lonely in the early days, especially before I was able to find employment but over the years there were happy times as well.

The gay situation doesn't bother me. I think the church spends too much time bothering about these things and not reaching out to people. We are supposed to be preaching the Gospel aren't we?

FLORENCE

FLORENCE'S STORY

'And so I made my commitment to Jesus"

I was born in 1943. My mother and father met during the war but my mother already had four children; she was widowed when she was very young. Then she met my father and had me and two years later she had my brother, so I've only got one brother but I had two half-brothers and two half-sisters. When I was born my father was actually in Burma and missing, presumed dead. Then he turned up and came home when I was two. The story is, and I don't know whether I actually remember it or it's because I've just been told it, my father and I talked about it not long before he died, apparently he came in the front door and I was at the top of the stairs and I just looked down the stairs and said "Daddy." So that's the story, that I obviously knew who he was, but I don't know whether I really knew.

My father had malaria several times when I was a young child. He wasn't a prisoner of war but he was actually behind Japanese lines. They were in Burma and had got behind enemy lines and they were stuck. They were trapped but eventually got out. I don't know how because he never talked about it. I wish now that I had talked to him more about it but he never ever initiated a conversation about it.

We lived in a council house in Bedford and we moved from there to another council house in Bedford that I don't remember a lot about, but the one I remember most was also in Bedford and we lived there until I was sixteen.

When my father came out of the Army he went to work as a storekeeper for a company that manufactured rubber cushions. He was there for a great many years. He was actually very clever but lazy, lazy in the sense that he didn't use his brain. He was very bright and he knew a lot and apparently when he was a young man he wanted to go into the Ministry but there wasn't the money around in those days, so he went into the rag trade with his brother. He had one brother who was younger than him. My mother had a very hard life, she was widowed very young. Her husband died of TB. He was only in his early twenties. She went into service when she was fourteen and married her first husband when she was about sixteen, so she had a very hard life and did basic cleaning jobs. She used to clean at a cinema in Bedford called the Empire and she used to take me with her. In those days you had to pick up all the rubbish and do all the cleaning and things and I remember going with her to do that.

I had a fairly normal sort of childhood, I think, there wasn't a lot of money, there wasn't a lot of extras, we never went on holiday. I've never been on holiday with my parents. There wasn't a lot of emotion in my house but there was a lot of trouble. One of my older brothers was very troublesome, he caused a lot of trouble and there was a lot of violence. My parents were not religious at all. I went to Sunday school on my own, I think I went on my own initiative, I don't think my parents would have told me to go but they never came with me. I used to be a member of The Lord's Day Observance Society. I wore a badge and basically it was about what you couldn't do on a Sunday. When I think about it the Sunday school must have been two or three miles away, actually in Bedford and we lived on the outskirts of the town. I remember it was in a dark little hall but I can't remember any of the teachers really; but I used to go along to church as well. I always believed in God I think and when I was young, certainly before I went to the High School, I always thought I would be a missionary. I wanted to be a missionary and I wanted to be a doctor.

Anyway when I was eleven I passed the Eleven Plus and went to Bedford High School. I think it was a very difficult time for my parents. I think they were very proud of me and didn't quite know what to do with me and to be honest, I think, the years I was at the High School I became a bit of a snob. I think quite honestly although I had quite a few friends none of them keep in touch now and they all came from quite wealthy families and there was a sort of envy in me in those early days. Also it was a bit of a shock to find that whereas I'd been the king-pin at the Junior school and just sailed through, when I actually got to the High School I had to work hard because everybody was just as clever as me and even a lot cleverer. That was a bit of a shock.

However, there was a friend, Amanda, who lived across the road to me, who was three years ahead of me at the High School and she used to cycle six or seven miles with me to go to church in Goldington. This was because we wanted to go to the Youth Club, they had a really good Youth Club on a Friday there, but we had to go to the church on Sunday if we wanted to go to the Youth Club. We did that right through our teens until we were sixteen and I was confirmed, having done my Confirmation classes at Goldington church. The actual ceremony was at St. Andrew's in Bedford with a lot of girls from my school when I was about thirteen. I always believed in God. I can always remember having a discussion once with a boyfriend at about thirteen when we were out for a walk one night. We were looking up at the sky and he was arguing that there was no God and I was saying "Well who made all of this?" "Oh well it just happened." "But I can't believe that it just happened." I remember that quite clearly.

Anyway when I was sixteen we moved house and moved out to a village, five miles from Bedford, into another council-house. They were always council-houses obviously and we never had a car. Then I met my husband, when I was sixteen. We went out together. He was an apprentice on a farm. He didn't come from a farming background but he had always wanted to be a farmer. I left school half way through my A levels. Part of it to be perfectly honest was because I had met James and didn't relish the thought of going off to university and leaving him behind; but part of it, as I say, was that I found the environment at the High School quite difficult, seeing people who had so much and I had nothing really. It was a great struggle for my parents, even though I was a scholarship girl and got grants towards a uniform but there was never enough to buy me clothes outside of school. There was one thing that tipped the balance, it sounds very silly but remember I was a seventeen-year-old. Once a year in the sixth form we had to do tea for the mistresses and we had to wear a day dress. We were not allowed to wear skirts and jumpers but I hadn't got a dress. My mother sent for one for me from a catalogue and it didn't come in time, so I just took the day off sick and I think in some ways that's the thing that really tipped it for me. I felt 'I can't bear this any longer. I'd rather go and get a job.'

The local council did this scheme whereby you could go for an interview and have a look at all the departments and decide basically which one you wanted to work with, it was that easy really. When I went along for my interview the town librarian said "You're just the girl for my library." I went on the understanding that I could do my Library Association training the following year. Unfortunately when I got there two of the other girls who were already working did it and they said I would have to wait until the next year by which time the Library Association had stopped part-time training and there was no way that I was going to agree to go back to college full-time, so that went by the board. I stayed there for three years and the year before we got married went to work for Texas Instruments, as their assistant librarian, a very high-falutin title really. I worked for the education officer in charge of the library but unfortunately he left and it all got far too technical for me, it was beyond my scope of understanding. I left and went to work at Unilever where James was working by this time for their research unit into pigs after a year away at college. I worked as assistant librarian. We had a normal sort of courtship that went on quite a long time.

My husband's parents were Scottish and they belonged to a Presbyterian church in Bedford, where his father was very involved with the drama group. They weren't particularly religious, we never talked about religion, we never talked about God, I certainly never talked about it with James but we used to go along to the Presbyterian Church. It was very much a social thing. That's where we got married when I was almost twenty-one. James was just a year older than me, all but a week. We were married in church because I believed it was the right thing to do. I would never have considered not getting married in church.

My parents were fine with James but his family were quite different. They were very middle class. His father was a draughtsman and worked for a company in Bedford. They had actually come down to England in 1941 after they got married in Scotland. His father was in the Home Guard because he was in a reserved occupation. He was sent to Farnborough as a draughtsman. They were quite different and lived in an old Victorian house in Bedford. In my home we never sat at the table and talked, there was always somebody coming in and going out. They would eat their meal and go off and all the rest of it. In James'shome one of the things that I loved about it was that we would all sit down for a meal together and we would sit and we would talk about what happened and all sorts of things. When we got married and had children we really valued that and wanted to continue because it was so important. We actually lived in a couple of rooms at the top of James' parents' house when we first got married because we didn't have any money. Four years after we got married James decided he wanted to go back into farming. He wanted to go back to the land really. He was a research assistant at the time, so it was a bit different. It was still outdoors and it was pigs but it wasn't actually farming. We were living in Northamptonshire and we didn't go to church at all then.

In 1968 we moved to the Cotswolds, where he was a farm worker. We had a tiny little thatched cottage, which was beautiful, it was lovely, but we were as poor as church mice. The job was an absolute disaster. The farm belonged to a schizophrenic and it was run by somebody who was supposed to be his carer, supposed to be some sort of psychologist or psychiatrist, but he was a horrible man. His wife expected me to do her housework and he expected his workers to work from noon till night and we were only there for about fifteen months. During that time our son was born and then we moved to Worcestershire, between Tewkesbury and Ledbury. We lived again in a tied house but this time it was much better. James was much happier and we stayed there for three years. I couldn't work at all, there was nothing for me to do.

When we lived in Gloucestershire where Andrew was born, it was a tiny little hamlet. There were only about half a dozen houses. He was born at home but there was no telephone, the nearest phone box was about a mile away. The nearest shops were about five or six miles away, but I loved it. In Worcestershire also we were quite isolated, the nearest shop was about seven miles away and there was no telephone again. It was there that I started going back to church, to the Anglican Church, simply because there was nothing else to do. James never came with me but I took Andrew who was just a few months old when we moved there. While we were there I had a daughter, Louise, who was born in 1970. So I started going back to church but it was more for social reasons than for anything else.

Then in 1972 we moved to Essex. James was offered a job setting up a pig unit in Essex. We moved into a pre-cast bungalow in the middle of a field and the pig buildings were in the field but that was it. I had to put my 'wellies' on to hang the washing out. I had two small children, Andrew was two and a half and Louise was one. But the boss was very good, a business man with a breeding unit for pigs. Basically James was breeding pigs for selling all over the world.

I hadn't been to church there, simply because the nearest was about three miles away. One Sunday morning in May a young couple knocked on my door; they were Jehovah's Witnesses. I was making bread at the time and I invited them in. They talked to me and I thought 'I've got to look into this.' I really thought 'perhaps I should be a Jehovah's Witness and go and knock on people's doors and all the rest of it.' I was really impressed by them when they talked to me. They were a young couple and they seemed to know exactly where they were going and what it was all about. So I invited them back and to cut a long story short they came back to see me a couple of times. During this time I started to look at my Bible and started to think 'well actually I don't think my Bible says what they are telling me,' and I got myself into a bit of a stew. Eventually one morning I drove into the village and went to the church and there was nobody there. A little old man was riding past on his bicycle and I said to him "Could you tell me where the vicar lives?" I had seen him at a coffee morning so I knew what he looked like. The old chap said "Oh yes, he lives across the green."

I left my car at the church and took Louise with me, who was about eighteen months old and as I walked across the green I saw the vicar running towards me and said to him "Please can I talk to you?" By this time I was in floods of tears and he said "Yes of course, come with me." He took me back to his home and his wife took Louise off to play with her and we sat and talked. I explained what had happened, that the Jehovah's Witnesses had been to see me but I didn't believe what they were telling me and I didn't know what's what. He said "Well I'll tell you Florence why I think they are wrong and why I think I'm right." He then explained to me what the differences were between the Jehovah's Witnesses and the Christian faith. Brian, the vicar, got to the end and then said "Florence, what you need to ask yourself is what does Jesus Christ mean to you? That is the question you must ask yourself and think about. Why don't you come along tomorrow night? We have a Home Group meeting at the vicarage, where I could introduce you to a couple of young mums like yourself."

So I went along and it was very weird because it was a discussion about baptism and I had absolutely no idea. It was a very heated discussion because a chap called Trevor was very 'anti' Church of England infant baptism. But Jill, his wife and another lady, Chris, were young mums like me and they invited me to their homes for cups of tea and they talked to me about Jesus. They talked of Him as if He was somebody that they knew, that they loved and was so real to them. It was mind-blowing really in that sense because I'd never experienced that before but at the same time I thought 'No, it all sounds too easy really.' I said "No, it's all too easy. I must have to do something." They said "All you've got to do is believe that Jesus is who He said He was, invite Him into your life and let Him take over basically."

Then I began to read the Bible and all I can say is that there were certain things in the Bible like 'Behold I stand at the door and knock, if you invite Me in I'll come' and 'No one comes to the Father but by Me, I am the way, the truth and the life' and as I read these things all I can say is that it all made sense, it just made sense. I thought 'This is what I've been looking for' because when the Jehovah's Witnesses came and I got in such a turmoil, I can't explain why, but it felt as if God was saying to me, "Come on, you've got to make a decision here, you've got to make a stand, don't sit on the fence all your life, either you're for me or you're against me." I don't think it was quite that plain but looking back on it that is how it seems to me. And so I made my commitment to Jesus and I can remember saying to my husband "I can't believe that I can be so excited about this," and him looking on and thinking 'Well, if it makes you happy'.

I started going to church in the village and for a few weeks I went to a House Group at Jill and Trevor's. The summer holidays were coming up and they said "How about in August, instead of you having to keep asking James to baby-sit, would it be all right for us to come to your house and then we don't have to ask him to keep looking after the children?" So I asked him and he said "Well that's fine, as long as you don't expect me to be there." I said that was okay. He said "I've got lots of jobs to do outside." He went down and sat with the pigs really. Anyway after about two or three weeks he got a little bit curious and he would come in at the end of the evening with us and it was quite astonishing really because it was only a few weeks. He says himself that he didn't know what he expected but he didn't expect these people to seem normal. He thought Christians were all a bit odd. But actually he found that they were quite normal and they certainly had something that he didn't have. He said to me one night, and he knows exactly when it was, "I'm going to ask Jesus into my life." He knelt down and said "I don't really know what I'm doing but I just feel this is the right thing to do." So that is what he did.

From that moment on his life changed. He didn't feel any different immediately, but on the Monday morning when he had his coffee with all the builders on the pig site, who used to sit around and tell dirty jokes, he suddenly felt 'I can't do this, I can't sit here and listen to this now,' and he walked away, he just really felt it wasn't what God wanted for him. He started coming to church with me. He's never changed, with James what you see is what you get. He's not one person on a Sunday when he's preaching and another person on a Monday at all. The vicar Brian, who had started my journey to the Lord really, at the time had a group of lay preachers who went out in twos to little churches where they didn't have vicars because there were five or six churches to deal with and James used to go out with one of the men and that was the start of it.

Then in 1975 we moved again. He was still working for the same person but he wanted James to run another unit in Hertfordshire, as well as another one in Essex. So we moved to quite a big village, to a thatched cottage, a tied house again. Two or three things happened the following year and I started working part-time as what was then a District Nursing Auxiliary. I used to go round washing old people and all that sort of thing, not the sort of thing they do now at all.

In 1976 we were still going to the same church in Essex five or six miles away. We had tried the local village church but felt it wasn't for us. There was a House Group and a Bible Study Group that would occasionally meet in the village pub. On one particular night we couldn't get a baby-sitter, so James went and heard a young chap talking from Africa, from Rwanda. He was at a place called All Nations' Christian College at the time, with the sister of Chris's husband, (Chris who had originally led me to the Lord). She had brought this young chap Alfonse along to the meeting to talk to them. James came home and said "You'll never believe what he said, he was fantastic. He said 'You people need Jesus.' This All Nations place sounds fantastic." I said "Oh does it.?" Anyway that was kind of the end of that.

In the September of that year Brian the vicar said to the congregation "We have a couple who are at All Nations and living along the road and if anyone could offer them hospitality for a meal at the week-end or something that would be great." They were Clive and Elizabeth. He had been an airline pilot. I can't remember what she did but they had just started at All Nations. They were living in a tiny little flat and they came to supper with us and James said "This place sounds lovely, this All Nations." Clive said "Why don't you come over for the day James? Come over with me and have a look round." They asked me if I wanted to come but I said "No, I don't want to come." They went off to All Nations on the day that James had decided he was going to breed chickens because there was space where we were living and a hundred day-old chickens were delivered. When he came home there was I in the sitting room with all these boxes of tiny little chickens and I said "Why didn't you tell me they were coming today?" But he said "I really feel that God is talking to me and this is something that we should explore." I wasn't keen, I'd just got this job and I couldn't see how this was going to work. I couldn't envisage going to college with the two children. So I said "Well, that's fine, you go and I'll stay and work and whatever."

All Nations is a multi-denominational Christian College in Ware in Hertfordshire. It takes students from all over the world and sends them out to all nations of the world. It's basically a missionary training college. They said "We will take couples but never would we take one without the other." So we went along eventually. I got there kicking and screaming because first of all we had to fund ourselves, secondly they didn't have anywhere for us to live at the time, so it all seemed to be a non-goer. Friends were saying to us "If God wants you to go there He will sort it out." Somebody who was supposedly in the know told us that there was no way we would get a grant from the local authority to go to a missionary training college. Anyway we went along to Hertford and had an interview with them and then got a letter which said they would give us both full grants for the college fees because we had never asked for one before. This was going back to the beginning of 1977 when my husband was thirty-five. Then we had a letter from All Nations saying that one couple had pulled out and they had one cottage on the estate, would we like to go and have a look at it, so that was sorted. Then Brian, the vicar, came to see us and said certain people in the congregation had pledged to pay our rent for the two years we would be at college, so that was another obstacle removed. We had a Labrador at the time and she had, unfortunately or fortunately, got out when she was on heat and had been mated by a pedigree Labrador along the road and we had the puppies. We were unable to take animals with us to the cottage because it was on a farm estate and pets weren't allowed because of the pheasants. We had another couple of friends, who agreed "We'll have the dog for you and we'll have the puppies and see what we can do." They sold all the puppies which paid for all of our books.

The children were fine. Andrew was eight by this time and Louise was nearly seven. It meant changing schools and it was poor Andrew's third school and for Louise it was only her second but she was much more adaptable. They had a wonderful time when we were at All Nations, they loved it. We spent two years there with the plan that we thought was God's plan for us. We were going to go to what was Zaire and is now the Congo. At the time the Church Missionary Society had a project, planning a farm, a church and a hospital in Zaire. During our second year there we went along to a Selection Committee for the CMS and much to our surprise and theirs, to be fair, they decided that they didn't think it was right for us. We stayed with them, with a lot of other couples from the Monday to Friday and during that time we ate and talked with them and did a lot of these psychometric tests and all sorts of things. Then at the end of the week, they all got together and prayed, to help them decide what they felt God was saying for us. On the Friday morning they told us that they had done something they had never done before, they had actually gone to bed the night before without having made a decision about us, so decided to leave it until the next morning. They felt that God was saying "No" for our family it would be wrong to go to Zaire. The children would either have to be left in England at boarding school or they would have to go to school in Kenya, which at the time was a very uncertain place, so they felt it would be wrong for us. We couldn't understand it at all, we thought 'what next?' and then we were asked to go and see the Director of Ordinands.

Just before we'd gone to college somebody had said to James, "James, have you ever thought about the Anglican Ministry?" He said "Good heavens, no." It had never really entered our heads but while we were at college we had been seconded to a church in Hertfordshire, so we spent every Sunday there. The students went to all sorts of services, non-conformist etc., it just so happened that we went to an Anglican church. So we went to see the Bishop and the Director of Ordinands with the idea that James should go forward with the Anglican Ministry. Much to our surprise they told him that they wanted him to go forward for ordination but first he would need to study with a tutor for a year. The Principal and his wife at All Nations offered to tutor James for that year and they had already offered him a job on the maintenance team and said we could stay in our house, so that is what we did.

A year later in 1980 we went off to Oak Hill College in Southgate, North London for ordination training. That was in many ways the hardest for Andrew, our son, because he had to start at Secondary School then and he spent two years at Southgate School, which was not a good school and he was quite unhappy. It wasn't a happy time for him, bless him. The last thing I wanted was to be a vicar's wife and also I didn't want to live in London. When it was obvious that we were going into the Anglican Ministry, I said to God, "Please don't let me live in a flat, I don't want to live in a flat." Well, then we had a letter from Oak Hill to say that they had accommodation for us and it was 52a and I said "Oh no, it's going to be a flat!" We decided to go over and have a look and found it was a detached house which had been built in a garden to the one next door, so that was a real answer to prayer. We went along for this two year training but it was very hard. It was much, much harder academically for him. I worked as a sort of secretary for the Bursar which helped financially. Oak Hill was a totally, totally different experience to All Nations. All Nations were more like a family, with lots of young people, including young women from all nations and the kids had a whale of a time. At Oak Hill the emphasis was very much on the male but it is much better than it used to be. Some friends we knew who had been there years ago said in their time, in those days, no women were allowed to be there at all, so it was better for us.

Towards the end of our time there, we started looking for somewhere to go obviously and went to see Jim and Jane Willett at a church near Chelmsford. Jim was looking for a curate and it was such a blessing. They were wonderful, wonderful people. When we talked to other couples who had left Oak Hill and gone for their first curacy and heard some of their experiences, we realise how blessed we were. Jim was such a lovely gentle Godly man, very, very strong in his faith and not prepared to compromise at all. He asked James what he wanted from him and he said "I want someone to love me like a father and teach me." James always says that is exactly what Jim did. And I said to him "Jim what do you expect of *me*?" I was by then nearly forty and this was all totally new to me. I was also a bit of a rebel in that I couldn't stand it when I saw what I called 'play-acting' in the Church of England, in the sense that when some people get up into the pulpit immediately their voices change, so what is all that about? Jim said, "I don't expect anything of you, except that you support your husband, I don't treat my wife like an unpaid curate and I don't expect you to be one." For me that was the defining moment in that I kind of felt no matter what other people expected of me it would be okay because there are a lot of expectations of wives in the Church of England.

There was no training for students' wives as such at Oak Hill but the Principal's wife led a group once a week where we would talk about expectations in the Ministry, what people would expect of us. Were we going to be the sort of 'vicar's wife' to get involved in everything or be more independent? Were we planning to work or not work? From time to time ex-students' wives would come back to tell us how their experiences had been. We would discuss topical issues that were in the news and how we would deal with things. It was a very useful time but I did sometimes think that it was negative in the sense that there was more emphasis on what you couldn't expect rather than what you could expect. One of the things that kind of always puzzled me was that you can't have friends in your parish, you can't have good friends. But as time went on, when James did have his own Living, when he wasn't a curate any more, I found that you do have to be careful because a few people will find it quite difficult if you are friendlier with some than others. At the same time, some people are far more willing to share with you. There were some very hospitable folk that would invite us for meals and there were others who would never do that. There is a kind of sense of awe that surrounds vicars in a way. I'm not sure now that that is as true as it was twenty years ago but it is still more noticeable in the older generation. Some youngsters don't even seem to know what a vicar is these days but the young people who are in church now don't have that same sort of sense of it that older people did. Just as an example, when James was doing his curacy, I worked for a while at another library in the town and the librarian there was a very clever person who would command respect and acknowledgment of her profession. But one day she said to me a very strange thing. She said "I really envy you your standing." I said "I don't know what you mean." "Well, people look up to you because your husband is a minister."

I found this strange because it wasn't a job that you took up because it had 'standing' or some sense of being better than others. I found this quite difficult but as my life has gone on and I have met more clergy I can understand where she was coming from. Some clergy I have met think they are God's gift to men and women and feel they are above reproach. When they've got their collar on or their cloak on, then they are not to be disobeyed or whatever and I find that very difficult.

James and I have always felt very, very blessed that he was older when he was converted and then went into the Ministry and especially for our time at All Nations. All Nations was international and for people from all walks of life and everyone had one common aim and that was to serve God, do what God wanted them to do and be the person that God wanted them to be. I don't want to make sweeping generalizations but I think that far too many of the clergy that I have met have gone from one academic background to another and sometimes I question why they are doing what they are doing. I felt we were blessed but it certainly doesn't make us better than other people, in fact I sometimes say to God, "Did you really know what you were doing leading us this way?" We were talking a couple of nights ago and remembered an old friend we had at All Nations who said "If I hadn't become a Christian, I would probably have become a criminal," and although I haven't got any real criminal leading, sometimes I feel that about me. I just am so thankful but it hasn't been easy, it's been a hard old way and I've said "God, what are you doing? I don't want to do this any more! I don't want people thinking I should do things because I am the vicar's wife."

In our first curacy the vicar was wonderful and his wife was working part-time. When we'd been there for three years the Bishop said we could stay there because James was older. Usually after a curacy of three years you move but because James didn't really want to do a second curacy it was agreed that he could stay, as long as he took an outside interest, which he did but that is another story. It was at that point that I decided it was the right time for me to start my nurse training because the children were older and didn't need me to get them up in the morning, so I started my training at Chelmsford. That was good, everybody was very supportive but I remember one of the young mums in the parish was very cross one day. She said to James "Florence should be doing the crèche on Sundays. The curate's wife has always done the crèche." He said "Well, I'm sorry but the curates' wives up to now have always had young children and have taken them to do the crèche, but our children are not young children and Florence isn't going to do the crèche." There were people there that were very supportive but there were one or two people who I found very difficult to contend with. They expected a lot, more than I was able to give, emotionally, spiritually and socially. But as I say, especially when we met other ex-Oak Hillites who'd gone into curacies where they didn't get much support, or any support at all from their vicars, we were blessed and so thankful to Jim and Jane, they were wonderful. Anyway towards the end of James' time there Jim actually retired, a new vicar was coming in and we knew it was time to move. In fact Brian, who was the first vicar I went to in 1972, asked James if he would consider going to a parish near where we had been living in Essex but James said no, he felt it wasn't the right time. He then asked us to go and look at another. One of the things that I had asked God, when I knew we were going into the Anglican Ministry was "If I've got to be a vicar's wife please could I have a nice big house?" because we used to live in tiny little cottages. In fact we used to laugh because all our friends were going upwards and progressing into bigger places but we seemed to be going into smaller places. So tongue in cheek I had said this to God.

Anyway then Brian asked James to go and look at a parish where there was a vicar who had been there for thirty-eight years. The church was all but dead and he had retired but wouldn't move out of the house. If you had the Freehold in those days you could stay there as long as you wanted basically, but it has changed now. Anyway we went along to meet the church wardens; there were two churches at the time and we were really impressed by them and what they wanted and all the rest of it. They asked James to go there but were convinced that he would turn it down. Because of what I'd said to God beforehand "Please could I have a big house?" I wouldn't look at the house, it wasn't vacant anyway and the incumbent made it very difficult. In fact I said we'd make the decision without seeing the accommodation. We decided that 'yes' we would go, James felt that it was the right thing to do. It was then that the Archdeacon or Bishop insisted that we were allowed to see the house. It was absolutely full of antique furniture.

Apparently the vicar's wife was a very wealthy woman and nobody from the parish had been into the vicarage for years, even when they had garden parties they weren't allowed in the house, but managed with a little greenhouse outside. Anyway we looked and it was a six bedroomed house, Georgian front and Victorian back with a biggish garden. I just couldn't believe it was in such a state, nothing had been done for donkeys' years. When the vicar and his wife eventually moved out, my son and James camped in the house to do the painting and something like forty gallons went on the walls. We were still near Chelmsford and actually moved out in 1988.

I was training as a nurse, so I was full-time basically. On the day we moved I went to work from our house near Chelmsford and went to the house in the new parish in the evening. By this time everything had been moved in and the place was in chaos. James lit a fire in the dining room and one of the church wardens and his wife, who was a Cornish woman, came along with a big basket of Cornish pasties and a bottle of wine, so we sat on a rug in front of the fire and had our supper. The house had central heating, not terribly effective central heating, but it had these wonderful fireplaces in these two big rooms downstairs. There was a third room that James had as a study which had a fireplace but we never had a fire in it.

We were there for ten years. It was a time of great joy and it was also a time of sadness in some ways, in both personal and parish ways. Hubert, one of the church wardens, died two or three years later and that was a very sad time and the other church warden and his wife moved away to Scotland. When we moved there I met a wonderful lady called Letty, who was a German and before we moved she and some of her friends who were Christians, walked round the boundaries of the parish claiming the parish for God. Nothing had happened spiritually in that parish for such a long time and Letty was a great support to me.

We used to get together, pray and all sorts, then she and her husband moved away and I really felt that God at one point was taking away from me all my props, all the people that were so important to me. Our daughter was actually married in the church in 1996 but sadly that didn't last very long and there were marriage break-ups and all the normal things that happen in parishes to cope with really.

Both of my parents died while we were there; James' mum died very suddenly, with my parents it wasn't quite so sudden. She died a year after we moved in. We got a call from his sister up in Yorkshire at five o'clock in the morning to say she had had a heart attack and they had taken her to hospital but she seemed to be rallying. We 'ummed' and 'ahhed' about whether we should go up and said to Nancy "Okay we'll come up at lunch-time and get the morning services out of the way."

It was a Sunday, and I was supposed to be going to work, in those days you worked all the time as a nurse. So I went off to work and at nine o'clock I got a call from James to say that his mum had died, so I went home and James took the services, bless him, and then at lunch-time we went off, up to Yorkshire. There were lots of sad things, we'd basically lost all our parents, James' father had died quite a long time before that in 1973 but as I say there were lots of sad things that happened while we were there.

My daughter was by then nursing, she'd moved out. When we left Chelmsford my son stayed with a friend, George, because he was working for Marconi's at the time. Then George was getting married so Andrew had to move out. He came to live with us for a year and then bought a place in Colchester. Louise did her nurse training and then moved out to work in Saudi Arabia in 1994, which is where she met her first husband. We did only have two children but when I was at All Nations I did have two miscarriages. That was a sad time but they were very supportive. We decided we weren't going to try any more, perhaps God only wanted us to have two.

We were at our first Living for ten years. When we were at Chelmsford and I was a curate's wife, I started a Bible Study group in the morning because I wasn't working the first year we were there. We lived then in a semi-detached in what I called a 'Skimpy Wimpy' a nice little house but it wasn't very big, the stairs came up out of the lounge and sometimes there would be thirty or more of us and there would be ladies sitting on the stairs. It was a wonderful time and I got involved where help was needed in the parish but it wasn't so easy when I started my nurse training.

When we went to N....., on the night of his induction, which was in February and it snowed, two little ladies came scurrying up to me and said "Oh, we are looking forward to you becoming our enrolling member" and I said "I'm really sorry but until I've done my final I'm not going to be doing anything in the parish. And after that we'll just wait and see what God wants me to do." They were obviously very put out by this. We had this awful place for meetings next to the church called Church House which was in a terrible state of disrepair, so James stopped people using it because it wasn't safe. At the time the Mothers' Union crockery was all locked away in a little cupboard and nobody was allowed to touch it and James asked one of these little ladies one day "Could we borrow the cups and saucers?" "No," she said, "you wouldn't let your wife be our enrolling member." It was nothing to do with James, it was entirely my decision.

The church was a very high profile in the village because it was old, it had a nine hundred year history, it was a very historical building and the village itself had a lot of history attached to it. There was a Historical Society and because the church had this very high profile, when the Parochial Church Council wanted to do some alterations which involved moving the pulpit, suddenly the whole of the Parish Council appeared in church. They got all sorts of people involved to say "No, you can't do this." That is what I find so difficult sometimes, particularly in the Church of England, although I don't have a lot of experience of other churches.

In 1998 we moved to a seaside parish in Essex, this wasn't an easy ride either. There were of course some wonderful, wonderful people and many were genuine, but again what I've always found most difficult in the Ministry, is the appearance of people who do not support the church normally and don't profess Christian commitment but think they have the right to dictate what the church should be doing. This time there was a great furore about altering the front of the church. There was even a petition in the town, which was started sadly by somebody who I think is connected with the church. People signed who didn't even live in the town, let alone come to church. That was very difficult.

When we went there, basically, the Bishop had said to James "We need some change, otherwise in ten years time there won't be a church." James often jokes that he said "We need you to go and spill some blood." The man before us was a lovely, lovely man who had started to try and change things, then had kind of backed off a bit. Then we came and certain people thought they were going to bully James into doing what they wanted him to do, but they discovered that he was quite a different sort of person who wasn't going to be bullied.

One of the things that had been mooted before we arrived was moving some of the pews and having a coffee area at the back of the church. This had been abandoned but James decided that was what was going to be done and got enough people on his side. After it was done everybody said it was wonderful. Now I've heard from a friend recently they even have things like messy church there and he was saying they don't know what they would have done without this useful bit at the back of the church. Also the whole of the front of the church has now been altered as James planned many years ago.

The other thing that caused a lot of arguments or opposition at the time was the church hall, which was away from the church down the main street. Part of it was leased on certain days of the week by the library and they actually wanted premises to have a permanent library. James was the 'leading light' or the 'guiding hand' and the library took over the whole of the building and made it into a permanent library. It is wonderful because they don't own it but rent it and have a full repairing lease, so they are responsible for everything being done. We had already gained a hall next to the church where the congregation had dwindled to almost nothing. It was given to the church for a pound or something ridiculous. It has now all been renovated since we left, so James started all of these things.

We were there for seven years. James retired early when he was sixty-three following heart surgery, although he hadn't intended to for a good many years. He always felt that he had left a lot undone but I think James is very good at instigating change. I've always worked to pay the mortgage for here to retire to because we never had any money. When James' mum died she left us a few thousand and a couple of years later we decided perhaps it was time to think about getting somewhere for our retirement, so of course I had to work to pay the mortgage.

In that parish we had a nice house opposite the church and it was much more modern with four bedrooms, quite small for a clergy house but after we had moved in we were told that they would put in a downstairs toilet and a separate entrance into the study but when we got in, of course, there was no money so they couldn't do that. Fortunately then we had a new Archdeacon, who was such a lovely man and he agreed it was ridiculous. There were so many elderly people in the parish and when we had an elderly couple for Christmas lunch, Tom the husband had Parkinson's and he had to crawl upstairs to go to the toilet.

Andrew found it very difficult when James went into the church, he was aged thirteen at the time and he used to say if James went to pick him up from school "Dad, don't wear your collar." Louise who was eleven at the time wasn't bothered at all and we always tried very hard not to make them feel that they had to behave in a certain way simply because James was a clergyman. In Chelmsford there was good youth work there and they were more than happy to be involved. As they got older the thing that made difficulties was that they resented the time that other people took of their parents, particularly their father. I have to say that as the years in the Ministry went on because I was working full-time and James was always busy at week-ends friends would come to us for a meal but we never felt we could go and visit friends. I love entertaining and have always done a lot but I did feel that it would be nice to have someone to a meal that I didn't feel obligated to. But even with people you felt it was a duty to invite, it turned out to be a lovely time because a lot of people are great really.

I used to be very anti-women priests in my younger days. When we first went into the Ministry I felt that it wasn't right but as time went on somebody said "Florence, is it worth going to the cross for?" Jesus did so much to uplift women as it were and I think He would have been quite happy about it. I don't know whether Paul would be but I think Jesus would be and therefore I accept it. I have always said and I still say that if the Church of England gets to the point where they accept openly gay practising priests, then I will leave the Church of England. I am not homophobic because I would never, ever, ever be against somebody because they were gay.

As I look back over the last forty years I am amazed at the way God has led us. There have been some very difficult, testing times, both in the role of Ministry and outside it, if the two can ever really be separated. But we have come through them by the grace of God.

The Church of England, a bit like the NHS, relies heavily on the goodwill and commitment of its priests and their families. But just as there are nurses who are less caring with their patients than others, so are there clergy who are not 'all things to all men.'

I am thankful that we have been privileged to meet and serve some wonderful people and when some others really got up my nose or became too frustrating, I had to remind myself that we were doing it all for God and He never lets us down.

WENDY CARR

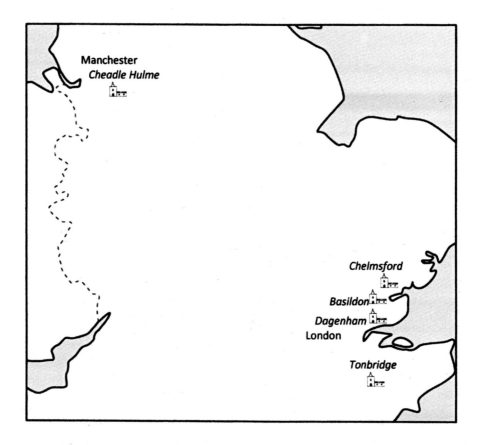

WENDY'S STORY

'I've got to go the way of the Lord'

My name is Wendy Carr and I now live in Rayleigh, Essex. My maiden name was Wendy Jackson. I wasn't from a religious family but my parents sent me to afternoon Sunday school which was huge with eighty or more children. That was the era when parents were quite happy to send you off on a Sunday so that they could have a snooze.

My parents were amazing. My dad was a plumber, so he was in and out of work really; but during the war, because of hearing difficulties, he was in munitions work in Liverpool. My mum did go and see him because she thought "If I want a baby, I'd better go and see my husband," so that was where I was conceived. It was quite difficult really because we lived in Morden in Surrey which is just South of Wimbledon. They both came from there and knew each other as youngsters and then married at twenty-seven years old in 1936 and then waited a while for me to come along because, as I say, they were split up quite a bit during the war. I know my dad had three houses destroyed during the war, family houses belonging to his father, all over England. We lived in Morden which my parents remember as quite a country place. It became built-up during the two World Wars.

I have a brother who is three years younger than me. He is still alive and we get on all right, he lives in Surrey. I had a very happy childhood. My dad was in and out of work but we had a house; he was buying the house and his three brothers, who all had good jobs,were all renting. I think the house cost about three hundred pounds and after the honeymoon they said they were absolutely broke. They got a solicitor's bill and said "Where shall we get it from?" They were very enterprising but my mother never worked until after my brother went to school but then she went to tailoring classes and made all our clothes. After that she went to work part-time for Triang Toys in Wimbledon as a shorthand typist which helped financially quite a bit. I decided that's what I wanted to be from when I was quite young and which I did eventually become.

My parents never went to church. My father never went because he thought it was very sissy for a fella' to go to church. My mother couldn't abide going because when she was a child she used to have to go three times on Sunday. Her parents were Victorian and had three girls and two boys and sent them all off to Sunday school and church, then she sent me off when I was about five years old and I just loved it. I came to know The Lord when I was about thirteen. Even when I was about ten I went to a holiday Children's Club and something was said that made me think 'I've got to go the way of The Lord' even though I was ten. Then when I was thirteen they had 'Outreaches' and things and we were challenged and I know it was then that I gave my life to the Lord. There was a Crusade when Tom Livermore was the Rector of Morden.

Then I went to Pathfinders and went on to be confirmed, but not until I was eighteen. I didn't want to do it earlier. Immediately after confirmation we had a course for becoming a St. Andrew's Sunday School teacher, which I attended and started teaching at eighteen. I had already left school when I was sixteen where I had learned to type and went to work in a bank in Old Broad Street in the City of London. I enjoyed that and was there for seven years, still teaching at Sunday school.

We were lucky because Morden had four churches, four big Anglican parish churches. One I saw being built. My husband went to one and I went to another but we met up at a Youth Club. My parents were happy for me to marry a clergyman but my father would not allow me to be engaged until I was twenty one. So we got the ring at Easter. My birthday was in August when we were engaged and had a party. That was good fun. John went to College that October and most of our courting was done by letter. During the holidays he managed to get jobs. At Christmas he was a postman and during the summer he got his old job back at Phoenix Insurance Company. The grant was three hundred a year, which was all we had to live on, but I was working and still living with my parents. I started at six pounds a week which wasn't a huge wage. John went to college in 1963.

We were allowed to marry before John was ordained, only because my father was dying of leukaemia. We had to apply to a bishop to get married who said "Because the girl's father is ill, I will allow them to." That was bishops in those days. Quite a few of the students did get married that year. They did allow it but they weren't that happy because they wanted them to be single. We had a lovely flat in Winchmore Hill, with a lovely landlord and lived at the top of his huge house. He was in his middle eighties. John was at Oak Hill College and he had a scooter. I worked five-and-a-half days a week and we were teaching in Pathfinders on Sundays as well, so we didn't have much time and only occasionally saw our parents.

My father died a year after we were married, which was quite traumatic. He became ill and died in the August of 1966, just before we were going to move in the early September. I left work in the August of '66 and we moved down to Tonbridge in Kent for our first curacy. It was traumatic because my landlord also died and I was leaving my job after seven years. After we moved we went on a holiday during which my father died whilst we were away. We came back

*Our old cottage
in Tonbridge*

to his funeral and John was ordained. We were in Boscombe on holiday in a Christian guest house and Mum said "Don't bother to come back," because she had her sister and there was nothing we could do. My brother was away as well. Mum coped amazingly well and lived to be a hundred. When she was left on her own she retired down to Seaford to be near her sister, so she was at Seaford from 1970.

For our first curacy in Tonbridge we had a very, very old cottage, getting on for a hundred years old. It was right next to the church hall and the church and we loved it but it was so damp. At one time John got his suit out and there was green mould all over it. It had night storage heaters in one bedroom upstairs and downstairs in the lounge and dining room which were separated by a large kitchen, so in the winter we had to have paraffin heaters and realised there was condensation from them. We were very happy there with a very good vicar and his wife and there was another curate who became a bishop eventually. When we wanted another storage heater we saw one secondhand and when John spoke to one of the members of the PCC he said "Yes, you go for it, it sounds very reasonable." But when two other members of the PCC heard about it they were furious and said "You should have come to the whole PCC!" We were only spending about ten pounds. They knew about the mould and in our last year Rentokil had to come to put in a damp course and re-plaster the walls.

Before we were married Oak Hill College was very good. They had fiancés' and wives' evenings once a month. There we were spoken to by various people. Maurice Wood was the Principal. He and his wife would give us talks on such things as how to run a Bible Study and how to do flower arranging. I remember one of the girls was not impressed, she said "I'm not going to do flowers." It stood me in good stead in a way because in our second curacy we went up to Cheadle Hulme in Cheshire and in my first week or two this woman came to the door with a bunch of flowers and said "I pay for the flowers, you arrange them." "Oh right." So I did my best but I hadn't done a lot of arranging. I didn't work during the first and second curacy because I didn't want to commute to London. When I left work I was earning sixty-two pounds and John's wage was only fifty pounds a month but then we had somewhere to live, which we didn't have to pay for so that it evened out and I was quite domesticated in those days and quite good at budgeting.

We went to Tonbridge in September '66. I had my first daughter in October 1967, so I was a year without the children and expecting. My mum of course was thrilled about that, she was still in Surrey when Rachel was born and she came over. Then I had Stephen in 1970, we were still in Tonbridge. I had him in the little cottage but Rachel was born in the Maternity Unit and in those days you stayed in bed for ten days.

At that time I was teaching in Sunday school and spoke occasionally at meetings. I went to Young Wives' and spoke at women's meetings. Even when I was expecting Rachel I was in a Ladies' Choir. We had just a little group and we were learning the Youth Praise songs. We used to go to one or two Nonconformists' afternoon groups and sing and really had a good time. I don't think we had a Mothers' Union group, if we did I didn't join it.

Stephen was born in the March and we moved up to Cheshire in the October of 1970, just before Rachel was three. I remember when we moved it was pouring with rain. In our tiny car we got on to the wrong bit of the M1, because the M1 and the M6 weren't joined up then, so we found ourselves going to Leicester. Rachel wasn't feeling too well and she was saying "I wanna go home." "So do I," I said. We got there eventually and stayed with friends. It was John's second curacy and was a team Ministry. We had a vicar and the curate was Priest-in-Charge of Emmanuel Church.

Our detached house in Cheadle Hulme, Cheshire

We had our own little detached house right next to the church. It had a lot of ground as well. Because of the flower arranging I was fortunate that in the local paper it had an advertisement for a local club that would be holding a course for flower arranging for six weeks. I thought 'that sounds a good idea.' It was because of that course that I got interested in growing vegetables and we had a lot of land really so I grew loads and loads of vegetables, I was also on the committee as well of this local group. I enjoyed experimenting with vegetables and it was a big area for the children to play in. I did do the flower arranging with other people.

When we got there and moved in, one of the ladies came round a couple of days later and said "Oh, you weren't at the committee meeting for the Young Wives'." Of course I didn't even know anything about it "I have only just moved in you know!" Some people are so insensitive, I'd just moved two hundred miles but I did end up taking the Young Wives'.

I felt the expectations were just part of the life and I could deal with it. I thought that's what curates' wives did. They have to be involved and really it stretched me; I was doing things that I never thought I could. I ended up speaking at meetings and found myself enjoying it. I was still able to do a lot of typing, writing up the talks and all that. I didn't earn any money at that time, except when I did some typing for a clergyman who was writing a book.

We were there for over eight years and after six and a half years I did work for the church Play Group and was paid two pounds a session. My children went to a lovely Nursery School where Clergy were allowed to pay only a quarter of the fees. Both my children started at three years old and were there every morning. Rachel went there soon after we arrived and then when Stephen was born he went there later as well. It was cheaper to send them there rather than to the church Play Group. We had to be so careful about money and in The Manchester Evening News a judge had ruled that a couple could exist on so much a week for housekeeping, so I said to John that I could cope with much less than that. I naïvely wrote to the Manchester Evening News and said I could manage on so much by growing my own stuff, making my own yoghurt and making my own biscuits etc. Well the abuse I got from people I didn't know! One woman rang up and said "If it wasn't for us putting money into the offering you'd bloody starve." Then I had a very rude letter from someone saying that I had no right to say things like that and then the conversation carried on in the local paper about how much people could manage on. People in the church were fine but I couldn't believe the abuse I got.

We didn't do much about relaxation and we hardly ever went out for meals like we do now. We eat out quite often compared with those days. In Tonbridge in those four years I think we only ate out about four times. When we were in Cheadle Hulme we would have our holidays down South, seeing John's mum in Morden and my mum in Seaford, or seeing friends or relations and on the journey we always took sandwiches. Even sandwiches were expensive for us at that time. Even now we think 'can we afford two pounds for a scone?' I think not! So I'd get the sandwiches ready and we'd leave about five o'clock and round about seven o'clock they would say "Can we have a sandwich?" So, that's how we did it. I knew that we'd never be very rich, I didn't expect to be when I married him but we made the most of what we had. It was a nice three bedroomed house in Cheadle Hulme and then it was extended while we were there, we then had a room over the garage and a utility room and John had a study upstairs. They did that wonderful extension in six weeks but it had been quite tiny, the dining room was only eight by eight and after we left they extended it even more and they had a downstairs study.

We stayed there eight years and then went to Chelmsford. John was Rector at St. Mary's Widford with the Church of the Holy Spirit. We had another quite nice house on an estate. It wasn't huge but it was right next to the church. The council estate was the other side of the road but ours was a private estate house.

While we were there it was extended again, so I was quite good at coping with workmen in the house. We had the study extended and they made the dining room larger. It had a medium size garden, so it was quite nice. The salary went up a little but not much at that time. The children were both educated there. They started off at the Cathedral School in Chelmsford, Rachel was almost eleven, she had an October birthday, Stephen was seven.

We moved in '77. Rachel was just there for a few months until July then she had to leave and go to Senior School. Stephen stayed there until he went to Highlands, the Comprehensive in our parish, so they could just walk there. I didn't go to work until both my children started work at Lloyds Bank. Rachel went there first when she was nearly seventeen.

Then Steven started when he was sixteen and then I thought 'These kids and my husband are earning money and I haven't got any.' To get anything I would save all the coupons I could find in magazines and save my birthday money and Christmas money and anything like that and I bought a camera, a single lens reflex camera for ninety pounds with what I managed to save up. I used to make chocolate caramel squares and sell them at the Town's Women's Guilds.

Our house on an estate in Widford

I never had any money of my own, if I wanted anything I had to ask first, John was very good and would let me have it but I had to eke out everything. I even bought my own microwave in 1983 after saving up; I was thrilled to bits and I only got rid of it when we came here because it wouldn't go in my kitchen. Then my aunt left me another one.

In 1981 we bought a canvas trailer tent and in 1982 we bought a different one and went to a family camp in Wadebridge, on the North coast of Cornwall. It was a proper site with special events for children; we went there three times at least, the last time was with a caravan because the previous time we left in a force ten gale, when even the Ark Royal lost its anchorage and it took five people to get our tent out. The next time when we went in the caravan it rained for seven hours, I remember it vividly, so after that I said to John "Never again. I will camp but I am going to have a hot holiday, I am fed up with holidays that are wet and cold." So he said "Well, you will have to go out to work then."

By this time both the children were at work but I hadn't worked for twenty years, all I could do was type, so I went on a course in Chelmsford and learnt the basics on a computer. I then applied for a job in Marconi's, which was quite big then and I got one immediately and started in an office in October 1986. I had such a wonderful boss, but there wasn't a computer to work on, it was an electric typewriter. I worked full-time and could get there in six minutes. I loved it, the fellows were good fun and the other people made me welcome. Then John had another job to go to after three months of me being there. His mum died just after Christmas in 1986 and we moved in the January of '87.

We moved down to Dagenham, Essex, in the snow. It was another evangelical church, St. Thomas'. We just had the one church. We had only cold water. They found out that the plumber had put a nail through one of the copper pipes and the water went through to the newly decorated study, the parish had painted just two rooms. It was an enormous house with fifteen rooms including the downstairs toilet, built in 1926, I loved it. I absolutely adored this house because there was room to move.

There were two halls, a small one next to John's study. There was a little porch and you entered this wonderful big hall space with parquet flooring. There was a wider than normal staircase, the kitchen was twenty-one foot by thirteen and we had all these rooms. I had a lady to help me clean; she did two hours upstairs one week and two hours downstairs the next.

The children were still with us. Rachel thought it was a bit too big but they had plenty of room for their friends to visit. The children were okay about coming to church until they were about sixteen but once we moved to Dagenham they didn't come to church any more. Rachel had just met her future husband as we left Chelmsford; he lived in Leytonstone. They started courting then and married in 1990.

Our house with fifteen rooms in Dagenham

Stephen stayed with us a bit longer and he would go up to his large bedroom and play his guitar like mad! Queen! He didn't have any friends in Dagenham because he'd been brought up in Chelmsford. He did have friends at work and would meet them up in London. I had left work in January and as only the two rooms had been decorated we decorated the other rooms. We did the small hallway, not the big one but every other room. Then I thought 'I'm going back to work,' even though the garden was half an acre. I went for three interviews and was offered three jobs. I joined a small company in Stratford part-time, doing two or three days a week. I learned how to use a computer and the telex thing, it was a good learning curve. John's mum had left us some money so he bought me an Amstrad computer and printer which jointly cost a thousand pounds in those days. He didn't start to use a computer until we moved to the next parish.

We were very happy at Dagenham with lovely people in the church. It was a rest cure because we only had one church instead of two; it was a team Ministry but John didn't have much to do at the other two churches. I was at work but no one in the parish resented me doing that so I was very fortunate. I did the flowers occasionally and Bible Study and Sunday school.

We had some lovely parties in that house when my son was eighteen and on my husband's fiftieth. I was fifty the year that we left there and we had a Barn Dance out in the garden. We had to do a lot of gardening there. When we went there the place had been empty for a long while and it took my husband ten hours to cut the grass initially and then every week it would take him at least two and a half hours to mow the lawn. At the far end it took us eleven months to clear the bindweed and bramble. After that we grew vegetables and had a lovely greenhouse which I had brought down from Chelmsford, it was a wooden one that I also took to the next move which was in 1993. We were at Dagenham for seven years under contract for that time, so then we moved again. It was a bad year for me because I started to have an over-active thyroid gland. I went on working. In 1989 I had decided to go full-time and moved my job to Aldgate East to work for P & O Containers. I worked with lots and lots of people and did computer work and that was great fun. But in 1993 I felt like death warmed up until they sorted me out. My mum was also ill and had developed Crohn's disease at eighty-four. She was in hospital in Eastbourne where they took away her bowel and she had an ileostomy and came out looking like a bag of bones. Her sister, who was two years older at eighty-six, lived round the corner and she looked after her, she was amazing.

We were considering a new parish in Basildon whilst we were visiting Mum for over ten weeks. The parish didn't know whether they wanted John or not. There were two churches, Holy Cross a fourteenth century tiny church and a 1950s St. Andrew's. They took quite a few months to decide whether John was suitable or not but I won't say much about that. We did go there and moved in September 1993 to a medium-sized house with four bedrooms.

My fiftieth birthday was in August, so we had a Farewell Barn Dance in our garden with good weather. Then we moved in the September. In October I immediately had to have radioactive iodine treatment and was isolated for ten days and could not meet anybody.

As I was working in Aldgate East I was treated in Whitechapel, at the London Hospital just down the road. I had to swallow a capsule and then went into the depths of the Whitechapel Hospital and you see all these things coming down from the ceiling containing lead and afterwards you can go home but you mustn't be longer than two hours with anybody. I got to the train station at Fenchurch Street and the train was delayed of course, so I was walking up and down the platform because I couldn't be with anybody that was pregnant. There was a girl at work who was, so I couldn't work for a fortnight. Before the treatment I couldn't run for buses, I could hardly climb the stairs and irritability was part of it. There was one fellow at work that I couldn't stand. So my excuse was "I'm irritable with you because I'm ill!"

*Our house
in Basildon*

When I walked into the kitchen at home my son and his dad walked out because I had to be in my own little room; the phone was used a lot. One of my friends sent one of these contamination notices 'Danger'. But we got through that and at the end of November we went to Germany for a week to stay with friends but by this time my hair was falling out in clumps, my long curly hair I had in those days. It was in my food and everything.

When we came back John found out that the local press was against him because he wanted to tidy up the church yard, get rid of curbs to make it possible to mow. A couple had objected to this and had got seven hundred people to sign a protest. My hair was still falling out, so I rang my doctor and a consultant rang me back and said "You are under-active now, get yourself on thyroxin". So Christmas Eve I had my first lot of thyroxin, which I have every day and I've now got thyroid eye disease.

The house was quite ordinary with its four bedrooms, it was a nice detached house with a medium-sized garden but I needed that. It was next to the church and the neighbours were lovely. At Basildon we had a lot of aggro, not particularly from the church people, although the first year we did. One divorced woman came who wanted to be married and that was before you could get married in church if you were divorced. She said "I don't come to church but I expect you to do what I tell you to do." It was the churchyard that caused a lot of aggro. John was just obeying the Chancellor's rules for churchyards but people didn't like it and there were special meetings with the Chancellor and these people were against him but rules are rules. I got very close to striking one fellow who was swearing on my doorstep, shouting and screaming and that really got me angry. "How dare you swear on my doorstep?" "I'll f***ing well swear where I want to!" Oh dear it got very close. Churchyards bring out the worst in people and he'd got someone buried there. It did go through, we changed it and the Chancellor was on our side but he was operating for the diocese so we picked up all the flak. First of all John wanted to tidy up the churchyard because we were relying on volunteers to clean it up. It became very difficult, especially when you'd got trees stuck in the middle of graves where they shouldn't have been and people were leaving artificial flowers, which they shouldn't. In the end John said "I'm right and it will be so." So we just had to put up with all the flak, John being the vicar. On the whole the congregation were with us for that but it was an open churchyard and they were not just church people buried there. But while we were at Basildon it became a closed churchyard and the Council looked after it regularly, so there was less hassle. It was our last parish; we were there for twelve years. Then we came to Rayleigh for our retirement when John was sixty-five. He had done thirty-nine years. I had already got redundancy from P & O in 2002, I'd been there twelve years and the deal was that for every year you got a month's salary, so I landed up with a year's salary for doing nothing and I was going to leave at sixty anyway, so that went towards buying a house.

We've been cruising since we retired with P & O. You go on Standby and you are told about a week in advance or two days. We could have gone whilst we were still working but it was too difficult to be on Standby because of the weddings John had to take. The perk still stood after retirement but sometimes it's not as good as you can get from another cruise company. We did go to the Caribbean and that was a wonderful perk two years ago.

Whilst we were working we could have holidays because I was earning good money, so we went to Australia to stay with a pen friend I'd been writing to for thirty-eight years, and had nineteen days in New Zealand seeing friends. We went to China in 1993; that was the year I became ill. I just went out to work to have holidays really, it had to be earned and I enjoyed it.

On the whole I enjoyed my church experience. I think it was a privileged life really. We've had a variety of homes but when we came to our retirement house, although it is so small, we enjoyed designing our first kitchen and owning it and we could have exactly what we wanted in our small kitchen. I've got my own craft room as well. I make my own greeting-cards, I've been doing that since 1998. I do altered books, you get an old ordinary book and cut it and stamp cut-outs on to it and I still do my flower arranging. I go to a craft class once a month and we both help out at 'church opening'. In Rayleigh we keep the church open every morning. We're there from ten o'clock until twelve thirty. We go to a House Group once a fortnight. My daughter is in Billericay, we've got two lovely granddaughters and Stephen is in Leigh-on-Sea with a boy and a girl. We live in the middle of them, so it's worked out very well.

I've seen many changes. I'm fine with women priests. It depends a lot on the person. In my opinion there's quite a lot of male priests who are not worth it, so it does depend on the person, good and bad, male and female, it doesn't worry me at all. I've known lots of women who had been deaconesses and some became priests and I think that is brilliant. I'm not keen on gay bishops but it doesn't affect me now. I'm glad I was able to follow my calling and go with my husband on the way of the Lord.

MARGARET

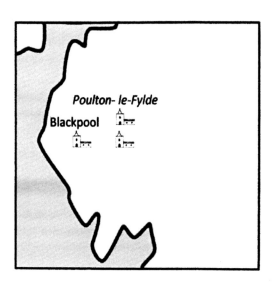

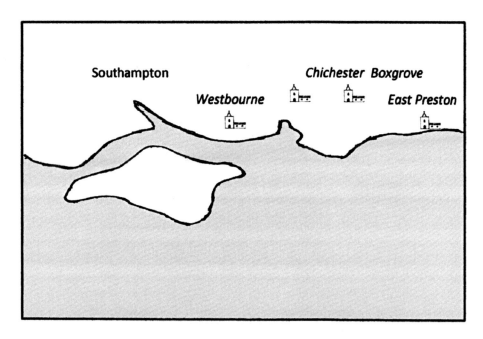

MARGARET'S STORY

*'I think what I've always tried to be
is a good church-woman'*

My name is Margaret and I now live in retirement with my husband in Boxgrove, a small village near Chichester. I am an only child and was much longed for. My parents were married for over ten years before I came along. I was born towards the end of the war, to a working class family.

Both my mother and father had to work to make ends meet, but they were determined that I should have an education. My father worked at the armaments factory during and after the war, which as you can imagine, as a teenager I was desperately against, but that was his job, it was just one of those things. My mother was eventually a cook in a day nursery nearby. They both worked hard all their lives, both of them coming from Lancashire starting their working lives in the mill, but they tried to get out as soon as they could. My father was born in South Lancashire, where during his childhood there was a terrific pit explosion killing over three hundred men and boys. His parents were 'cotton not coal' but within two years of that accident they had migrated to Canada. He and his mother and sister were abandoned in the outback when his father joined the Army, when he had no need to do so.

My grandfather fought in France and then after the war they had the Spanish 'flu which affected everybody, and they came back to England and opened a chip shop. In a way their family was probably better off than my mother's family. The two of them met in church, the Methodist Church, and the two of them would walk out together after the evening service.

I think my parents' religious affiliation grew because when I was about twelve years old we had a very good priest who came and guided us all. They were Church of England even though they met at the Methodist Church because in the North of England church and chapel were very mixed up together. I went to Sunday school but I rebelled against that because they used to read Enid Blyton stories to us, which I had already read. I couldn't bear it, so by the time I was ten I used to go to Matins, sitting with a lady who was a member of the Parochial Church Council. She was a headmistress and she used to bring out her Bible in French. She made me follow it, but it didn't mean anything to me whatsoever. Mum was a stalwart member of the Mothers' Union. When I went to college, my father's words of wisdom were, "Don't come back with a curate." It was a joke but of course I did come back with a curate in the end.

I went to Saint Katharine's College in Tottenham, which was a church teacher training college, which amalgamated with another institution to become the College of All Saints. I made a college friend in Lancashire. My teacher had arranged that another new student and I should travel to London together. We got on like a house on fire, and she thought that her cousin, also a student in London 'would be just right for me.' And so she introduced us through a blind date, believe it or not to go to church together with her and her boyfriend at All Saints, Margaret Street. Her cousin Bryan was also training as a teacher and we found that we had an awful lot in common. When I met him he had already decided that he wanted to be ordained and had already put out feelers. Within a few months he had an interview to come to Chichester for his training to become a priest. We had so many similarities in our backgrounds. His father was an electrician, but his mother was at home more than mine. He had one brother who was my age. They were a split family. On Sundays his mother was 'church' and his father was 'chapel' and each went their own way. Bryan used to go to the 8am Communion service with his mother and occasionally to the Methodist chapel with his father. When he wanted to become a priest I think his mother was quite pleased but his father thought he should become a headmaster. At least that's what he had in mind, so the Church of England wasn't quite the thing.

My mother fell in love with Bryan the minute she met him and there was always this joke that if ever we split up he would go home to her! It was wonderful because our two sets of parents became friends and even after we were married they would go to tea with each other; so I got on well with my in-laws. I met Bryan in my first year at college, so we had two terms together in London before he left to go to Chichester, after which we only saw each other once a fortnight. I was living partly in college and partly in digs with a lovely landlady who was a Congregationalist, now United Reformed. I shared a room in her house with a college friend.

Bryan and I were not allowed to become engaged. Bishops and college principals had an unwritten agreement that this should only happen after college and preferably after the diaconate. I was always made welcome at the college where the Principal invited me to social events and I came to Chichester two or three times a term. They gave me no training of any sort and in fact the end of my time at college coincided with the end of Bryan's time at Chichester. We returned to the Blackburn Diocese for him to be a curate in what had been a middle class market town near the coast called Poulton-le-Fylde. It was really a commuter place for Manchester and Blackpool. Bryan was very happy there.

I had gone home to work in a village very close to where I was born. I was teaching seven-year-olds. The parish didn't want us to be engaged as there was no house for us, so no immediate prospect of marriage, but as soon as the vicar Father Jim Stretch met me, he decided it would be all right. Father Stretch was one of the first people to enter Belsen at the end of the war and his wife was as wonderful a role model as anyone could need. What she did was to love people, she was a former nurse and a very warm person. Every three weeks I would go and stay at the vicarage on Saturday evening with the encouragement and at the invitation of the family. Bryan was in lodgings, earning nine pounds per week, five of which went on his full board, but his hosts were a very nice couple. The vicar's daughter was away from home and I think I became the daughter of the vicarage. Although engaged, we could not marry until we left that parish, but suddenly the Senior Curate was given a Living, and the vicar said "Well, you'd better get married and have the curate's house." It was a tiny house with very small rooms. We were married in my own village church by my old vicar, with Bryan's vicar celebrating the Holy Communion.

We were only allowed four days for a honeymoon, as the vicar always had his holidays at a certain time, and in those days the curate always did what he was told. It was not a question of having any rights, but Bryan could not have had a better trainer for his future Ministry than that good man. I'd had no instruction or guidance at all. We went to the Forest of Dean for our honeymoon.

When we returned a friend came to see me and Bryan was already seeing someone in the sitting room, there was no study in the house there were just two rooms, one off the other. Just then another person came with papers to be signed, so I had to put him into the dining room and take my friend into the tiny six feet square kitchen. Believe it or not at that moment the telephone rang and another caller came to the front door and I thought, 'Is this what it's going to be like?' But it was all right. It was wonderful because the parish welcomed me and I suppose in a way mothered me.

After a year we moved to Blackpool when Bryan became Priest-in-Charge of a daughter church of the large parish of Holy Trinity. It was St. Nicholas' Church at Marton Moss which was next to Blackpool Airport at South Shore. It gave him a bit more independence and continued his good training. It was good to be in a second curacy with the back-up of another supportive vicar in a very large Blackpool parish. The parsonage was a house built during restrictions after the Second World War. It was bigger than the one we had before but with a solid fuel stove which bad to be fed in the kitchen. It was fine, most of our furniture was passed on or secondhand, but it was fine.

Father Stretch, Bryan's first vicar, made sure I joined the Mothers' Union. At the time of our engagement the Bishop of Lancaster's wife took me on one side at a parish function and said, "My dear I'll give you a bit of advice, keep your mouth shut and your door open." I've always tried to follow that, and it's been very good. We've always had an open door policy and parishioners have always been made welcome in the house. It has amazed us when we've often gone into places where people have never stepped inside the vicarage.

When we first went to Blackpool the previous vicar said, "You'll get a lot of tramps because we are the first place of call in the town. They'll always have a mother in hospital in Fleetwood and will want the price of the tram fare, the cost of two pints of beer! If you say to him, 'I'm just going in that direction, I'll take you there,' you won't get him further than the end of the road."

We left that parish after two years which was the usual duration for a second curacy at that time. I was in hospital having Richard, our first baby. I was extremely ill, very badly dealt with and carelessly treated. They didn't check that all the afterbirth had come away, and after a few days my temperature rose and I told the nurse I had lost two big lumps like liver. "Oh, don't be silly," she said, but within two more days I had an operation to cleanse my womb. It really was quite a horrid time and the poor child cried and cried; Bryan and I had to take turns at going to bed alternate nights. I wanted to breast feed but my own doctor's wife had bottle fed so he wasn't interested and there wasn't the help there is now. I had been ill and the baby had colic. That was a struggle.

While I was still in hospital Bryan went to see the vicar of a neighbouring parish who was the patron of several benefices. He had said, "I have just the Living for you. Come and see me." It was an industrial village attached to a nearby market town, a bit on the wrong side of the tracks (it was a railway junction!). There was only one factory and many rows of little dark brick houses, and people who lived there worked away. Bryan came to visit me in hospital and told me about the parish. There was a large geriatric and acute mental hospital of which he would be chaplain, and a well-established church primary school, and since he was a teacher be thought that would suit him fine. I asked, "What was the vicarage like?" "Oh, I forgot to ask!" was his reply. But the Lord shone on us; it was a beautiful house, possibly the best we have ever had! I had time to recover because we didn't in fact move until the summer and our son was born in January.

All was fine, but the only sad thing was that my mother died just then at the age of fifty-six. It was a terrible shock. The baby was just five months old, but she saw him, and she had helped us prepare the vicarage for our move. She died of heart failure. It was really a very tragic time for us.

Of course by then I had stopped teaching, and no way could I have gone back to work. I didn't feel fit for work, and in any case I didn't particularly want to. So I didn't work while we were there, and we had our second child, Paul. He was born in the vicarage, and everyone, including the locals, was thrilled. When we had been there a month or two Bryan invited the PCC and their wives and husbands in to have a cup of tea, and most of them had never been inside the vicarage before. Incredible!

It was very different for me there because I was expected to be the enrolling member of the Mothers' Union. Although there was a secretary and a treasurer,

I was expected to write all the letters and engage in everything that had to do with leadership. It was a community of Indians without chiefs. All the church officers, Church Wardens, PCC Secretary and Treasurer, school Head Teacher and his staff, all came from outside the parish. It was not an 'educated' village, and our time there was a real hard slog. It surprised us really because we thought that, coming from our background, we would have understood and coped with it better than we did. It was quite an eye-opener. The vicar and his wife were expected to do everything themselves. The people were just there in the pews. It seemed strange to us.

I had never been a member of a PCC but I started a Young Wives' Group, and just got that going before we left. I had to do all of the letter writing for the Mothers' Union, fixing speakers and arranging meetings. I appointed a secretary but she said, "I'm all right being secretary, love, but you'll have to write the letters." You couldn't really take offence at it or anything. She did try to take the minutes of the meetings.

One community thing I did was in connection with the local open prison. Every Saturday three prisoners came to look after the churchyard and the vicarage garden, no officer came with them. Bryan had to supervise them and we decided we would feed them properly. The prison expected them only to have a sandwich and a mug of tea in the garden but we had them join our family meal in the kitchen with our children. This was quite illuminating. Many of them had families at home and they appreciated sharing an ordinary home while doing their time. One of them claimed to be innocent of his charge and after he served his sentence he became a Methodist minister.

When we had been there about four years, Bryan thought that he wanted to get back to teaching. He'd never particularly wanted to be a parish priest and when he went for selection for the Ministry he had said he wanted to teach and be a school chaplain, which with certain conditions was accepted. Things don't always work as we intend them but he saw an advertisement in the Church Times for a Priest-Vicar at Chichester Cathedral, and Chaplain to the Cathedral School teaching Divinity and Latin. Well, he had thoroughly enjoyed his time at the theological college in Chichester, so he applied for the post and was appointed.

I went very, very reluctantly. I knew we could not stay in our Lancashire parish for ever but I didn't want to move South, I didn't want to leave the north where we had our parents and lots of friends. I also had a cousin who was as close to me as a sister and we knew all the local young clergy well. We knew each others' children and we had parties and social gatherings, with good support systems and post-ordination training for our husbands. I went unwillingly, thinking it would only be for three years, as that was the length of the contract. I thought, 'well, it's a contract, so we'll come back to real life after three years at the cathedral.' One rather nasty thing was when one of the local clergy wives said, "Oh, you'll hate it, I don't know why you are going, they will be snobbish and catty and it will be horrible in the Cathedral Close." That didn't help, but do you know, we found it could not have been nicer. It was wonderful.

We lived in a flat in the Cathedral Close and discovered a youth we never had, because Bryan became a vicar at twenty-nine. By the time I was twenty-five I had one child and was enrolling member of a Mothers' Union branch of more than eighty members. It was a small flat to start with but then the two ladies who lived below us moved out and we were given the whole of two floors. It was an eighteenth century house with large rooms. It was sparsely furnished but we had space. Originally there was a garden but that was taken over by what became the Cathedral Cafeteria. The Bishop's Garden nearby became a public park, so we could put the children in their push chair and walk round there.

Bryan was effectively vicar of The Close, and was the Precentor in all but name, singing all the services, editing the cathedral newsletter, visiting the sick and taking Holy Communion to housebound members of the cathedral congregation. It was much like the work of a parish priest. In addition he taught two-thirds of a full school timetable, twenty two sessions per week in the cathedral school. He taught Latin and Divinity as well as acting as chaplain to the school, preparing candidates for confirmation, with occasional boarding duties when other teachers were not available. The role was officially Priest-Vicar of the cathedral, seconded to the school. He took a cut in stipend because the Chichester Diocese paid less than the Diocese of Blackburn. We lived on his stipend alone and to say that we were hard up was putting it mildly. With two small children I wasn't working and when the washing machine broke down Bryan asked the bank for a loan of two hundred and fifty pounds and we were refused. The Bishop's wife heard of our plight and the following day a cheque from the Bishop was posted through the door with a note saying 'Just pay it back when you can.' The car failed its MOT and we were due to go on holiday to stay with friends in Exeter. Without the car and being unable to afford the rail fare for the whole family, we were about to cancel the holiday when an anonymous benefactor from the cathedral congregation put an envelope through our door containing the rail fare in cash. People really are wonderful. I know we see the bad side so often but there is very great kindness in people.

When we normally had holidays we exchanged houses, mainly with our brother clergy, but we had two holidays in Wells-next-the-Sea at a special clergy holiday home, and we always spent at least a week with Bryan's parents in Clitheroe. Holidays were always rather make-do-and-mend but we usually managed three weeks in the summer. We became so hard up that when a friend whose husband was chaplain to Bishop Otter College asked if I would like to help by cleaning the students' hostel, I went for two mornings each week. I didn't resent this poverty because it was what we had to deal with together.

Me with my class at Prebendal School, Chichester

I didn't resent it but I was cross about it. The children just didn't get the sort of things the others did. At Christmas we received many gifts of alcohol but I used to make biscuits to give to people because we couldn't afford to buy anything else. When the opportunity arose for a teacher at the cathedral school for the first form children, I jumped at the offer. I found it quite difficult because I had to do one night each week until eight o'clock. When Bryan came back from Evensong he was able to deal with our children that night. I also had to work Saturday mornings, as did Bryan, and two or three times a term I had to work Saturday afternoons or the whole of Sunday supervising the boarders. The one great advantage was that the classes were small.

My children were at the local primary school and eventually went to the church comprehensive school in Chichester, it did work out extremely well in the end. In the cathedral we started a crèche during the services and I helped with teas for the meetings they had, just the usual sort of things. It was a happy time there.

We were there for seven years. They renewed Bryan's contract twice, but then the Dean said "I think for your career you ought to look at moving on." Not that Bryan has ever been a career clergyman but from then on he began to look, and within eighteen months the Living of Boxgrove and Tangmere became vacant with the vicarage in Boxgrove. Although we had been brought up low-church, the theological college in Chichester where Bryan trained was Anglo-Catholic and we both had leanings towards higher churchmanship. It was quite strange, because Boxgrove was 'bells and smells' and Tangmere was quite 'happy clappy'. Bryan said, "I just change my hat as I cross the A27." It was no use trying to force his views in one place or the other but we did a lot of mixing up. The Bishop wanted it to be all one parish and although we had joint

*St. Mary and
St. Blaise, Boxgrove*

all-age learning days that could not happen. We always gave an annual lunch to each PCC, mixing up the two parishes by invitation, but there remained two administrations. The parishes now have each its own incumbent with very different regimes indeed.

We were in Boxgrove and Tangmere for nine years, after which we moved to Westbourne where we remained four and a half years. The Rectory house was awful. It was brand new. The previous rector had looked at the plans which were measured in millimetres. He gave his approval because he thought the measurements were in inches and the house was 'nice and big' (his words). In fact it was tiny. The study would only take a couple for wedding preparation. If a meeting was held in the vicarage I had to retire to the kitchen or go to bed. Just before we moved in Bryan brought the Archdeacon to see the principal bedroom, because its dimensions were too small to allow a bedside cabinet at each side of the bed. When we got up together, one of us had to go into the other bedroom to dress! It was disgraceful that such a building should ever have been approved.

It was a parish that needed nourishing. There had been a succession of parish priests who had faced unfortunate difficulties and there was a need for some calm and consolidation. The parish was not receptive to Bryan's encouragement, and he began to feel himself in need of more spiritual nurture than was forthcoming from the parish. I was still working at the Cathedral School, as it was easy to get to Chichester. By that time Richard was at university and Paul said "I can't stop here for long, Mum." It was a bit early, he was nineteen but he moved out to be with friends in Chichester. Although some of the divisions in the parish were being healed, Bryan took the opportunity to move to another Living offered to him by the Dean and Chapter of the Cathedral, the parish of East Preston with Kingston, on the coast between Littlehampton and Worthing.

This turned out to be an excellent move. The house there was built in 1914. It had five bedrooms and two attic rooms, all centrally heated. With me working, I wasn't so worried about the expense. I'm sure if you do work you subsidise the parish. You're bound to but I don't regret that at all. Obviously they give your husband expenses for various outgoings but it wasn't until we actually got to East Preston that the PCC said, "Because you are having all these people in to your house for hospitality, we will give you a monthly allowance towards the cost." Before then I had just done it because I thought that was what we ought to do. At East Preston we had a regular Bible group and Lenten and study groups met in the vicarage.

I think what I have always tried to be is a good church-woman, supporting my husband all I can and be a good mother to my children. The rest is extra. Certainly I have never had anyone say, "You should not go out to work." I have never done anything about church flowers. At East Preston we had a lady who believed herself to be an expert and if I had gone there I would have caused more trouble than I was worth! I have done things like reading and intercessions, whatever was needed like that. I didn't have a Mothers' Union here in the South, as it was not as popular as it had been in the north. Bryan never expected me to do things. He never said, "I think you ought to be doing Sunday school." When I was teaching full-time I didn't want Sunday school as well. We always had teachers in the vicarage for meetings and that was all right, but I did not want to be involved in the actual teaching. I used my skills in helping with the Youth Groups and Confirmation classes, taking them on study week-ends, pilgrimages to Walsingham and visits to our link parish in Normandy.

We rarely had a Sunday to ourselves at the vicarage. If we were not entertaining a visiting preacher, we would often have parishioners to lunch, but we were fortunate to get Wednesdays off together. This began as a half day

Farewell family service at St. John's Westbourne

Opposite: St. John the Baptist, East Preston

for me in lieu of Saturday morning school, but this gradually built up to me having all my free periods on Wednesday morning, so that we could have a full day together. That was a source of conflict for Bryan because I wanted to potter around and catch up with jobs at home and he wanted to get out of the parish for the day. We compromised and it worked out well because we always had this little window in the middle of the week.

I like gardening and we always had to deal with our big garden ourselves but at East Preston our grass was cut by the man who looked after the churchyard, so that was nice. I've always made friends in the parish but realise that you do have to be very careful that you don't become too partial towards one person. You have to welcome everybody. You only realise when you leave a parish the ones who are your friends you can keep up with.

We were at East Preston for seven and a half years. It should have been longer, but Bryan became ill and had to have a triple heart by-pass. Our doctor said to him, "I know what you are going through, because your parishioners are my patients. They tell me how hard you work and this must not go on if you are to recover properly. You must retire now." So two years earlier than would have been normal he retired on grounds of ill-health. It was a trying time. He had his surgery at Guy's Hospital in London, and my school was very good in arranging things so that I could leave at lunch-time to go up to London by train to visit him. It was quite stressful, but all went well. We knew just before then that our present house had been left to us. This was such a help, because the thought of having a sick husband and having to leave your home must be a nightmare. We had a little money saved towards a house, but nothing that would have provided a home like our present one here in Boxgrove.

We would never have thought of returning to the parish to live in retirement but as the house was bequeathed by a former parishioner it was wonderful.

However, Bryan felt quite strongly that he could not return without the agreement of the present vicar, having previously held that Living himself, although it was some fifteen years ago. There had been another incumbent in the meantime, but we knew the present parish priest well, because he had been a student at the theological college when we were at the cathedral, and he was one of our many student baby-sitters. At first he was a little doubtful but after some reassurances he was happy with the idea.

As Bryan had now been a canon of the cathedral for several years, that would be our spiritual home in retirement. The vicar told the PCC that we were returning to the village, and we were made very welcome with good relationships all round. I am the one who is busy now!

I help with a village lunch club for the Over-Sixties. We cook a meal for about twenty five people each week, and about once a month Bryan and I cook an evening meal for the residents of a local night shelter for the homeless. Bryan takes occasional services in this and other parishes as the need arises.

Looking back, we realise that our children were inclined to be a bit devious at times, as children can be. We said, "While you are home this is our life, and we expect you to come to church with us." Richard was quite orthodox and took part in things.

Paul was a bit more rebellious. He was lucky in a way, because our young Church Warden and his wife became like his second mum and dad. When vicarage life got too much for him, be would go to spend time at their house, they had two sons slightly younger than ours. He grew his hair long and had dreadlocks but he grew through that phase. Both our boys say that life at the vicarage gave them people skills and in spite of the 'niggles' they recognize that they have lived in nice houses in interesting places. On the whole they would say that they have benefited from their experience.

On one occasion we returned from a church meeting to find them entertaining a tramp in the kitchen. We had 'gentlemen of the road' in every parish. Bryan always spent time with them. Some were prepared to do work for us, but that wasn't very often. Mostly they wanted money. Bryan had an arrangement with the local railway station to provide rail tickets at his expense, without any money going into the vagrants' hands. It was all about the dignity of the person and not being taken for a ride! We had one tragic case of a chap in the care of the community who frequently turned up without a jacket, and freezing cold. He was schizophrenic and needed specialist help, which he certainly was not receiving in community care.

Bryan was not convinced about women priests, not because he didn't think women could be priests, but because he didn't think the Church was sufficiently prepared. The debate in Synod took place on a Wednesday and was televised in full, so we spent that day watching and listening. In the end, we felt that it was an honest debate and the right decision was made. In fact Paul's godmother was the third woman in the first ordination in Bristol cathedral.

Although the bishops of this diocese will not ordain women, one of them had a sister who is a priest, and another has a daughter who is a priest. Our present parish is served by priests who all subscribe to Forward in Faith, but the parish itself is not yet committed one way or the other.

Gay priests are a difficulty within the Church and I have gone through problems with that but we do know a number of gays who are wonderful priests. I think the Church ties itself up in knots about sex when there are far more important things to be worried about. You obviously have to guard against things like paedophilia, but it is no more likely that a gay priest will be a paedophile than a straight one. I think we always have to say, "What would Jesus say? How would He judge this man?" We know wonderful people in high office who are in a relationship, but who will never be promoted.

There is a similar problem with divorced clergy. We say marriage is for life, but social patterns have changed over the years. You become wiser with experience and deal with people in their situations. Neglected love dies and marriages come to an end. Then the only answer is to bury it decently. Divorce will still remain for some people the worst possible sin. I don't always think this, because fallible human beings sometimes make mistakes. Nobody wants easy divorce and easy marriage to be thought of as something that doesn't matter. It is a matter of deep concern. I feel very sad for Roman Catholics who, if divorced, can no longer receive Holy Communion.

Bryan and I are quite lucky to be 'people' people, so we have always joined with our parishioners and shared their lives. We were privileged to be sharers in their joys and sorrows. It was a very, very good life.

MAUREEN

Maureen's Story

'I used to scream at God sometimes'

My name is Maureen, I live in Suffolk and I was brought up in South London. My parents weren't religious when I was first growing up but came to faith when I was ten or eleven years old. They were converted through friends who started going to church. They were very good friends and the wife said "Why don't you come along with us?" So that is what they did. Our lives from then on were very involved within the church. I had one sister who was also converted, she is older than me. During my growing up a lot of things were involved with the church environment. From then on my parents had a very strong faith. I went to Sunday school; even before they were converted they sent me to the Baptist Sunday school when I was very young.

My father was in the Royal Air Force during the war. I don't think he ever went abroad because he was working on the aircraft, so he didn't actually go abroad. My parents were separated a lot of the time but it wasn't quite the same as him serving overseas. I had an uncle who was in a concentration camp, so obviously that affected the whole family. Their involvement in the war did affect them but I think they liked to look at the good times. I was born after the war, so I wasn't personally affected by it.

I did okay at school but I was never brilliant. I held my own but can't say I did particularly well in exams and all that sort of thing, I was always very apprehensive. In actual fact I left school without any qualifications because I left at fifteen and didn't take any General Schools' Certificate Exams or whatever they were. I left school and walked straight into a job. I was always clerical. I worked up in Oxford Street for a large company. When I left there I went to work in Council Offices and worked for the Electricity Board, always as a clerk, never anything major; but I've always had work and been quite happy with that. I lived with my parents until I got married, that was the thing that was done then.

I met my husband when I was out in a park with my cousin. We were walking around and just started talking to these chaps; it went from there really. We took their phone numbers I suppose. He also lived in London, in North London, a different part from me and we just started talking to each other and my cousin went out with his friend. He was working with his father as a manual worker in the food industry, so he didn't have any qualifications either. He then left that and went to work for the Gas Board as a manual worker, outside not inside work.

He changed that work with a view to us getting married and was able to come over to South London, which was better because when we decided to get married it would have been very difficult to keep up the other job. So he decided to get to my side of London and managed to get a flat which we moved into when we got married. He stayed in that work until he went into the Ministry and I went on working until the children started to come along about four years later.

My husband Phillip had never been a church-goer and for a while I stopped going to church and I missed it. So I said to him if he wanted to see me on a Sunday he would have to come to church with me. At first he wasn't very happy about it but he obviously did get used to it and just before we got married he became a Christian which was lovely. He was confirmed and that was lovely and we went to the church my parents were at. His parents were not religious at all and I think they thought he was a bit mad really. They couldn't understand it at all. They knew he was going out with this girl who was a bit strange but I got on all right with them.

We went to Bible Study together with other young people. I wouldn't say we were over-involved but our lives revolved around church because that's where our friends were and our faith was central to that. That was where our life was and everything sprang out from that. Our life just carried on in an ordinary way and there is nothing exciting to report about that time. We started to have a family after four years and had three children.

We'd moved around by this time and were living on the outskirts of London, more to the east and it was during our time there, after the birth of our third child, that Philip felt the call into the Ministry. We had a few problems with my third child, he was quite ill at times and really the church was so supportive of us, so it was a wonderful time as well because we got closer to God through it. I think all things work together don't they?

Anyway it was after the birth of our third son that my husband felt that God was calling him into the Ministry. I wasn't very happy at the beginning, I liked the life that we had and all my friends and things like that. Life was very good and straightforward really. So it was a surprise for us all I think and a bit of a struggle perhaps to begin with. We accepted having to give everything up to follow his calling. He had to prove himself academically before he went to college, so he did knuckle down to do his studies, which was very hard because he'd never studied before so it was very difficult.

He went off to theological college. I couldn't work because I'd got the children and we went to the accommodation near the college. It was tough but I think in those days that's what you did. Our church was very supportive of us. If it is what God wants you to do somehow you get through don't you? It was tough, we were short of money but we coped and survived and we got through.

It was a very difficult time for my husband at college because it was such a different environment for us both. There again you're in an environment where you are all Christians and you support one another and help each other through. Our church was very supportive when we left and my family in particular because they were all Christians. We could keep in touch with them and they would all visit. He didn't really get any qualifications before he went to college but he had proved that he could study. When he was ordained Deacon it was wonderful that he had actually achieved that.

We had two curacies with a house but we never had a lot of money, that is the daft thing but I expect clergy get more now. Our friends from our 'home church' as we called it were still good to us and sometimes took us on holidays and things like that so we did extremely well. It always seemed that if we were in need, something came up. In our first curacy we were just in a terraced house in a road full of terraced houses. There was no heating in it but we didn't expect an awful lot and the house was fine. We'd never had heating and there were enough rooms and we were comfortable. My husband had a study and we had a dining room and we were very happy.

I got very involved, my husband was the one who was ordained obviously but we both thought we were in this together. I took on the Young Wives' in the first parish and from that I did a Bible Study. We had a very open home and were always having visitors and things like that and having people round for meals. I like to think we got alongside people. There were always people with problems, so we were there for them and helping and supporting them if they needed anything done. We got alongside folk.

We were 'low church' and got involved with family services and all that because obviously we'd got a young family as well. Our children did all the usual things. They had to keep changing schools when we moved which must have been very hard, but I think you realise that more when you come away from a situation. When you're going through it you just get on with it and almost expect them to get on with it, but I think it was definitely hard on them as well. You have to do the best you can with the circumstances you've got. The children always seemed to fit in fairly well. On the whole I think they did fit in, make friends and get on with things. Obviously it was tough on them but I don't think we realised at the time how hard it was for all of us; but you're all in it together aren't you? For the second curacy we moved out of London and into Essex, which wasn't so far away. We didn't stay quite so long there, two and a half years then we moved again but still to a Living within Essex. I don't think I noticed the money going up much but during the second curacy the children were at school so I was able to get a little job. I worked part-time in a shop.

I loved being a vicar's wife. I thought it was such a privilege because people share their lives with you. You can get alongside people, help them with their problems and be there for people. It was my calling really, being alongside people. I liked doing things for them in a practical way, chores around the house, the ironing or taking children to school. That's how I saw my calling. I never wanted to be at the front but very much supporting in the home.

I led Sunday school. We didn't have Young Wives' or MU but I always led Sunday school and had groups in our home. It was just an open home, people felt very much they were able to call and come in. I used to visit the elderly and things like that. That's where I felt my role was; I'm very much a 'people person'.

We only had the one Living and were there for five years. That is where things really started to go wrong. We were in a church that didn't want change, a very small church and we came in as a family that wanted to welcome families into the church and open the church up more. The people within the church found that very difficult. They wanted my husband to be 'the vicar' and to perform. We weren't like that. We were just ordinary people who loved the Lord and wanted to share Him and wanted to show people that we weren't any different to anybody else. God welcomes all sorts and if the children wanted to run around in the middle of the sermon it didn't matter. When children came to the church I think the older members found that very difficult, they were very set in their ways. I think that was very hard for my husband because they weren't allowing him to be the person that he was. They weren't responding to him as an ordinary chap that God had called. They didn't want that, they wanted him up there performing and that wasn't his Ministry.

The parish was on the edge of a town. We had three churches, all very much separate ones, but they weren't large congregations when we went there. They did work together in some ways but they did like their own identity. We amalgamated them more because we had things in our home for them, so perhaps we brought them together a bit more than they were before. For my husband it was hard because they wouldn't let him be the person that he really was. He wanted to get alongside people and they wanted this man up there doing all the right things and saying all the right things and performing in the right way. He then started to be the person they wanted him to be, rather than being the man that he really was, whom God had called. It produced a lot of conflicts for him and then things became difficult for us. I could see a bit of what was happening but perhaps I didn't see enough; I'm not really sure but we had a difficult time in our personal life.

You get so involved. I'd got the family, I was still working a little bit, I was trying to lead Sunday school, visit people, help people and so we hadn't time for each other, perhaps, as much time as we should. He was having these difficulties, trying to be what they wanted him to be, that is where the rot started. Perhaps we weren't giving each other enough time, we were so involved with everybody else. But I still always felt we were very happy, well I was happy. I'm not saying life was perfect but I thought we were happy.

This is where it gets rather difficult. In all of our parishes we got alongside people who had needs. My husband was very good at talking to people and they did respond to him and perhaps he got closer to some than I realised. Obviously in our last parish that definitely happened and this person talked to him and gave him time and she also had problems of her own. She responded to my husband and that is how it all started I guess. We actually left the parish and my husband went into other Christian work. Although we moved away and left parish work it didn't get any better, he didn't end the relationship as I thought he was going to and over a period of time it developed. I thought once we moved away it would all finish but I think I was a bit naïve. From then on the marriage did break up even though I didn't want it to.

We separated and I went to live in a house belonging to a friend of mine, she had moved out and it was going spare, so I went to stay and the children used to come to me and stay with their father as well. They were divided between us. By this time two of them were working and one was still at school. Schooling and everything had to carry on, but lots of people didn't realise that I was no longer living with my husband. They just thought because of our children's circumstances I was spending the week in the house and at week-ends we were getting together.

I didn't tell anybody. We were a distance away but not too far and that carried on for a long time actually. When it did dawn on people that something was not quite right a lot of people felt that it was my fault because I loved being in the Ministry and parish life and because he'd come out of it, it was me that couldn't cope. They felt it was my fault and a lot of people blamed me for the break-up of the marriage, it was mainly people we had known before, not my closest friends. I had stopped going to church for a while and they thought it was my fault because I was the one who had moved out into the other house. It took a long time to come out, but I did wonder why people weren't over-friendly and kept their distance a bit from me, those I had previously known, Christians! It took a long time for people to come out and say that they thought I was the one who had left.

I still didn't tell anybody that my husband was having an affair but just said "That is far from the truth, that wasn't the reason," but I still didn't tell them why we had separated. It was up to them whether they accepted or not but I knew the truth. I still didn't tell people that there was anybody else and no one ever knew. I'm sure my husband knew what was going on. I don't know what their full relationship was like, they moved and I had very little contact with them. It was only because of the children that we had any contact but I think his partner didn't like me seeing him, so it was really very difficult. I was very lonely although I had loads of friends and I did see people and I had my own family, I'd still got a mum, but it was lonely and very tough.

I was renting but eventually we did manage to buy the house my friend was renting out to me. Financially my husband was very supportive of me and I was doing quite a few little jobs and earning money. I was in my late-forties and early-fifties when this was going on. It was hard and I was lonely and I used to scream at God sometimes. For a while I didn't go to church because I couldn't bear watching the minister, it broke my heart, so I couldn't keep that up. I couldn't really get involved in church life for quite a long time.

We were finally separated for about ten years before we got divorced and I think that is when I started going to pieces at the final. I found it very hard. That was the end. It wasn't something that I wanted or expected. I always thought we had been happy. After ten years I never really thought we would get back together but that was the end, the final piece of paper, it was very painful. I didn't break down but I did go to pieces a bit, it was quite hard. I think by then people did know that I was divorced but they didn't know the reason why and a lot of people today still don't know the reason why.

Most of the time I was on my own, my son went to live with my husband, he'd moved around a bit as well. The other children had got partners by this time and most of the time I was on my own. In the early days I had two out of the three children living with me but they slowly moved out, went to live with friends and got partners. They were always very close to their dad, which is good because I never ever ran him down or wanted to spoil their relationship. I can't blame them if they didn't always understand where I was coming from. Obviously they knew there was something going on because their dad was with another woman, they knew that. He lived with her before we were divorced. They knew that.

He was still working for the church within an organisation but he eventually went back to the Ministry with her as his wife. I have reason to believe that the church never knew he'd been divorced. He didn't have a lot of contact with our past friends, he moved to another area.

I got on with my life. I went back to church because I missed going but for a long, long time I never really got involved in the church. I would go as the service started and would never hang about after. I went on my own, felt very lonely and didn't want people to know too much about me. I often used to cry at communion because I did find that really painful. I still find it very painful. I've never got over it, I still love my husband. I still miss being a minister's wife because I did think it was a very privileged position. People did respond to me and I'm still in touch with various people, so I don't think I made a complete hash of it.

I think you always take on a lot of guilt. I suppose I felt I had let my husband down; I wasn't a good wife to him but you can only do the best you can at the time and I always felt we were happy. I thought I was a dutiful wife really, I was doing what I was asked and what I was told and I didn't fight. I didn't stand up. I did challenge him obviously but I should have fought.

I very much did what he wanted me to do but I feel I should have stood up to him more. Perhaps fought for our marriage more, rather than just doing what he wanted me to do, which enabled him to carry on with what he was doing. He wanted me not to say anything, to keep the secret. I wanted to protect my children too. They had some idea as they got older but perhaps not in the early days. They all drifted away from the church and were making their own friendships and doing their own thing. It wasn't as vital as they got older, but whatever their age I wanted to protect them. I think with any broken marriage the children's lives are spoilt, there are always divided loyalties and I think that is hard for them, even now it is hard . . Oh yes, whatever age they are it is always hard on the children. I thought I did my best to protect them, to ease the pain, but I always think I let them down and have always felt a failure. I think I always will.

I don't know where I would have been without God, lots of times I wanted to die. I kept that inside my head for a long, long time because I felt so lonely. I just wanted to die but I wouldn't do that to my children and I did always know that God was with me. I don't think I could have coped without a faith. I came pretty low at times but God was always there and there were times when I was screaming at God. I cried and cried out to God but I don't think He minded me screaming at Him. That was okay, He understood and that in a sense was a relief, to scream at God. I think He knew how lonely I was and what a failure I felt and I was able to tell Him.

I loathed Sundays. It was the most lonely day of the week, even when I was going to church. When you're a minister's wife everybody knows you, people want to know you and you are essential to them. I guess in a way I did enjoy that, but then going to church as a single person on your own is different. You've lost your status and you're getting older. You're not this young thing coming to church, you're this older middle-aged woman and there are a lot of older middle-aged women in church. You're breaking into relationships that have perhaps been going on for years and so people aren't always so friendly and forthcoming. Going to church on a Sunday increased that loneliness even more and I loathed Sunday afternoon, it was always a difficult day.

I met my present husband nine years ago through a dating agency. It was very painful because it was never something that I wanted to do, or ever felt I could do. Friends wanted me to go and paid for me, they obviously realised, they were a lovely family. In my naïvety I thought that you had to meet everybody that wanted to meet you. I met one chap in a pub and he couldn't understand that I didn't want to see him again. I came home and sobbed my heart out and felt I had reached the pits.

Fortunately I started writing letters to another, then we rang each other up and eventually we met and I knew I wanted to see him. From the word go we were able to talk about our past and our partners, his wife and my husband and I think that was a good start to a relationship. So really we've gone on from there and we are happy but I still have that in the back of my mind that I'm not good enough. He's a dear. He's really lovely and puts up with an awful lot. I'm never lonely now, that's one thing I realised not so long ago. We often do our own thing but I'm never lonely, even when he is out. We go to church as a couple and we've got involved in the church and we love it here. It's a completely new start, nobody knew us. He has children and I get on well with them, I love them. I think it's different for them because they lost their mum and my children still had a dad, so he can't be a dad but they get on well and the children are pleased for me.

Life is very good now and I am very happy but always with regrets because we both realise that we would not have married again, we would both like to have been with our first partners. My husband would rather have been with her and I would rather my marriage hadn't failed. I don't think my first husband realised how lonely it was for me when we separated, he thought I had lots of friends and we didn't have a lot of contact. But I'm very happy with my present husband, although he knows I love my first husband and he still loves his wife. That's where we are but we also have a love for each other. I can't imagine not having him now.

I think I saw myself as a traditional clergy wife. It was what I felt called to do. I think in our first church I was asked to lead the Young Wives' but I don't think anybody told me this is what you've got to do. I'm useless at flowers but I'm a much more practical person. I wasn't sure about women in the Ministry but now I'm fine about that and I think if you read the Bible that it is fine for women to be in the church. I've got friends who were clergy wives and now they are priests, but I'm not happy with gay priests. I don't feel that that is what God intended. I can accept some people are gay and that is how they are made and that's fine and they can be priests but not in a relationship, I can't go along with that. I'll accept them as people because that is how they are, none of us are perfect when we are born, we are all different but not to go into a relationship and certainly not within the church. They are not following God's guidelines and to me it seems very clear but you can only do what is right for you and be true to yourself and we should not judge others.

My ideal was one man for life and that is why it has been so hard. I thought I was married for life, I truly believed that. Now that my husband has died I still wish I could speak to him when problems come up. I read once there are worse things than losing your husband to death, losing him to life hurts more. My husband died to me when I divorced.

MARY NAGEL

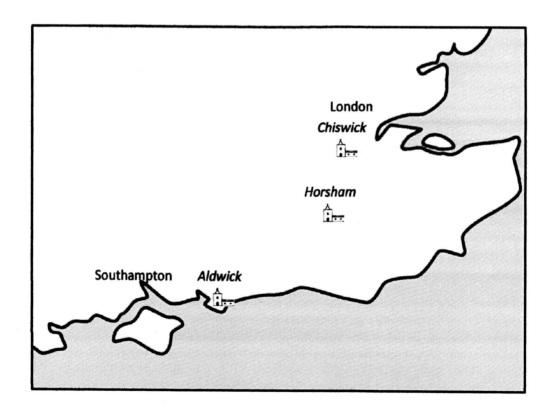

MARY'S STORY

*' I had a pretty good idea what it
would be like married to a priest'*

My name is Mary Nagel, my middle name is Phillipa. I was named after one
of the Sisters of The Holy Name with whom my parents were very friendly.
I live now in Aldwick, we've lived here for twenty years. My husband is vicar
of St. Richard's. We moved here from Horsham where we were for five years
and before that we were in Chiswick where my husband served his title at
St. Nicholas. We were there for three years.

My maiden name was Thomas and I was brought up in a vicarage.
My father was a priest and he came to England from Australia for two years'
parish experience and stayed here for the rest of his life. He met my mother in
Coventry where they married before moving to Sussex and I was born there
a year after they married. They moved then to Roffey near Horsham. He was
vicar there for nine years in a large old rambling vicarage where my sister Helen
was born and then my two brothers were born in '58 and '59.

We were as poor as church mice, typical of clergy families, but we never
went hungry. We were always well-fed and well-dressed. My mother worked
very hard, she didn't go out to work, she stayed at home to look after us.
So were we poor? Yes I suppose by subsequent standards yes, we were poor.
It depends what you mean, it depends what you want in your life, we never
realised as children what a struggle particularly my mother had to make ends
meet but we lived a very blessed life, a very happy life, a very homely life so
I was very fortunate. In hindsight I think I was more fortunate than many other
people were. We were all very involved in the life of the church and, in a way
that I couldn't understand, that was a different way of life.

At school everybody insisted that I lived inside the church, I explained that
I lived in a house behind the church but they insisted it was all united. We ate all
our meals together, we played together, we worked together and there was never
any question about going to church, we just did. It's the same as my own family,
there has never been any question about going to church, there were never any
arguments and thanks be to God we all four of us kept our faith as we grew
up. My brother is a priest, my sister married a priest, and I married a priest.
My younger brother is a church warden on and off, he has a few years off and
then is church warden again. The church was very much part of our upbringing,
part of our life, part of the way in which we grew. To me it was quite natural.

My mother grew up during the Second World War, her brother was fighting abroad. He went off to war as soon as it started because he was quite a bit older than her. My mother's family was quite affected by the war because her father used to work in the motor industry and in the thirties he was very much out of work. Then the war came and the car factories became munitions factories in Coventry in the Midlands. Mum wasn't evacuated; she stayed in Coventry during the blitz and remembers Coventry Cathedral going up. The usual farewell at the end of the day at school was "See you tomorrow if you're still alive." That was the way it went. Very often there were spaces in the classroom the next morning when people had been hit.

It was quite natural for me to marry a priest and when people asked me where I met him, "I met him in church." It was one of those things, it wasn't through my parents that I met him because at the time I was living and working in London as a teacher. I lived and taught in the East End and then in Brixton. I met my husband when he was halfway through his ordination training in Salisbury but he had a flat in London. We got married just after he was made a deacon, which wasn't the easiest thing to do because we had to go through interviews with the Bishop to get permission.

There was an attempt to ask my husband to put off ordination or to put off marriage but I was twenty-nine and if I was going to get married I wanted to get married. It wasn't as if I was straight out of school or college but I felt I had my own mind and I think the Bishop realised that. He couldn't argue with me so we had permission and we were married during his deacon's year.

I was working as a teacher but gave it up when my first baby was born. I married in the August and I taught until the following April when I went on maternity leave. I knew I wouldn't return to teaching. Fortunately Maternity Benefit was quite generous in those days. I was quite happy to stay at home, I'd always wanted to stay at home and bring up my own family. I wanted to be as my younger daughter says "I want to be a stay-at-home-mummy."

We were married during Lawson's deacon's year

That was my intention because to me family life is more important than earning more money. It was the way I'd been brought up and it was a philosophy I think that is somehow true. When my younger daughter reached school age people said "Are you going to go back to teaching?" But I'd been out of it for long enough and there had been so many changes, I would have needed to go back and do a refresher course; but I wanted to be there and go and see them in their school plays and I wanted to support them. I had enough to do with a big house to run so I was quite happy to stay at home.

I had a pretty good idea what it would be like married to a priest, I knew what to expect. Things had changed over the years since I was young, since I was a child. Expectations were different; you weren't so much expected to be the unpaid curate as in my mother's day. I feel there is still a bit of the old school "You will help in Sunday school won't you?"

There's a little bit of that but I think I was a strong enough character to say what I was going to do and what I wasn't going to do. I suppose it was a bit different but then I think I moulded the role I wanted to play according to my own desires, my own thoughts and my own aspirations. But everything I hope I've done and everything I hope I do is moulded round family life and the church. That has always been my priority anyway, which is why I now do a lot of work for the church on a voluntary basis. When I first got married I became a member of the Mothers' Union. I used to go as a young members' family representative to Mary Sumner House, which everyone was very pleased about because I brought the baby with me. They thought that was wonderful and the secretarial staff spent the whole day looking after my baby and not doing their work while I was at the meeting.

I suppose the first thing I did think I'd do was to run a stall at the Parish Fair but I'd always done that ever since I was a child. That wasn't particularly new but I suppose the first new thing was when I was asked to do catering for the Fair, cook meals and so on. That was a bit daunting because the vicar's wife had always done it and she was a professional cook but she said one year "Mary, you do it instead." I wasn't a professional cook but I did that. I spent most of the time I was there having two children so I didn't take on a role as such. That came much later on.

I found it a privilege to work in the church, with the church, with the people. In 1994 in the early days of Ofsted Inspection I became a Denominational Inspector of Schools. I did that on and off for about ten years but it wasn't permanent, it was every two-or-three days now-and-again. I would be inspecting schools, Anglican Church Schools, it was called Section 23. I inspected the RE teaching and school worship and the ethos of the school and all that that entailed. Of course it fitted in really with anything the children were doing, it was only spasmodic. It helped a bit financially.

Ten years ago I was a Team Leader for the Census. Once done never again, thank you very much! It was much more work than I intended to do but the children all helped to sort things out and were put on the payroll, which wasn't bad, it meant getting up early to get the post. That was just a temporary job for about four weeks.

The church in its wisdom, back in the 1960s when I was a child, suddenly put up the stipends. They realised they were not keeping up with inflation I think, the stipends became easier as time went on. Since I've been married I wouldn't have said stipends were on that kind of poverty level as they were back in the '50s. The church is more realistic now about living. What I think a lot of clergy wives do is work to save money to buy a house for their retirement, but that is something I haven't done. Anything I did was just a bit extra to pay for holidays really. I suppose I could have gone out to work full-time, but I remember my mother once saying to my father "You should have let me go out to work full-time and then you'd have a house for retirement," but his reply was "But then the children wouldn't have had such a happy childhood."

In their retirement they lived in a Pension's Board house in Bexhill which was fine. My mother now lives in a retirement home for clergy in Lingfield. The reason they moved from Bexhill was to help me with the children because, although I didn't go out to work, I was elected to the General Synod in 1990. My parents said that if I was elected to the Synod they would come to look after the children when I was away every year. When we moved here it was just too far away from Bexhill, so they moved to the village of Felpham to be nearer the children and it was a great help to me to have them nearer and if I was away for those few nights they were there to look after the children. My father died in '96 but my children grew up knowing him. Then my mother decided she should move again because her eyesight was going and she needed to be somewhere that she would know her way around, so that's how it turned out.

When we married we lived in a curate's cottage in Chiswick, a small two bedroomed cottage. That was fine until we discovered that the cold water tank was outside on the roof, so it required climbing out of the bathroom window on to the roof to defrost the pipes with hair dryers because they hadn't been lagged properly. Then when we moved to Horsham we had a fairly modern house built in the seventies. It had four bedrooms, was purpose-built and easy to warm. Then we moved here in 1990 to a large seven bedroomed house which is on the Parsonage Board list as overlarge and expensive to maintain and doesn't come into their Green Guide.

Before we moved here there was an attempt to find a different house, but there was nothing suitable within the parish. But we came here and saw the house with four children and we loved it. It has central heating but what was originally the maids' wing doesn't have any heating; but then I don't heat the bedrooms. It wasn't a maids' wing when it was a vicarage. This is a house that was built like Topsy; it was originally a four bedroomed house.

The people who bought it were the main benefactors of the church and they had servants and so they built a servants' wing with a new kitchen and another bathroom, so that made six bedrooms. Then they wanted another servant, a chauffeur-gardener, so they built a seventh bedroom. It can be draughty. It was very, very draughty until they put replacement windows in twenty years ago. I'd had pneumonia before we moved here which was one of the reasons why we asked if we could have replacement windows and they upgraded the boiler for the part-central heating. It used to be oil but they put in gas which was done some years ago. The pneumonia was nothing to do with the house, it was a chest weakness which I had when the children were very little and Polly was still in her pram. My parents were there to look after the children, the neighbour was good, the doctor was good and the parish was very helpful.

You can't please all the people all of the time. I hope I keep an even keel, I think I do. You can't go twenty years in a parish with no problems for your husband or yourself. There are differences of opinion but hopefully as Christians you have to learn to live with each other and live with differences. Over the years people mellow and I don't think I'm the hot-head that I was twenty years ago. I'm still quite strident in what I believe and what I say but hopefully I can see a point of view without compromising standards. But that is the same for whatever kind of life you lead I think. Living like this with the people you do hear things from various points of view and sometimes it's best to keep one's own counsel and just listen. I've learnt to hear all and say nothing; I've learnt that over the years. It's a very public life as well and I was fortunate in that I was brought up in that life so it wasn't a great shock to me. I think for people who've not had that and get thrown in at the deep end, it must be very difficult. I was brought up to err…brought up to know how to answer the phone but I know that sounds a bit daft in these modern days. I was also taught how to deal with people at the front door. Because I was brought up to that I didn't have to learn or relearn something new but I had to do what anybody does as they mature, I had to learn how to cope. Things can be tricky but what I think I have learned is important to do is to love people for what they are, not for what you think they should be. Yes there can be problems, but the problems usually come from an outside force which I can cope with.

I had four children, my first Tom was born while we lived in that little house, he was born in Chiswick in Queen Charlotte's Hospital and twenty months later my daughter Lucy was born and three weeks after she was born we moved. I don't advise people to move just after they've had a baby but you just do it, it has to be done and it's done, you can't change things. It's just a bit tiring but my brother came to help me pack and that was helpful. So they were both born in London and when we lived in Horsham my second son Tim was born in Crawley hospital and then twenty months later Polly was born; they are all about twenty to twenty-one months apart. I didn't have any problems at all I was very lucky, very fortunate.

My family:
Tom, Tim, Lucy
and Polly with
husband Lawson

Tom started school in Horsham, in those days they didn't take children into school until they were five so he didn't start until three weeks after Polly was born; but he'd formed a very close bond with the baby. They are all very close together in age; there are only five years between the eldest and the youngest.

All four children went to church schools from primary to junior and then they all went to school in Chichester. Since then they went to university, Tom went to London University and he now works there. Lucy took theology at Bristol and is now teaching RE there, Tim went to Southampton University and did a degree in mechanical engineering, he now works in tax consultancy in Bristol and Polly my youngest has finished yesterday her final teaching practice and is to start teaching maths in Liphook, Hampshire. They will all soon be settled.

We're a bit like Derby and Joan, none of them are married, well the oldest is only twenty-seven so they are still quite young and I don't know of any immediate prospects. I didn't meet my husband until I was twenty-eight and got married at twenty-nine. They will enjoy working and finding their own way in life. One thing I am glad about is that they went away to university and they've gone away to work because I feel if you've been brought up in a vicarage you can still be seen as the vicar's children and I do believe that they have to make their own mark.

As I said before, we do live a fairly public life and they need to be able to become their own people, away from expectations of people in the parish. For example some people have sometimes said to me "Where are your children, why aren't they helping to keep things together?" Like things I had said to me when I was a child. So my answer is "Well they do have their own lives to lead." This is before they left home before they left to go on to higher education. They haven't been pushed out but I do think it's important for them to go away in order to create their own world, their own future. I think they can become stereotyped, I think that trend is not as common now as it used to be. I remember when I was young and working in Boots as a teenager, somebody said to me

"When you go away from home you will change." "What do you mean I'll change?" "You are only going to church because your father says you've got to, you only do this and that because of that." There is that feeling that vicar's children only behave because they've got to. Well actually I haven't.

There is another stereotype for vicars' children, they always want to be the naughtiest, a different kind of reaction. I wouldn't want my children to change because they are away from home but I think they've been able to develop independently from being the vicar's children and live their own lives. I think that's important, I'm glad they have been able to do that. We all have to work our own way in life anyway.

I don't think vicars' wives are stereotyped now as much as they used to be. At one time when a parish was getting a new vicar they wanted the Archangel Gabriel, someone in their early forties, with enough experience but not too old, with a family and a wife who can run a Sunday school and stay at home. I think there is now the realisation that they have a life outside the vicarage. It has changed since we've been married and I think a clergy wife has every right to work full-time and pursue a career. It is up to individuals what they do. It wouldn't be right for me; I was quite happy to be a vicar's wife but then I was able to do lots of church things like General Synod work, be on various committees including The Board of Education and things for the diocese and I have been the enrolling member of the Mothers' Union. I've been in charge of Action for Outreach for the diocese and I'm Governor to two schools but that is because I've chosen to do all of this, it is not because I was expected to do it. I chose to do it as part of my Christian life, part of service as I was brought up to be doing, services that make a difference to the world, I believe in it. When I look at the work my children are doing outside of their professional work I can see they are doing that kind of thing as well, various kinds of voluntary work because that has been their lives and what they have chosen to do.

Our vicarage in Aldwick with seven bedrooms

Opposite: St. Richard's Church Aldwick

With regard to women priests I'm a traditionalist in that field. I don't believe that the Church of England has any right to act unilaterally on matters like that unless we are in consensus with the wider church, the great churches of the East and West. I can accept that women have been legally ordained as priests, but I cannot accept their Ministry as priests. It has been said at various conferences that those who cannot accept this development are still loyal Anglicans. There are the two sorts of integrity and I belong to one of them.

With regard to gay priests, I have problems with people who do not stick to the rules of matrimony. I believe marriage is between a man and a woman and I believe in marriage for life. I know this doesn't always happen and things break down and sometimes it is for the best that things should be dissolved; but I actually believe that those in the church, particularly bishops who are pastors, should give a moral lead and if they are not married they should lead celibate lives.

I'm going to stick my neck out a bit because I don't believe that bishops and priests should be married, divorced and remarried. I could be shot down in flames but I do believe in the spiritual union that marriage is between man and woman and for life. If men are gay by nature then, particularly within the church, celibacy should be the norm. It's a big issue and it is not going to go away. I don't know what the answer is, I really don't. We had a report in the General Synod on human sexuality but it has never really been debated. We are trying to sort it out with the whole American business aren't we? I don't know what the answer is, we are in a bit of a mess in that we are going along different ways of thinking and I really don't know what is going to happen.

All I can say is that, from my point of view, we should keep faith with the scriptures and keep faith with the tradition of the church and keep faith with the holier life that I believe we should be living. Christians should keep the faith. Ordained clergy and bishops should set an example. They have after all been chosen for high office and should take a stand over the gay issue. In the present day world it seems to be "Do whatever you feel you would like to do, if it feels right for you." No I think we have got to have standards, I think we have got to have rules to live by.

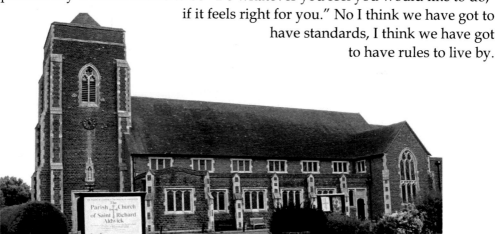

Our family now

It's not just me. There was something I read in the paper that I felt very sad about because it was about a couple who'd just had a baby, their third child and they weren't letting anybody know the sex of the child because they want the child to decide as it grows up where his or her orientation is. Personally I think that's child abuse and I know we mustn't stereotype children but this is awful, this kind of "We think we've got a better idea" or giving them no guidelines, just let them be, I find it all quite frightening really.

I think I've had a very privileged life. It's been a privilege to live in lovely houses, particularly this one. It's been a privilege to be able to share it with other people. I have meetings in the house, I have garden parties, and I have coffee mornings, all as it used to be. The trouble is now some vicarages are like little kind of boxes and you can't do this kind of thing. Some people don't want to do it in their homes but I like to open up my home to other people and share what privileges I have and do one's bit, if you like, as part of a Christian community. It has been a traditional way of life which I think is disappearing. It is sad really.

My sister is married to a priest. She works part-time but likes to be at home and does her turn at the coffee mornings, teaching in Sunday school and things like that. It is a bit different in South London because open house means the tramps come round. We used to have tramps but not so much now because even the tramps have gone more up market; it is really not like it was when I was a child. In the next generation it will not be the same anyway because now market forces dictate that women should work because of housing, to provide housing on retirement. We have to trust in God and the Pensions' Board but I haven't got that far yet.

CLERGY WIVES' STORIES

'They are mostly nameless and forgotten, the women who have supported their husbands' calling with so much piety, patience, and sense of dedication.'

(Margaret Watt, *The History of The Parson's Wife*. Published by Faber and Faber; Mcmxliii, page 166).

INDEX

PHOTOGRAPHS